Is There Sex after Marriage?

Other books by Carol Botwin

Love Lives
The Love Crisis
Sex and the Teenage Girl

Is There Sex after Marriage?

by Carol Botwin

FOREWORD BY HAROLD I. LIEF, M.D.

Little, Brown and Company

BOSTON   TORONTO

Second Printing

The author is grateful for permission to reprint the following copyrighted material:

Letter from April 26, 1983, Ann Landers column, reprinted by permission of Ann
Landers and News America Syndicate.

Excerpts from *The New Sex Therapy, The Evaluation of Sexual Disorders,* and *Disorders of
Sexual Desire,* all by Dr. Helen Singer Kaplan, reprinted by permission of the
publisher, Brunner/Mazel, Inc.

Excerpts from "Relations," *The New York Times,* December 21, 1981. Copyright ©
1981 by The New York Times Company. Reprinted by permission.

Library of Congress Cataloging in Publication Data

Botwin, Carol.
    Is there sex after marriage?

    Bibliography: p.
    Includes index.
    1. Sex in marriage—United States. I. Title.
HQ31.B726 1985   306.8′72   84-25073
ISBN 0-316-10350-0

DESIGNED BY ROBERT G. LOWE

MV

Published simultaneously in Canada
by Little, Brown & Company (Canada) Limited

PRINTED IN THE UNITED STATES OF AMERICA

To my husband

CONTENTS

PART TWO: THE HIDDEN DYNAMICS

APPENDIXES

FOREWORD

I AM NOT ordinarily fond of superlatives, but in the case of this book, I must drop my usual reticence and state flatly that Carol Botwin has written the best book about sex and marriage that I have read. Ms. Botwin's book is addressed to the general public with the hope that, through increased understanding of marital interactions, many marriages may be saved, many married people can have more fulfilling sexual lives, and many people contemplating marriage will have a clearer comprehension of what lies ahead. I believe she will succeed in influencing the lives of many.

We have had far too many sex manuals, too many how-to-do-it "sex cookbooks," with the authors' favorite recipes for getting with it, getting turned on, getting one's kicks, and, in the process, winning a gold medal in the sexual Olympics. This book is different. It deals with what professionals in the field call "marital dynamics" — the nuances and subtleties of what takes place in the lives of people hoping to find greater satisfaction and fulfillment with another person in an intimate relationship. While the author makes the decrease in sexual desire a major theme of her book, the content actually is a discussion of the life cycle of marriage and the changes that take place in marital relationships as people marry, have children, pass through various crises or turning points, and manage the problems of parenting, the empty nest, menopause, and aging. The influence of these life-cycle events on sexual behavior and gratification is admirably explained and illustrated with case histories.

The author's other major concerns are how people achieve or fail to achieve intimacy (one of the best parts of the book deals with the defenses against intimacy and the reasons why so many people are afraid of it), and how struggles around power mess up sex so badly.

The content of Ms. Botwin's book is anything but superficial. She is an excellent journalist (the reason I was happy to spend time talking to her), and she has taken the best ideas of many keen observers of the foibles of us humans and set them down in language that is so easy to understand that it is a joy to read. (How many people would be able to take the idea of "projective identification" and explain it in ordinary, nonjargonish language so that it is perfectly intelligible?)

The readability is enhanced by scores of case illustrations. At random, I selected twenty pages in the middle of the book and counted a dozen case histories. These are augmented by the cases supplied by her "panel of experts" and her thorough review of the subject matter. I hope this work finds a wide audience.

HAROLD I. LIEF, M.D.
Professor of Psychiatry
University of Pennsylvania School of Medicine
Specialist in Marital and Sex Therapy
at the Pennsylvania Hospital

ACKNOWLEDGMENTS

T HERE IS no adequate way to thank the experts I consulted who were so generous with their time. The knowledge they imparted to me during personal interviews made this book deeper and broader than it could have been otherwise. The wisdom of those who were quoted, as well as those who weren't, but who contributed in significant ways to my overall understanding of sex in long-term relationships, is the cornerstone of this book. They are, in alphabetical order:

BERTA ANAGNOSTE, M.D.; Clinical Assistant Professor of Psychiatry, New York University Medical Center; psychiatrist in private practice, New York City and Denville, New Jersey

ROMAN ANSHIN, M.D.; Clinical Associate Professor of Psychiatry, University of Southern California School of Medicine, Los Angeles; member, Board of Trustees, American Academy of Psychoanalysis

REBECCA BLACK, M.A.; private practice of psychotherapy and sex therapy, San Francisco

ERNEST BRUNI, PH.D.; private practice of psychotherapy, Los Angeles

HARVEY CAPLAN, M.D.; private practice of psychotherapy and sex therapy, San Francisco

JOSHUA GOLDEN, M.D.; Professor of Psychiatry and Director, Human Sexuality Program, UCLA Center for Health Sciences; private practice, Santa Monica, California

FRED GOTTLIEB, M.D.; Associate Professor of Psychiatry, UCLA; Director, Family Therapy Institute of Southern California, Los Angeles

HELEN SINGER KAPLAN, M.D., PH.D.; Director, Human Sexuality Program, New York Hospital–Cornell Medical Center, New York City; specialist in sexual disorders, New York City

OTTO KERNBERG, M.D.; Medical Director, New York Hospital–Cornell Medical Center, Westchester Division, White Plains, New York

HAROLD I. LIEF, M.D.; Professor of Psychiatry, University of Pennsylvania School of Medicine; Specialist in Marital and Sex Therapy at the Pennsylvania Hospital; private practice, Philadelphia

JAY MANN, PH.D.; Director, Family Program, Veterans' Administration Medical Center, Palo Alto, California (It was with great sorrow that I learned of the death of Dr. Mann soon after the completion of this book)

GAYLA MARGOLIN, PH.D.; Associate Professor of Psychology, University of Southern California, Los Angeles

EDWARD L. PARSONS, M.D.; Clinical Assistant Professor of Psychiatry, New York Hospital–Cornell Medical Center; psychiatrist in private practice, New York City and Westfield, New Jersey

RAUL C. SCHIAVI, M.D.; Director, Human Sexuality Program, Mount Sinai Medical Center, New York City

BERNIE ZILBERGELD, PH.D.; Codirector of Clinical Training, Human Sexuality Program, University of California, San Francisco

An enormous contribution to this book was made also by the many men and women I interviewed who, with remarkable honesty, shared the details of their sex lives with me. Because they were guaranteed anonymity they cannot be thanked by name, but my gratitude to them is herewith acknowledged.

Introduction

CHAPTER 1

The Problem So Many Couples Face

ALLAN and his wife Francine, both in their twenties, were sexually active until the birth of their first child, Laurel. Then Allan stopped wanting to make love with Francine. He now forces himself to every three weeks or so, but even though he reaches a climax, he finds the pleasure minimal and the act more mechanical than anything else. Francine complains that they don't have sex often enough. Allan blames it on his being tired because of his career efforts, but the truth is — although he doesn't know why — he no longer finds sex with his wife appealing.

Debbie and John have been married fifteen years. They have three children — two boys and a girl, whose ages range from seven to twelve. Although Debbie and John enjoyed sex together at the beginning of their relationship, their desire has gradually withered until now they have intercourse maybe once a month at most.

Larry and Tina have been living together for a year. Although they are happy and compatible in every other way, their sex life is driving Tina crazy. Everything was fine until Larry gave up his apartment and moved in with her. Then all of a sudden he lost interest in sex.

Ginny and Peter married three years ago. Sexual interest between them has gradually dribbled away since then. Though happy with one another in every other respect, they are living together asexually — like "a brother and sister who get along very well," as they describe it.

Charlotte doesn't understand why there's so much fuss about sex. She never enjoys it, and because of this, she avoids intercourse with Ron, her husband of sixteen years, whenever she can. He feels frustrated and angry, and for years has buried his sexual desires under a pile of work. Today, however, as he approaches his forty-first birthday, Ron is beginning to insist that Charlotte do something about their situation: he wants to lead a normal sex life — before, in his words, "it's too late."

These couples are suffering from the number-one sex problem in marriage today: lack of interest in making love by one or both partners. Leading sex clinics around the country have reported an upsurge in recent years of husbands and wives who, in one stage of their marriage or another, have confronted the fact that the sexual "charge" is going, has gone, or, in some cases, has never quite been there — and who want to know why.

In Manhattan, for example, at New York Hospital–Cornell Medical Center, Dr. Helen Singer Kaplan, who heads the sex therapy clinic, says that waning desire is the leading complaint of couples she sees. Dr. Raul Schiavi, director of the Human Sexuality Program at Mount Sinai Medical Center in New York, reports that both single and married people complain of other sexual dysfunctions, such as impotence, premature ejaculation, and inability to achieve orgasm, but *every* male patient in his program suffering from lack of desire has been married. At the Marriage Council of Philadelphia, a survey of patients with sexual problems revealed lack of sexual desire to be the leading complaint.

Some therapists estimate that 50 percent of their patients are turned off to sex.

Dearth of desire as a problem in committed, established, long-term relationships has become so noticeable that loss of libido has recently been given an official name — "inhibited sexual desire" — and classified, for the first time, as a sexual dysfunction in the *Diagnostic and Statistical Manual* issued by the American Psychiatric Association.

Recent studies back up the fact that infrequent sex is a relatively common phenomenon in marriage. One survey of 100 couples, published in the *New England Journal of Medicine,* discovered that 33 percent of the husbands and wives were having intercourse with their spouse two or three times a month or less. Another study, published in the *American Journal of Psychiatry,* revealed that among 365 husbands and wives, one-third had ceased having sexual relations altogether for long periods of time. Although the median period of abstinence was eight weeks, some of the husbands and wives had gone without intercourse for three months or longer.

Until recently, it was widely assumed that sparse sex and lack of desire would most likely be encountered in the marriages of older couples, but the surprising news is that libido can be lost in marriage at any time. Case histories from leading sex clinics confirm this and the *American Journal of Psychiatry* study makes the fact strikingly clear: more than three-quarters of the husbands and wives making do with little or no sex were under the age of thirty-eight — a prime time in life, when intercourse between spouses, on an average, takes place two or three times a week.

Most people being treated to restore a lagging or defunct sex drive are in their thirties and forties, but men and women arrive at sex clinics at all ages, these days, wanting to revitalize a dying sex life. Dr. Joshua Golden, director of the Human Sexuality Program at the University of California, Los Angeles, has successfully treated couples in their seventies. Dr. Helen Singer Kaplan and Dr. Harold Lief, the well-known psychiatrist and sex therapist who is now in private practice and who headed the Marriage

Council of Philadelphia for many years, have seen an increase in the number of husbands and wives under thirty who are concerned about their loss of interest in sex. Dr. Kaplan thinks that younger people, because they are more open about sex in general, often don't let lack of desire linger as a problem in their relationships the way older people do — which is fortunate, because the sooner you catch the problem, the better the chance to overcome it.

Dr. Lief and Dr. Kaplan, working independently, first defined interest in having sex as a separate, initial stage of the sex act. Desire has to be present before you can go on to intercourse itself. Dr. Lief and Dr. Kaplan were also instrumental in pinning down the fact that impairment of the sex drive is a sexual dysfunction in its own right; often, patients who couldn't reach orgasm or were impotent were found to be suffering primarily from lack of desire, which caused other sexual difficulties when they forced themselves to have sex anyway.

Although the problem of impaired sexual desire in marriage has "gone public" through reports of work being done at sex clinics, the population of patients seeking treatment probably represents only a fraction of a much larger group of married couples who lead lives of sexual estrangement to varying degrees. Journals, books, and papers by marriage therapists, psychiatrists, psychologists, and social workers have reported, from the time of Freud on, a wealth of case histories based on patients who for one reason or another have had trouble feeling sexual passion for their marriage partners. Dr. Edmund Bergler, the late, eminent psychoanalyst, once wrote that "the history of sex in modern marriage is, in general, the history of sex sparingly used."

Works of fiction, such as *Cat on a Hot Tin Roof,* deal with the problem. Broadway musicals have alluded to it; Stephen Sondheim, in a song from *Follies,* wrote revealing lyrics about "passionless lovemaking once a year." The biographies of public figures contain telling references to it. Freud himself stopped having intercourse with his wife at about the age of forty. Tolstoy hated sex so much that he was moved to remark, "Man can endure earthquake, epidemic, dreadful diseases, every form of spiritual torment, but the most dreadful tragedy that can befall him is and will remain the tragedy of the bedroom." He believed in celibacy in his own marriage.

There is no doubt, though, that the largest number of people suffering from loss of libido are those countless ordinary husbands and wives who continue to live together in marriages in which sex is infrequent or absent altogether, and who do so without ever seeking professional help or, sometimes, without even discussing the situation with each other. The aforementioned Dr. Lief, professor of psychiatry at the University of Pennsylvania School of Medicine and chief investigator of sexual-desire disorders for the American Psychiatric Association, estimates that about 20 percent of the general population suffers from inhibited sexual desire. Some of these people consider themselves to be happy anyhow; others feel varying degrees of distress about their sex lives but don't know what to do about it.

There is some debate among experts about the true state of life in sexless or sexually sparse marriages. Certain authorities believe that when sex is unimportant to *both* partners but they remain close and affectionate in other ways, they can continue to be reasonably happy. It is, they maintain, when husband and wife are on different wavelengths — with one still interested in sex, while the other is not — that a real problem exists in the marriage.

No one can deny the potentially devastating effect rejection can have upon a partner who is continually refused or ignored sexually. Some slighted spouses seem to take no notice, however. Indeed, if they have a sexual problem of their own, they may welcome the mate's lack of interest. They are happy they no longer have to be "bothered" for sex. It is far more common, though, for sexually ignored wives and husbands to feel rejected, inadequate, or unattractive as a result — as if, somehow, it is their fault that the partner has turned off. Many spouses feel very threatened. They worry that the uninterested partner may abandon them. There is often a sense of deprivation or anger. Frustration, bitterness, and resentment may grow over time. In addition, although such fears prove groundless in most cases, spouses these days may secretly wonder if a mate is ignoring them because he or she is a closet homosexual. It is very common for the rejected partner to become depressed, preoccupied, or obsessed about the mate's sexual rejection.

A forty-year-old woman in a large New England city recently described her reactions in such a situation. She has been married for ten years. Her husband is a lawyer with a very busy practice. Sex with him is great, she says — when they have it. At the beginning of their marriage, they used to have sex two or three times a week. The rate gradually fell off during the year after their wedding until it reached the point it is at now: they have sex once every three weeks or so. She is a woman with a strong sex drive and feels the lack of physical contact intensely. She has confronted her husband in the past about the infrequency of sex, but most of the time he claims he is too tired for lovemaking. He works hard, puts in long hours, and he feels that the way *not* to relax is to have sex. He regards sex as a chore.

This woman blames herself more than she blames her husband for their predicament. His lack of interest makes her feel humiliated and unattractive. As a result, as soon as the frequency of sex fell off in the relationship, she tried to improve her appearance, thinking that a new look might help to restore her husband's interest. Although she was not really overweight, she went on a diet. She watches her weight compulsively now. She also started to put on cosmetics the minute she woke up each morning. Her efforts produced no results, however: her husband remains unaroused. Sometimes she feels attracted to other men, but this makes her feel guilty and ashamed, so she fights her sexual impulses. Since she feels so unattractive, she hates to go to parties. She goes with her husband when she can't avoid it, but she suffers from a sense of inferiority the whole time. The sexual situation in her marriage is never far from her thoughts. She stays married to her husband because he is a kind, protective man who is considerate of her in every other way.

Of course, this woman was insecure to begin with — but most

of us are to some degree. Perceived sexual rejections generally feed into whatever insecurities exist or activate dormant feelings of inferiority. Consequently, "neglected" sexual partners tend to feel worse about themselves than they would otherwise.

Some spouses react to their partner's sexual indifference by pressuring the mate even more frantically in an effort to elicit a sexual response, which usually makes matters worse: the partner avoids sex even more. A more common reaction among sexually ignored spouses, however, is retreat. The partner who feels spurned eventually withdraws sexually, too, out of fear of further rejection or additional humiliation. As a result, sexual efforts on both sides come to a standstill.

The partner who has turned off may not be bothered by the fact at all except for the spouse's pressure tactics and expression of frustration. If a spouse does not complain, the indifferent partner may go without sexual activity for years on end without thinking much about it. But, in contrast, many people with impaired desire are very distressed. They may feel damaged, humiliated, or see lack of sexual interest on their part as a sign of aging. Often they think they are washed up sexually. Others interpret their condition as a sign that they no longer love their spouse.

Frequently, both the partner who is turned off and the one who remains interested in sex may try to "sit it out on the sidelines," waiting patiently, and somewhat unrealistically, for the problem to go away. Their hope is that the turned-off partner will just wake up one day and be interested in sex once more. "Fifteen years can go by in this way," says San Francisco psychiatrist and sex therapist Harvey Caplan, commenting on the number of women and men he sees who wake up late in the game to the fact that diminished sexual desire is a genuine problem in their marriage and that they had better do something about it.

Dr. Otto Kernberg — medical director of the New York Hospital–Cornell Medical Center, Westchester Division, and one of the most well known psychiatrists in the United States — takes issue with those of his colleagues who think that couples with little or no sex in their marriages can be relatively well adjusted anyway if they are not in conflict about lack of sex. "A couple can eliminate sexuality altogether and believe that they live very well," he says. "I think, however, that the lack of sex indicates an impoverishment in their relationship. It is an impoverishment that shows in other areas of their life. There is generally a severe restriction in the scope of their emotional life.

"If a couple in their seventies has sex once a month, I would like to know how they are doing. How is their sex? It may be satisfactory. But if a couple in their thirties or forties has sex once every three months, I consider this to be a serious sexual inhibition," says Dr. Kernberg. "I consider it to be a major problem, even if they don't. I have found, in my practice, that even people who have severe sexual inhibition haven't been aware that it is a problem. If they don't want treatment, I would leave them alone. I'm not saying everybody should have satisfactory sexual relations in marriage. You can't order people to be normal."

The well-known sex researchers John H. Gagnon and William Simon take a somewhat opposing point of view in their book *Sexual Conduct:*

> It is possible that we have assumed an important role for sexuality and the management of sexuality in the maintenance of the marital bonds because we have assumed that sex itself is an important part of most people's lives. This may not be true. Particularly after the formation of the marital unit, it is quite possible that sex — both as a psychological reward and a physical outlet — declines in salience. It may become less important than alternative modes of gratification (work, children, security, constant affection — any or all may become more significant), or the weight of these alternative modes of gratifications may minimize the effects of any sexual dissatisfaction.

The results of various surveys and studies that have explored the relationship between sex and marital satisfaction perhaps tell the story best. Time after time, these studies come up with the same findings: the couples who consider themselves most satisfied and happy in their marriages also lead enjoyable sex lives. The most recent of these reports was the *Love, Sex, and Aging* survey of over 4,000 men and women over fifty done for Consumers Union by Edward Brecher, which found that high enjoyment of sex correlated with happy, long-term marriages and low enjoyment of sex correlated with unhappy marriages.

This doesn't mean that a sexual dysfunction cannot exist in a contented marriage. It may, indeed. William Masters and Virginia Johnson, prominent authorities on human sexual behavior, have estimated that sexual dysfunctions exist in about 50 percent of the marriages in the United States. But in spite of a dysfunction, many happy couples still desire and value sex in their relationship. Having sex — even if it's not always perfect — seems to make life fuller and better for the overwhelming majority of husbands and wives at any age.

Nevertheless, as the pioneering sex researcher Alfred Kinsey and others discovered, sexual appetites differ greatly from one human being to another. Some people need a great deal of sex, while some seem to have naturally lower libidos. For example, although three-quarters of the men in Kinsey's landmark study had coitus in the range between once a week to a little over six times a week, there were also 7 percent who averaged seven or more times a week, while a little over 11 percent had sex only once in two weeks. There was considerable variation, in other words, from Kinsey's mean average for all men: 2.34 sexual experiences per week.

Statistics gathered by Kinsey, as well as those compiled by Morton Hunt for his book *Sexual Behavior in the 1970's*, indicate that the average married couple has sex between two and three times a week until their midthirties. Between the ages of thirty-five and forty-five, they have intercourse approximately once or twice a week, then once a week until their midfifties. At age fifty-five and over, the average is between once every week and once every two weeks. *But* there are couples who have sex once a day, year in and year out, and others who have always been content engaging in intercourse no more than once every two weeks or so.

According to Hunt's findings, married people are having some-what more sex today than they were in the 1930s and 1940s when Kinsey's data were gathered. He also found that women enjoy sex more and have a greater appetite for it in marriage than they did in earlier times and that frequency of sexual activity in marriage declines less with advancing age now than it did in the past.

Most experts hesitate to talk about what is average or to publi-cize statistics about frequency of sex. This is because people tend to compare their own sexual behavior to published statistics and try to live up to what they think is normal, and they feel deficient if they don't succeed. It should always be remembered that sexual practices among human beings vary widely. The person who wants sex once a day is no more "normal" than the one who wants it only once a week, assuming that no significant psychological, health, or interpersonal problems are interfering with sexual ex-pression. One generalization can be made, however: feeling *no* de-sire toward your mate is simply not a normal state in a reasonably contented marriage to a partner you still like.

"Throughout his life the normal person experiences spontane-ous sexual desire, and also has the capacity to be aroused by an attractive partner," writes Dr. Helen Singer Kaplan. "Even when a man and woman are happily in love, sexual desire normally fluctuates, so that interest in making love shows some variation. However, it never remains absent for long for normal couples."

The effects of aging, often falsely blamed for diminished sexual desire, are gone into elsewhere in this book. It is enough to note here that although passion may dim somewhat with advancing age, interest and sex drive never go away completely unless cer-tain medical problems intervene. Whatever effect aging has on sex occurs only very gradually over the years. The truth is, throughout most of our life — in youth and old age, in marriage and out — most of us are *physically* capable of much more sexual activity than we actually experience.

How can you tell, then, if something is wrong? How can you differentiate natural fluctuations in sexual interest from inhibited sexual desire? Let's quickly look at some typical circumstances that might cause a temporary loss of interest. At times of great tension or stress, you may lose your libido for a while. When conditions change and the stress lifts, however, desire usually returns spontaneously. The same is true of anger. If, for some reason, you are mad at your mate, you may not want sex while you are still upset. But once you stop being angry, your desire automatically returns of its own accord.

The sign that something is seriously wrong, though, is when your sex drive — or your partner's — *diminishes significantly and stays that way.* In other words, something is amiss if day after day, week after week, either or both partners want sex much less than they formerly did, or, for unknown reasons, don't seem to want it at all.

Experts find that impaired sexual desire takes two forms: global and situational. It is global if you are no longer interested in sex at all and are not aroused by anyone. ("I don't even look at pretty girls anymore," complained one man.) You no longer even fantasize about sex. ("Even Robert Redford wouldn't turn me on," joked a wife, bitterly.) You don't masturbate.

On the other hand, the lack of interest could be situational. In that case, you feel no sexual desire for your partner, but other people still ignite your interest. You still may have erotic fantasies or masturbate when you are alone.

It would be characteristic of situational loss of desire for a woman to feel romantic and turned on by a love scene she sees on television or reads in a book, but turned off the minute her husband makes a sexual advance. Similarly, a man with situational inhibited desire might get an erection while reading *Playboy* on the train coming home from work, or have sexual fantasies about a woman he sees across the aisle, but then feel completely unaroused by his attractive wife once he gets home. A person with this type of impaired sex drive could function sexually with a pickup with whom contact has been minimal, yet fail to be excited by a loving spouse who desires a close, sexy relationship.

Although this is out of the range of conscious knowledge,

spouses suffering from impaired libido often avoid pleasurable or erotic thoughts when their partner is present. At bedtime, for example, they may start to worry about problems at work, financial difficulties, or troubles with an aged parent or an unruly child. They might think about one of the spouse's bad habits ("She always leaves her shoes in the middle of the room," or "I wish he wouldn't expect me to pick up after him"); or they might concentrate on some unpleasant feature of the mate ("When she gets excited her voice becomes so shrill," or "He has black rings under his fingernails").

Sometimes, however, people with lowered libido can force themselves to engage in sex (often out of guilt toward their partner) and can even reach orgasm if their genitals are stimulated sufficiently, but in most cases the experience is not really satisfying and is not apt to be repeated. Dr. Kaplan likens it to eating when you're not really hungry.

The unerotic aspects of physical contact — hugging, cuddling, kissing — may be pleasurable to some people whose desire is inhibited, but others hate any kind of contact and avoid it — and sex — like the plague. Some who force themselves to engage in sex feel that they have to leave the partner immediately afterward to wash up or take a shower. Often, any attempt by the partner to interest or seduce the person with impaired sexual desire will either fail to produce any feelings at all in the partner or will produce negative ones, such as irritation, tension, disgust, the desire to escape, even sleepiness.

Partners who feel turned off to sex with their spouse generally try to avoid sexual situations through a variety of strategies. The most obvious one, of course, especially in the case of men, is that they stop initiating sex. Some people, particularly when anger is behind the turn-off, tell a mate that they are not interested more subtly: they engage in sex but do so in such an unenthusiastic way that their lack of ardor is obvious to the partner. (This acts to turn the mate off as well.)

Some spouses with impaired desire withdraw only sexually,

while others do so both emotionally and sexually. There is often the fear that if they show affection in nonsexual ways, it will lead to sexual expectations.

The use of avoidance tactics is universal. You come up with a variety of excuses such as "I'm tired," or the famous one — "I have a headache." You may have an allergy attack, or you may complain that the weather is too hot. You may throw all your energies into work so that you forget even to think about sex. You may bring a pile of work home from the office or watch TV until long after your mate has gone to bed.

You may sabotage. For instance, you may pick a fight, make an impossible demand, criticize or insult at bedtime or whenever you feel sex is a possibility. One wife told her husband when he started to make sexual overtures on a weekend afternoon, "The children will be back any minute now," which instantly dampened his ardor. Another wife, in the middle of intercourse, reminded her husband that he had forgotten to mail an important letter. A husband started to criticize his wife's handling of their young son when he thought she was getting amorous. Another husband continued to smoke his pipe in the bedroom even though he knew his wife hated the smell of tobacco.

A specifically sexual put-down can be used to sabotage. For example, you may let your wife know that you wish her breasts were bigger, which will make her so self-conscious about her body that she will be unable to have an orgasm or even want sex. Or you may remind your husband that he may not be able to "get it up," like the last time, which will create such anxiety for him that your reminder will turn out to be a self-fulfilling prophecy.

Lack of sex in marriage may currently be considered a symptom of a new sexual dysfunction, but as a subject it's old. It has been a topic of humor among men for a long time, with wives frequently being depicted in jokes as not interested in sex (they have "headaches") or so sexually passive that, since they just lie there, a husband could easily turn off, too.

One example of the wife-as-turn-off type of joke:

DOCTOR [to heart patient]: You must not get too excited
   during sex.
PATIENT: Oh, that's easy. I'll have sex with my wife.

The new wrinkle in the old game of marital sexual ennui, however, is that in today's social climate, with sexual expectations ris-
ing and women's roles changing, there is often a switch in the
roles partners play. Dr. Harold Lief finds that a great reversal has
taken place among the patients he sees. It used to be husbands
who complained that their wives weren't interested in sex; but
now, he says, the number of wives complaining about their husbands is "striking."

In the light of higher sexual and marital expectations for both
sexes in our society, it is easy to see that lack of sex in marriage,
whether it occurs early or late in a relationship, can be more disruptive today than it was in our parents' and grandparents' times.
It conceivably leads to more divorces and extramarital affairs,
both of which are on the increase anyway.

Nevertheless, there are countless husbands and wives who
choose to stay together, leading relatively sexless lives. Many of
them are unaware that help is available to them.* Indeed, as lack
of desire has become recognized as a specific sexual dysfunction,
sex therapists have found new, more effective ways of treating it.
The techniques now used in the sex clinics to treat inhibited sexual desire are different in some respects from those used to help
other sexual dysfunctions, such as impotence or inability to
achieve orgasm. Most sex therapy relies heavily on sexual exercises and assigned tasks that patients do in private. Although
these, too, may be used in the treatment of blocked desire, special-
ists generally emphasize psychotherapy — couples therapy, individual psychotherapy, or both, depending on what seems to be
causing the loss of libido. Some therapists have been using group
therapy, which brings together unrelated spouses with the same

*A list of sex therapy clinics can be found in appendix B.

problem who may find comfort in realizing they aren't alone — that there are other husbands and wives who also find themselves sexually marooned.

The chances of successful treatment are much higher today than they were in the recent past: one reliable source estimates that the number of husbands and wives whose libido has been restored in varying degrees has more than tripled.

The subject of failing desire, however, has another dimension. To understand it fully, you also have to grasp how sex fits into the life cycle of a marriage. At what points in a couple's history does sexual desire become more vulnerable and why?

Whether they realize it or not, when a couple join in matrimony they are entering a relationship that will go through a series of stages that are common to almost all marriages. At certain periods in every marriage there are predictable kinds of adjustments that have to take place, psychological problems that have to be resolved, and significant events such as pregnancy, child rearing, midlife crises, and retirement that enter into the picture. And biology is always simultaneously doing its work in the background as the clock of life slowly but ineluctably winds down. All of these things have a bearing on what kind of a sex life a couple will have as their marriage progresses.

Using surveys, statistics, sociological and psychological studies, and clinical evidence from therapists' practices, it is possible to predict, in a general way, at what points in the marriage cycle sexual interest will peak and when it will be at its lowest, as well as what kind of issues are liable to crop up that could create sexual problems. This constitutes "the natural history of sex in marriage."

Of course, not every couple goes through exactly the same sexual history in marriage in exactly the same way. For example, one person can have a midlife crisis, with its sexual consequences at age thirty-eight, while for another it may not strike until the age of fifty. Nevertheless, once the midlife crisis hits, it has recognizable sexual components. Or a couple might have children later than average in their marriage; as a result, sexual problems connected with pregnancy and child rearing may crop up further along in their life together than they do for the average couple, and midlife problems may have to be solved simultaneously with those that accompany new parenthood. And, of course, various individual problems identified by sex therapists (and discussed in the second part of this book) may come into play at any stage of a marriage. So, the natural history of sex as it is outlined in the pages that follow is not meant to be taken as an exact description of how a sex life plays itself out for everyone. Nor is it meant to be taken as the way things *should* be. It is simply a generalized model delineating periods in the marriage cycle in which certain events, with sexual consequences, commonly take place. As such it can help you to understand where you are sexually and emotionally — and why — at any time in your married life.

PART ONE

The Natural History
of Sex in Marriage

CHAPTER 2

Stage One: The Early Years

SOME sex researchers call it "the honeymoon effect." Others talk about it as "the Coolidge effect." The latter are referring to an incident that is supposed to have occurred when Calvin Coolidge and his wife were visiting a farm while he was president. Mrs. Coolidge, taken on a separate tour, was impressed by a prize rooster who was exhibiting remarkable sexual vigor, mating over and over again. She said to her guide, "Tell Mr. Coolidge about it." When the rooster's activities were duly reported to her husband, he asked, "Was it always the same hen?" Informed that the rooster was performing with a variety of hens, the president is reported to have said, "Tell Mrs. Coolidge about that."

Whether you call it the honeymoon effect, the Coolidge effect, or don't call it anything at all, you may recognize the phenomenon from your personal experience. Sex, which was frequent and urgent in the early stages of your relationship, fell sharply during the first year or two of your marriage.

In 1981 sociologist William James, analyzing data from the Kinsey Institute and other, later reliable sources, found that coital frequency in marriage fell by one-half, on an average, by the end of the first year, confirming what other experts have said: the sharpest drop in sexual activity occurs at the beginning of marriages. From then on, the decline continues over the course of the marriage, but in a less precipitate way. Other research, such as two United States National Fertility Studies, in which 5,000 women were questioned, confirmed a sharp drop in coital rates during the first year of marriage. Even when sexual activity has been cut in half, going, let's say, from once a day to two or three times a week, sex is usually more frequent in the first few years of marriage than it ever will be again in the life of the couple.

The honeymoon effect — the decline of sex from its early frenzy to a more sedate pace — actually can take place prior to the honeymoon, these days, if a couple lives together before legalizing their union, although, according to the recent study *American Couples,* conducted by Philip Blumstein and Pepper Schwartz, sex continues to be more frequent for cohabiting unmarried couples than for those who marry.

The wedding itself may give sex a whammy, according to Dr. Berta Anagnoste, clinical assistant professor of psychiatry at New York University Medical Center. She has seen numerous couples who get so embroiled in the preparations for a large wedding, and so full of tension as a result, that sex, which previously had a high priority, suddenly drops to a low place on their agenda. The engaged pair may, also, suddenly find themselves divided as a couple and fighting over issues involving the wedding because of pushes and pulls created by their parents. Sex suffers as irritations mount.

Although problems associated with the wedding tend to resolve themselves soon after the ceremony, high passion is generally doomed to simmer down permanently anyway, if not within the first year, as William James concludes, then by the end of the second year — which is Dr. Harold Lief's estimate. "The magic called love lasts for a couple of years," he says, "and after that there is some decline in frequency of sex, some decrease of desire, and sometimes, not always, a decrease of responsivity."

Dr. Helen Singer Kaplan thinks that the excitement associated with a new romance can persist a bit longer. According to her, "It lasts about two to three years or until a baby is born."

The *American Couples* survey found that sex during the first two years of marriage occurred three times a week or more for 45 percent of the men and women studied. It remained at this high level for only about 25 percent of the couples between the second and tenth year of marriage.

What causes the sharp decline in sexual activity during the first stages of marriage? Coolidge was not alone in suggesting that sex with the same partner was at fault. "One may suspect," writes sociologist William James, "that the novelty that wears off is not of sexuality itself but of sexuality with a specific partner. I suggest that the same rapid decline in coital rates characterizes each honeymoon of people involved in a succession of marriages."

In the animal kingdom, among lower mammals, various experiments show that the sexual appetite of male monkeys and rats diminishes when sex occurs with the same partner and picks up when new mates are available.

One research team, Michael and Zumpe, studied and recorded over a three-and-a-half-year period the mating activity of male rhesus monkeys paired regularly with the same female. They found that sexual frequency diminished each year. The rate of copulation shot up again dramatically, however, when, at the end of three and a half years, a new female was introduced. Sex returned once more to its former low levels when, after several weeks, the new female was removed and replaced with the old mate.

Such findings would seem to verify the novelty-wears-off theory of sexuality and make the honeymoon effect seem built in by nature, at least among males — the experiments tested male mammalian sexual preferences only. As yet, we have no way of knowing whether female mammals tire of the same old mate the way their male counterparts do. But even if they do, many experts argue that human beings cannot be compared to other mammals. Our intelligence and feelings complicate our sexual workings in such a way as to make comparisons to animals unreliable if not downright foolish.

The high frequency of sex in the beginning of relationships may actually be the abnormal state — caused more by other factors than by sexual passion per se. Dr. Harvey Caplan believes that the newness of the partner in the early parts of a relationship does, indeed, keep sex exciting and frequent, but for two reasons that are rarely recognized: (1) because with newness comes uncertainty and anxiety, and (2) because a new person represents a barrier that has to be overcome — he or she has to be conquered.

"I think a lot of sex in the beginning of a relationship has a 'proof' quality about it," he says. "Early on in the relationship, sexual interest is a barometer if you are not sure of one another.

"Two people looking for a permanent relationship like each other and then they want to win one another. They put a great deal of effort into the winning and a lot of it is expressed sexually," according to Dr. Caplan. "Sex, initially, is often an important determinant as to whether the people consider themselves to be in love and whether they care about each other. But after the caring has been established in a good relationship and the two people trust each other, then the need to prove it by sex goes down somewhat. Less value is placed on sex per se in the marriage and there is a general decline in desire and lower sexual frequencies.

"I really believe, as well," Dr. Caplan continues, "that sexual arousal, desire, and excitement has to do with overcoming certain barriers. The sexual drive is stimulated by some kind of resistance or tension. If the tension between two people that is there in the beginning disappears altogether and they become totally comfortable with each other, familiar with each other, are very predictable, and don't argue, they tend to have low sexual interest and frequencies," he explains. "If you accept the idea that mellowness between two people — a soft, tender, wonderful, easygoing, trusting relationship — is anathema to great sexual tension and arousal, then you can see how useful fantasy during sex can be for keeping sex exciting."

Dr. Lief agrees that the anxiety engendered in the initial stages of a relationship can be a turn-on — a theory backed up by a study published in the *Journal of Abnormal Psychology* in which subjects were purposely placed in anxiety-provoking situations. It was found that the greatest erotic arousal in the subjects was preceded by some degree of anxiety.

"Although a lot of anxiety interferes with sexuality," says Dr. Lief, "a little seems to turn some people on. That's why people often fall in love with another partner. The lover is more exciting than the spouse. Part of the reason is the anxiety."

According to Dr. Otto Kernberg, however, tension persists to some degree even in long-term relationships between well-matched couples. He maintains that there is always some mystery attached to a marital partner, that spouses can never completely know one another, and that that sense of not knowing is one part of what keeps mutual sexual interest alive in two mature people who are married to one another.

Dr. Caplan adds another dimension to the question of why sex is frequent early in a marital relationship then falls off dramatically. "Many people," he says, "operate sexually in the beginning of a relationship from a 'should' perspective — for example, I 'should' be selfless, I 'should' be highly aroused. Then, after a while, people like this get married and feel more comfortable in the relationship and their natural bent about sex comes out. 'Whew! I don't have to push myself so hard anymore,' they think, and sexual activity falls off. For some of them sex may not really be a very important thing."

In a published roundtable discussion, Dr. Martin Goldberg, current director of the Marriage Council of Philadelphia, told the following anecdote, which illustrates how a "should" perspective operated in one case.

A number of years ago I was seeing a young lady in psychotherapy. In the course of treatment she married. After a number of months passed, I asked her how the marriage was progressing. She said she had only one complaint. The amount of sexual intercourse that her husband wanted was excessive for her. They were having intercourse every night. However, she didn't feel comfortable in saying anything to him so she complied with her husband's overtures.

I asked her to have her husband come in to see me. I approached him indirectly, saying, "I understand that you and your wife are really doing very well sexually, at least in terms of frequency." And he said with a big smile, "That's right. We're having sex every night." I then said, using a bit of fabrication, "That's remarkable. You know that most people have intercourse only twice a week" — which is true if you average everybody, but it isn't necessarily true for a couple that's newly married. He sat back in his chair with a tremendous look of relief on his face and said, "Is that right? You know, twice a week would be plenty for me but I have been hearing a lot from the guys at the office and I got the feeling that I'm supposed to be doing it every night."

Other theories as to why sexual intensity fizzles have to do with what happens as a couple starts to live together. "There is a period of intense romantic courtship," says Dr. Helen Singer Kaplan, "then there is a consummation of the relationship. It is still very hot, very exciting, and very romantic for a few years, and this can last, albeit at a less intense level; but in some marriages, even if it is a very good, loving, cooperative relationship — a good partnership — they are not really a couple anymore. They become a pseudo-couple who give the appearance of being a couple. They are more like business partners or very good friends. They are not really that romantically interested in each other. The pulse no longer quickens when they see each other at the end of the day. An external network holds them together, but the internal bonds are not that strong."

Dr. Joshua Golden has his own explanation of the living-together process: "A lot of things are likely to happen when you get married. In addition to seeing your spouse now as potentially a parent, he or she is also the person you fight with over the cap not being put back on the toothpaste and how much money is going to be spent and whether you keep the light on at night or not. A lot of things happen all at the same time when you get married and that is what makes it very difficult."

The simmering-down process varies, of course, from couple to couple, but everyone seems to agree that in almost all marriages it is inevitable in the early years — and normal, provided that sexual interest continues. "Two healthy people living together, even if they no longer have a bond of high romance, should still feel desire for each other," says Dr. Kaplan.

"One characteristic of sex as it goes on in a relationship," says Dr. Golden, "is that people are less likely to be concerned with quantity and become more concerned with quality — another reason why it tends to be less frequent as you have more experience with it."

The problem is that many couples are not prepared for the normal changes that occur. "Most of us see it as if something is wrong," says Dr. Golden. "We become disappointed or fearful because we have no understanding of the natural process in marriage. People don't recognize that what they are experiencing is not abnormal but rather is part of the normal process."

"There is very little sex education in regard to what happens after marriage, throughout the entire life cycle," agrees Dr. Roman Anshin, clinical associate professor of psychiatry at the University of Southern California School of Medicine.

"Romantic love lasts about two years, but in movies it is shown as lasting forever," notes Dr. Lief. "We are brought up with the idea that it will last forever. That's why it is a rude awakening when it doesn't."

Couples today who have a long love history with various partners before marriage may have a particularly tough time, according to Dr. Gayla Margolin, an associate professor of psychology at the University of Southern California. "I think the simmering-down process is hardest for people who have been in and out of a lot of relationships and are used to a lot of initial sexual highs," she says. "When things sort of calm down, they think something is wrong. There are a lot of people in their thirties and forties today who have been in a lot of intense relationships and they get used to that intensity. They aren't used to the intensity dying."

Another thing that many couples are unprepared for is the ebb and flow of sex that occurs throughout a relationship. People tend to think of good sex as being a constant. "If it is really good," they think, "I should always be horny and the sex should always be terrific." The truth is, the sexual aspects of the relationship are affected by the rest of a couple's life together — by crises, tension, fatigue, worries, jobs, money, illness, anger, depression, lack of privacy, and a myriad of distractions of various kinds. One of the things a new couple has to get used to in marriage is that there will be times when interest and even responsivity will fall, and there will be other times when passion will flare up again and burn brightly before simmering down once more. For the most part, in a "normal," happy marriage, sex will be nice but not great.

Dr. Kaplan also mentions what she finds to be a relatively frequent occurrence among women who "save" sex for marriage. Despite the so-called sexual revolution, a good number of these women still exist. The noted sex researcher John Gagnon has estimated that one-third of the females in the United States who marry are sexually inexperienced.

"A woman like this often has had tremendous desire in the preliminaries," says Dr. Kaplan. "But the first time she has intercourse, she turns off. Permanently."

"Often young women expect their first sexual intercourse to be a major success, and are profoundly disappointed by pain, ineptitude, and the like," writes John Gagnon. "If the mark of an early unsuccessful experience is not washed out by later, more successful practice, a woman may retain her first impression and find future sex unpleasant."

Dr. Golden comments that "in the natural history of sex in marriage, at the time when passion and excitement are greatest, we are ordinarily most ignorant (assuming most of us tend to marry relatively early in our sexual careers). That's changing somewhat and I think it is beneficial, but for almost everyone of my generation and for most people of the current generation, the initial experience with intercourse is disappointing: it doesn't match their expectations."

Dr. Golden thinks it would be helpful if couples would approach each other with the following attitude: "Although we are attracted to each other, don't expect too much in the beginning. Sex probably won't work well the first time, or two or three. In fact it may take us several weeks or months before we get to the point where we can reliably count on our parts to work and find pleasure in it. But if we are willing to struggle with it for the length of time necessary to learn enough about each other, it should be pretty good in a few weeks."

"I think if people communicated in this way," he explains, "they would not be disappointed by their experiences, nor would they be so likely to think there is something wrong with them and suffer silently."

Unfortunately, in early marriage, if new spouses are not able to reach a climax, or suffer from other sexual problems, sometimes they keep the resulting sense of failure or disappointment to themselves rather than try to communicate and work at the problem jointly. Because they don't address the problem directly, they end up with an unfulfilling sex life that may continue to be unsatisfactory for the rest of their marriage.

"If a couple is committed to the relationship and they can learn to trust one another and talk about sex, as well as other things, then they'll do just fine," says Dr. Golden. "Unfortunately," he adds, "for many people it's considered wrong to talk about sex. It's considered wrong to tell your partner what to do or be told by your partner what to do."

If inexperience isn't an issue, there may be others. Sometimes, for instance, the husband starts getting anxious about his ability to keep performing sexually in the consistent way that he imagines marriage demands. Or a sexual dysfunction that one or both partners ignored or hoped would get better upon marriage looms larger. As the couple settles into domestic life, the sexual problem can no longer be overlooked or the couple recognizes that it is not going to be cured by marriage after all: the premature ejaculation persists; the impotence does not go away; the wife, no matter what her husband does, rarely, if ever, achieves orgasm.

It should be noted that new wives have been found in various surveys in the past to have the lowest rates of orgasm of all married women. Although the rates have probably increased somewhat in recent years, Kinsey's finding that one-quarter of the wives in his survey had not had an orgasm in the first year of marriage is still pertinent. Morton Hunt mentions in *Sexual Behavior in the 1970's* that the younger women in his survey were having more orgasms than women thirty or forty years ago, but that they were still not as orgasmic as older women. Most experts agree that women flower later than men sexually. Even though coital rates drop as the marriage progresses, the female orgasm rate tends to increase.

INCOMPATIBILITIES

In addition to the sexual dysfunctions a young couple may have to face, other kinds of incompatibilities that may not have surfaced during courtship can turn up in the early part of the marriage.

"As sexual honeymoons end, idiosyncrasies, physical problems, and small repulsions may appear," says Dr. Anshin. A wife may suddenly find her husband's habit of coming to bed in his boxer shorts abhorrent. A man may find that strands of his wife's hair on the bathroom sink are a turn-off as he prepares for bed. One woman described "going crazy" after three weeks of marriage because her husband always threw the pillows onto the floor in the early stages of lovemaking. "I kept worrying that my new pillowcases would get dirty on the bare floor. I hadn't chosen a rug for the bedroom yet. I also started reacting badly to what I began to see as an obsessive ritual on his part." Another wife remembers her husband not wanting to cuddle her anymore in the early days of their marriage because he found her body temperature was too hot for his taste.

One partner may want sex more often than the other; one may want to experiment more than the other; one may like sex at the end of the day while the other prefers it in the morning. Statistical and clinical evidence indicates that a sexual disparity is likely to exist based on gender alone. "A young man's sex drive is usually much higher than his wife's," explains Dr. Helen Singer Kaplan. "In young couples it is often the husband who doesn't feel as if he is getting enough sex. He may want sex every night, while she may want to be left alone once in a while."

Sexual patterns, in general, get set — sometimes in stone — within the first year or two, around a variety of issues: Does each partner feel free to initiate sex or does it become the husband's role only? Is the wife able to refuse sex if she isn't in the mood or does she always go along with her husband's desires? Will a husband insist upon sex even if his wife is not in the mood? Will sex be used as reward or punishment for matters that are not sexual? Will the couple try to conduct their sex life as a thing apart from the rest of their relationship — will they have sex routinely whether they are mad or glad, happy or sad with each other? Will they become inhibited within marriage so that a formerly free expression of sexuality becomes ritualized into only one or two positions and only at certain predictable times? All of these issues, often in an unspoken way, are settled very early in a marriage.

Other sexual concerns in the early part of married life often have to do with reproduction. Birth control choices, fear of unwanted pregnancy, and inability to conceive can all interfere with the full expression of sexuality. The National Fertility Studies found that sexual frequency rises or falls according to the method of contraception employed by the couple: Higher frequency rates correlate with the surer methods of contraception, such as the pill. The riskier the birth control method, the less sex a couple has; those using the rhythm method or douches showed the lowest rates of intercourse.

Couples who do not fear pregnancy — those who decide to have a baby and abandon contraception altogether — have the highest coital rates of all in early marriage.

The need to find a balance between work and the love relationship comes to the fore, perhaps for the first time since the couple met, soon after the wedding. A married person must learn to juggle marriage and a career without neglecting either — a balancing act that many spouses fail to master. They often end up giving too much time and priority to a job, creating resentment in their mate that could easily reverberate in the bedroom. Or they may sacrifice career goals for the sake of the marital relationship. Generally, it is women more than men who consciously or unconsciously start to give their family relationships priority over their career upon marriage.

Companionship — shared activities versus independent ones — also starts to become an issue for the couple who did everything together during courtship. Sociologists have found that companionship is usually highest in this early stage of marriage and that it gradually disintegrates as the marriage progresses. This is true of communication as well. Researcher Harold Feldman at Cornell University found that newlyweds talk to each other more now than they will later on; typically, marital communication dries up after the first stage of marriage.

These are significant matters in terms of sex. If, as most important surveys indicate, sex declines more and more during each succeeding decade of marriage (more than the biological decline due to aging warrants), a major contributing factor may be that the couple no longer enjoys either regular companionship or good communication. As husband and wife grow more distant from one another, there is a great tendency for sex to cool off also.

It is in this first stage of marriage, too, that the limitations of one's own personality in terms of sex are faced, perhaps for the first time. Marriage is the surest test of whether we have the capacity to integrate sex and love over the long haul.

Dr. Otto Kernberg classifies human beings along a continuum in this regard. Starting at one end, there is the mature individual who has the ability both to enter into emotional relationships of depth and to fully enjoy sex without guilt with a long-term love partner. Sex and love continue to be fine and fun in marriage for a person like this.

At the second stage along the continuum is the person stuck at the Oedipal stage of development. Spouses like this are capable of having very good emotional relationships but may soon become inhibited sexually in marriage. They suffer from very strict consciences, which prohibit them from fully enjoying themselves sexually. Dr. Kernberg says these individuals are ideal candidates for psychoanalysis, where the Oedipal problems are unraveled, consciences become less strict, and sexual freedom becomes possible. He says, too, that people like this often do very well in sex therapy because they respond positively to a person in authority — the sex therapist — giving them permission to enjoy themselves sexually.

The third kind of person along the continuum may be uninhibited sexually but is unable to relate in a sustained, deep way, in or out of marriage. For such a person, sex becomes "a substitute for relating emotionally," according to Dr. Kernberg. People like this are stuck at a very early, infantile stage of development. "They have trouble having an integrated concept of themselves or others," says Dr. Kernberg. "They can't join loving and hating aspects of themselves or others." They have a poor sense of their own identity and tend to think of themselves and others as either all good or all bad instead of having a combination of better and worse qualities. They are naturally promiscuous, and if they marry, they generally have affairs, which frequently begin soon after the marriage.

Finally, at the opposite end of the spectrum from the mature individual who can be free sexually in a loving relationship is the person who has no capacity to have either sexual relations or emotional ones. Fortunately, people like this are relatively rare, and since they are isolated individuals, the question of whether marriage will reveal their capacity to combine sex and love never arises: they never marry.

The other levels of relating along the continuum show up, however, very quickly in the first few years of marriage and continue to influence the course of a couple's sex life all through their years together.

CHAPTER 3

Stage Two: Let's Make a Baby

THE EFFECTS of pregnancy on the sex life of a couple are significant and they often begin before conception. The husband and wife who decide it is time to have a child generally rev up their sex life — they have sex more frequently in an effort to bring about their wishes posthaste. If the pregnancy does not occur within a reasonable amount of time, however, a cloud begins to envelop their eroticism. They worry, first secretly, then out loud. Is there something wrong? Will the wife really be able to conceive? The couple begins to wonder if they are cursed by infertility.

If the desired pregnancy does not come about after a great deal of time, then, with panic and trepidation, the wife, often followed by her husband, generally rushes off to medical authorities to track down the reason. If no medical problem seems to be preventing pregnancy, a well-meaning doctor will often prescribe a routine of temperature taking to determine the woman's time of ovulation and will instruct the couple to have sex at the peak of her ability to conceive. It is at this time that disaster often over-takes formerly pleasant sex lives.

What happened to Jill and Jimmy is typical of what can occur. Jill, an account executive at an advertising agency in the East, was thirty-nine when she married Jimmy, a successful forty-six-year-old life insurance salesman. Since they both had married relatively late, they decided they wanted children right away.

After six months of trying to conceive, Jill talked over her desire for motherhood with her gynecologist and he suggested the temperature-taking routine. Unfortunately, Jimmy responded badly to Jill's rushing in every month after taking her tempera-ture and announcing: "It's the right time. We have to have sex to-night!" He called it "sex on order" and found not only that he couldn't perform, but that he resented the whole process so much he didn't even want to try. This led to accusations by Jill that he really didn't want a child, quarrels, and the end to what had pre-viously been a good sexual relationship. Intercourse according to a doctor's prescription instead of the partners' own inclinations can endanger a couple's sex life.

Barring this kind of complication, sex for the average couple trying to conceive will generally continue to be more frequent until the wife announces one day, "Darling, I have some news for you," and proceeds to tell her husband that she is pregnant. If the pregnancy is desired, there will be exultation over the impending parenthood, but the pregnancy will also have other, unexpected consequences: it will depress the couple's sex life — for some, for only nine months; for the majority, permanently.

Masters and Johnson researched the effect of pregnancy on sex-uality and reported that sexual frequency and satisfaction de-clined during the first three months, picked up somewhat between the third and sixth month, and took a nose dive between the sixth month and delivery. Other researchers — Solberg, Butler, and Wagner, in the *New England Journal of Medicine* — reported a de-cline in sexual interest and activity that continued from the be-ginning to the end, disputing the sexual oasis that Masters and Johnson found midway. The finding was confirmed by Tolor and

Di Grazia, who distributed a questionnaire to 161 women in varying stages of pregnancy and found a characteristic "decline both in sexual interest and activity as the pregnancy progressed." In 100 interviews, still another researcher, Pasini, confirmed the steady erosion of sex in the life of soon-to-be parents.

Solberg, Butler, and Wagner discovered not only that sexual interest and activity decreased, but that even when sex took place the majority of pregnant women had fewer orgasms during intercourse than they did before conception (although a small percentage reported an increase).

Sex may lose its thrill for the pregnant woman, but close physical contact becomes more important. Studies show that there is an increased desire simply to be held — probably a reflection of a growing feeling of vulnerability and a need for reassurance on the woman's part.

Women who have positive attitudes about their pregnancies have better sex lives than those with negative attitudes, according to Pasini. Masters and Johnson, and others, found that sexuality declined much more during first pregnancies than during subsequent ones.

Almost one-half of the subjects studied by Masters and Johnson continued to have low levels of sexual interest three months after giving birth. Another study found that the rate of intercourse was still lower than prepregnancy levels seven months after delivery. In addition, many women report more difficulty in achieving orgasm after having given birth than before.

REASONS FOR THE DECLINE

As the pregnancy progresses, a myriad of adjustments have to be made, many of which will have repercussions on the couple's sex life. A lot will depend on how the woman is feeling.

"Some women experience their pregnancies as the ultimate fulfillment," writes Dr. Alexander S. Rogawski, a training analyst at the Southern California Psychoanalytic Institute. "Their physical well-being and their enhanced self-image increase their sexual receptiveness and their loving attention to the needs of their husbands. Both spouses enjoy the freedom from concern with contraception, and some marriages experience renewed sexual vigor especially in the early stages of pregnancy." Physical symptoms such as nausea, heartburn, and fatigue during the first trimester often create the opposite effect, however: lack of sexual interest on her part, reluctance to disturb her on his.

The wife's changing physical appearance may affect each spouse adversely. She may feel physical discomfort during intercourse or not feel sexually attractive anymore, and act accordingly. A new worry may gnaw at her: "Women fear that the physical changes of pregnancy will temporarily or permanently interfere with their husbands who may turn to other women for excitement," says Dr. Rogawski. There is some justification for the fear. Masters and Johnson reported a good number of husbands who felt turned off by the ballooned-out abdomen or swollen legs of their pregnant wives.

Very important in terms of sex for both husband and wife is an unfounded but common fear: that lovemaking can hurt the developing embryo. Worry about harming the fetus may make either or both partners reluctant to engage in intercourse. Even when this fear does not prevent a couple from having sex, they may feel inhibited if, on some level, they feel that they no longer are alone. "Each sexual overture is a reminder of the growing baby present in the wife's body," says Dr. Berta Anagnoste.

Frequently, husbands feel sexually turned off to a pregnant wife without understanding why — which may make them feel guilty and create negative resonances in the relationship. Sam Bittman, coauthor of the book *Expectant Fathers,* has acknowledged that he lost sexual interest at one point during his wife's pregnancy. "It's a pretty frightening thing," he told a reporter for the *New York Times,* "and it has a ripple effect when the issue is not discussed with your spouse. Then everybody's threatened by it. My poor wife felt she was no longer sexually appealing to me. In fact, nothing could have been further from the truth. It's just that there were so many new feelings." The feelings that the father-to-be may be experiencing are often unconscious ones. He may be viewing his wife as a mother now that she is pregnant, identifying her on a subterranean level with his own mother or feeling the nonsexual kind of emotions a son is supposed to have toward his mother.

The wife may be grappling with similar unconscious reactions. She may be feeling motherly in her pregnancy and less sexual as a result. On the other hand, there are pregnant women who feel more erotic than usual, at least in early pregnancy. This is generally true for women in their second or third pregnancies rather than their first.

The pregnant wife may, at times, become anxious or preoccupied with her impending motherhood, worrying about her own safety or health, or the well-being or normalcy of the growing baby. "Almost all pregnant women have moments of anxiety or depression relating to concerns over motherhood," write Dr. Dennis Munjack and L. Jerome Oziel, Ph.D., of the Sexual Therapy and Marital Counseling Clinic at the University of Southern California Medical Center in Los Angeles. As suggested earlier, the wife may worry about being abandoned by her husband — and "not all the fears of pregnant women that they may be abandoned are without foundation," says Dr. Rogawski. "Some men, repelled by the physical or psychological changes in their wives or by the meaning their pregnancy has for them, do turn away and become involved with other women," he writes. "Some young men, unable to respond to expectant fatherhood as a new phase of personal development and a new opportunity for self-realization, see it as a trap interfering with their life plans. The sense of being caught in an inescapable dilemma," he continues, "combined with feelings of exclusion and estrangement from their wives, inhibits their enthusiasm for sexual intimacy and may lead to impulsive acts of infidelity with subsequent guilt and remorse."

In general, the wife's concern about her husband's reactions may trigger withdrawal reactions of her own. "Women who feel unsupported by an ununderstanding [sic] husband or who are preoccupied with concerns about the future become introspective and emotionally labile, and are given to mood swings," writes Dr. Rogawski. "They seem to withdraw emotionally from their husbands and show little sexual interest or appetite." This, of course, may make a husband still more resentful or distant.

Clearly, the issues discussed above could create a growing sense of estrangement between spouses who are expecting a baby. Indeed, such polarization often occurs, despite the common mythology that pregnancy is a time when couples grow closer. This, of course, does not mean that all couples draw apart. Many find pregnancy a time of joy and bonding. Pregnancy can be an acid test of the relationship. "Pregnancy and parenting in a good marriage brings people closer together," notes Dr. Harold Lief. "In a bad marriage it drives them apart."

Many doctors, including psychiatrists, have chided obstetricians in print for, as a matter of course, banning intercourse six weeks prior to delivery and six weeks after. These critics call the restriction unnecessary on a physical level and frequently destructive to the couple on an emotional one. "The traditional six-week period of abstinence before and after delivery, with its potentially damaging influence on the marriage, is . . . unnecessary," according to Dr. Rogawski. "Intercourse can be permitted until shortly before the due date, and again as soon after the delivery as the vagina is healed."

After delivery, postpartum vaginal dryness, the result of a sharp decline in estrogen levels, can last up to three months, and it may make intercourse so uncomfortable that the woman avoids coitus or loses sexual interest altogether. Alternatively, the man may misinterpret the lack of lubrication as sexual indifference on his wife's part. Husbands and wives should keep in mind that there may be a lack of natural vaginal lubrication at this time. The condition is temporary and self-curing, and until the dryness disappears, a water-soluble artificial lubricant can be used to alleviate any discomfort that may occur during intercourse.

Nursing mothers often have additional problems. Although it has been found that breast-feeding causes contractions of the uterus that speed up the healing process of a new mother, nursing may also, to her surprise, stimulate sexual desire. Many women feel guilty about the erotic feelings they experience during breast-feeding. Persistence of low estrogen levels throughout nursing may make intercourse difficult if genitals and breasts become overly sensitive. In addition, the nursing mother tends to retain extra weight gained during pregnancy longer than the woman who chooses not to breast-feed, or is apt to gain even more weight during this period. This may turn off a husband who is sensitive to physical appearances. Lactation, which frequently accompanies sexual arousal, can do the same.

Since breast-feeding duties cannot be shared, the nursing mother may feel particularly tired and overwhelmed by her new responsibilities and, as a result, say Munjack and Oziel, "resentful toward her husband." Resentment can translate itself into lack of interest in sex. One thirty-two-year-old woman remembered her experience as a new mother: "I felt that I was servicing everyone — the baby, then my husband. It got so I started to refuse sex just to reclaim my own body."

Dr. Joshua Golden notes that he frequently sees this kind of reaction. "There is ordinarily a great deal of energy that goes into care of an infant, particularly when you're nursing," he says. "A relatively common thing for women to say to me is that they have a feeling that their body is being used by other people. The baby is nursing on it, they have to get up and feed the baby and clean this and do that. When you are tired and you feel your body isn't your own, you are not necessarily eager to provide it for the pleasure of your husband. Or yourself. Of course," he adds, "other women feel differently about it. They feel, 'We have created this wonderful creature together,' and they feel more loving."

In some women, moreover, the scar from an episiotomy, the surgical opening made routinely these days to facilitate vaginal delivery, can cause pain or discomfort for up to six weeks after delivery and interfere with intercourse.

"Sometimes," conclude Munjack and Oziel, "sexual activity has been so disrupted by the pregnancy that couples may feel embarrassed and unsure when attempting to resume coitus. The partners sometimes have to go through an exploration and adjustment period all over again."

It is an adjustment period even more complicated than the first one, for it takes place with a disruptive third party in the home: the new baby.

CHAPTER 4

Stage Three:
And Now We're a Family

THE ARRIVAL of a child may be a blessing to a couple in many ways, but sex is frequently not one of them. Studies reveal that childless couples have considerably more sex than parents do. Since sex and other aspects of the marriage are inextricably interwoven, it is significant that, according to various studies, marital satisfaction, in general, declines from the time the first baby is born to the time the last child leaves home. Women, in particular, report a lot of negative feelings about their marriages during the child-rearing years. Karen Renne, who studied a representative population of a large West Coast metropolitan area, found that "contrary to popular belief, childless marriages are more satisfactory than others."

As mentioned earlier, some couples reach a sexual impasse, even before the arrival of the child, during the wife's pregnancy. "In some marriages the sexual relationship between the couple is not reestablished after delivery," say Munjack and Oziel. Dr. Martin Goldberg, in an article in *Medical Aspects of Human Sexual-*

ity, talks about "the pattern so many couples fall into: having once gotten out of the habit of a good sexual relationship, they allowed all sorts of reasons — good, bad, and indifferent — and all sorts of alibis and rationalizations to prevent them from resuming an active sexual life."

"For many women, the years of childrearing are years of relatively low sexual desire," writes Dr. David Kupfer in the same journal. Data from the United States National Fertility Studies reveal that women in the postpartum period have some of the lowest rates of intercourse in marriage. And sociologist William James, in a study of middle-class college-educated women, found that in the nine pregnant women among his subjects, "the arrival of babies in all nine cases seemed to depress (apparently permanently) their parents' coital rates."

It is a relatively frequent phenomenon for a new father to react to his own baby as a rival and to feel as if his position in the marriage has been usurped. The hidden rage he feels may make him withdraw sexually and emotionally from his wife, who he sees as cheating him of love and attention. Wives, on the other hand, often become resentful and turn off if they feel that their husbands don't share enough in child-rearing duties. They may also react this way when angered by a new emotional coolness or preoccupation with other matters that they sense in their husbands. Disenchantment with a mate, for women, according to sociologist Alice Rossi, often begins with the arrival of children, although for men it typically starts even earlier.

A working wife may find herself more conflicted than she anticipated — preoccupied and guilty about returning to work and leaving the child in the care of strangers — or trapped and resentful if she decides to give up her career for a while and stay home with the baby. The husband may find himself attacking his career with a vengeance now that he has shouldered the responsibilities of fatherhood. He may also deal with his ambivalent feelings about his child by starting to overwork. If he devotes more time and attention to work and less to his wife, she often feels neglected or emotionally abandoned at a time when, overburdened and feeling vulnerable, she is in greater need of his help and emotional support. Bad feelings and misunderstandings, which reverberate in their sex life, frequently arise between spouses over these issues during the early child-rearing years.

Another factor that can work against good sex once children are on the scene is the fact that intercourse often begins to take place only at night, after the infant has been put to bed. As a result, playfulness and spontaneity get lost. The mother may also be distracted during sex, participating with one ear cocked for sounds from her baby. Crying and even cooing or gurgling can ruin things for one or both parents. The sound of children in the background, whatever their age, may interfere with erotic fantasies that enrich sex.

As the child grows, parental sexual inhibitions often increase. Parents frequently worry that the child will overhear them making love or will barge into the bedroom. "Men and women who fondle each other sexually in the privacy of their home without children commonly restrict such intimacies to the bedroom when children are around," writes sex researcher John Gagnon in his book *Human Sexualities*. Sex tends to become more and more ritualized once it becomes restricted to only after the children are asleep and only in the bedroom.

Actions that used to rev up sex in other ways are often stripped away by the arrival of children, too. "Children also take up time, space, and money formerly used for the pleasures of the couple," explains Gagnon. "Parents find that they cannot take vacations or go away as easily. Vacations were erotic and pleasurable events and allowed sex to be 'like it was before marriage,' exciting and detached from daily responsibility. Having sex with a spouse somewhere other than the bedroom also served to increase the erotic character of the relationship."

The lack of spontaneity or opportunities for sexual renewal, fear of being overheard or intruded upon during lovemaking as the child grows older, the growing disenchantment with each other that is common between the partners (as pointed out by various studies), the erosion of both communication and companionship once children are on the scene (also revealed by studies), and disputes that frequently arise over child-rearing methods all may account for Jay Mancini and Dennis Orthner's findings: all through the child-rearing years, the desire for sex declined among husbands and wives, who expressed a preference for a variety of other kinds of activities instead.

Apparently, the first child has the greatest adverse impact upon the sex life of parents. Statistical evidence indicates that parents who have only one child have sex less frequently than parents with two, three, or more children. It seems that it takes a while to get the hang of parenthood and combine it, in some reasonable manner, with sex.

THE AGE-THIRTY CRISIS

Other things besides children intrude upon the couple's sex life during the early child-rearing years — and throughout the other stages of their married life. At the same time that the spouses jointly experience potential crisis points such as pregnancy and the birth of children that can impair sexuality, they are also undergoing periodic individual crises, at approximately ten-year intervals, during transition periods from one stage of life to another.

If husband and wife marry at traditional ages — at the beginning of their twenties — they can expect to go through the so-called age-thirty crisis while they are still raising young children. The adult crisis at thirty is really what the famous seven-year itch is all about. It is then that the sense of immortality common to young people begins to wear off. The passage of years is felt as threatening for the first time. "I am getting old" becomes a mental refrain. With this in mind, spouses start to reevaluate themselves, their goals, their marriages.

Husbands often become much more openly critical of their wives. Wives become more dissatisfied with their husbands. Eleanore Luckey studied couples who had been married an average of seven years and found that they described their mates in less and less favorable terms as time went by.

The age-thirty crisis period is marked by a restlessness. There is a desire to expand horizons: often, in the early thirties, people begin to think of their present life as too confining. Husbands married to women who stay at home and take care of the children may start to think of their wives — and their own lives with them — as boring or stultifying, particularly as they eye career women who seem to be more interesting or exciting by contrast.

"You see this very often," says Dr. Lief, "in marriages where both partners started out in professional careers, but the wife has given up hers to rear one or two children and she's not growing intellectually at the same pace as he is. If she has never had a career," he adds, "this is even more true. He finds her dull and boring, which in essence means that his interests are not hers. Her sense of femininity is threatened, so both of them may act out their frustrations in adulterous sexual relations. He does so because he is bored with his wife, and she does so because she needs reassurance about her femininity."

Wives at this time often become very unhappy with their husband's lack of tenderness, emotional expression and communication — all of which have been drying up throughout the period of early parenthood. Or they may increasingly nurse a sense of loneliness and feeling of deprivation: they brood over not being nurtured properly, and over the man's neglect of the family in favor of work. A wife at this stage often looks back nostalgically on courtship and the days that one woman wistfully calls "B.C." (before children). Her husband used to talk to her and want to be with her then. He used to express affection. Where has the man she married gone? she wonders.

As during pregnancy, there is often a gnawing fear on a wife's part that her husband may abandon her, particularly if he is becoming more and more critical or aloof. If she has stayed at home, she is probably feeling unable to take care of herself; studies reveal that housewives feel more dependent and less self-assured with the passage of time. Her insecurities may fuel her concern about being left on her own. What she feels about herself may be in direct contrast to her husband's growing sense of self-esteem, which has been augmented by his accomplishments in the workplace. At this stage in life, many men feel more self-confident than they did as young bridegrooms.

Wives who are busy tending to their growing children may resent husbands who start to pressure them to go back to school or get a job. "Curiously, we sometimes also see the husband pushing the woman into a dual career," Dr. Lief remarks. "He's bought a distorted notion about women's liberation, which makes him denigrate rather than respect the homemaker role." The wife often thinks that she is already doing plenty and becomes resentful, or she interprets her husband's pressure as a desire to get rid of her and becomes insecure.

Other mothers take a different tack and begin themselves to wonder about personal fulfillment. They may have dreamed originally that all they ever needed to be perfectly content was love, marriage, and motherhood, but once they have accomplished these goals they discover that life, after all, does not begin and end with housework, cooking, and child rearing. They start to consider going back to school or work. Wives who knew all along that they were only going to spend the first few child-rearing years at home start to put into motion their original plans to return to work.

Although many husbands support their wife's career wishes, others fight them. A large group are openly in favor of the wife "doing something with herself" but inwardly feel threatened and as a result either unconsciously sabotage the wife's efforts or send out confusing double messages. This may create resentment or paralysis if the wife is herself ambivalent about returning to work.

Working couples without children, on the other hand, may start to feel a lack in their life: they may miss the roots that children provide. They often begin to think seriously at this time about starting to raise a family. This can sometimes become a source of disagreement.

As you enter your thirties, concern about not making your mark in a career may surface strongly as well, starting you on a path of renewed effort in the workplace over the next decade. Or, you may start to question whether you have embarked on the right career after all.

When the age-thirty crisis manifests itself, increasing internal dissatisfaction or growing disaffection between husband and wife may show up in the bedroom. "In the context of such marital strains you see all kinds of sexual problems," notes Dr. Lief. "Men often become impotent. Women who have been orgasmic early in the marriage no longer are. Women around the age of thirty suddenly don't get 'turned on' to their husbands. There's a wall that's built up because the husband fails to appreciate her or doesn't meet her expectations. Similarly, the husband may feel that his wife is not fulfilling his hopes. There is a decrease in sexual interest, and relations become infrequent and unenthusiastic."

Those who married early and without much previous sexual experience may begin to feel that they have missed out on something. The thought "I need more sexual experience" buzzes in their heads. Afflicted with the seven-year itch, some scratch it by experimenting with an extramarital affair or two (or more).

"We find a lot of extramarital sex going on at this time," according to Dr. Lief, "almost as if people are testing themselves in other relationships that will give them more pleasure; they wonder if somebody else will be a better companion, as well as a lover. They begin to ask if their spouse is the person they want to spend the rest of their life with."

Others start to want to change things sexually at home and put pressure on a mate to be more daring, effective, or provocative. "Why don't you wear low-cut black nightgowns that show something!" one husband kept hollering at his modest, inhibited wife. A thirty-one-year-old wife in the Southwest, feeling a typical desire to make sex better at this stage in life, finally confessed to her husband that his technique had been inadequate all along. She had been faking orgasms and she wanted him to do things differently so that she could climax genuinely. He was devastated by her revelation but tried to do what she wanted. When she felt that his efforts to improve his performance weren't good enough, she started having an affair with a man with whom she found sex to be exciting and fulfilling. She let her husband know about the affair. She refused to give up her lover, her husband became impotent with her, and the couple finally separated.

Divorce all too often seems the answer to restlessness, dissatisfaction, and the desire to try things a different way. According to the National Center for Health Statistics, more marriages break up during this stage of life — at the age of thirty for women and thirty-three for men — than at any other time.

"In the past people were pleased just to make ends meet and be responsible parents. Now there are new goals — personal actualization or fulfillment, to use the jargon of the day," Dr. Lief told an interviewer. "Even though their devotion as parents may be no less than a generation before, they are more apt to separate and divorce in order to pursue self-centered concerns."

Another common response to the malaise that attacks partners around age thirty is to see it — the questioning of one's own goals, the irritations toward a spouse or life-style, the desire to change things or break out — as a sexual matter. Rather than fully examine internal problems or trouble in the relationship, one or both spouses concentrate on sex instead. Marriage and sex therapists are accustomed to couples who come in and blame sex for all their problems these days. "If only sex were better," these patients think, "everything else would be, too." Occasionally, sexual technique or some inhibition does, indeed, turn out to be the problem, but more often the couple exhibiting the seven-year-itch, age-thirty, first-decade-of-marriage symptoms has to be made aware that they are making sex a symbolic scapegoat for other dissatisfactions that lurk either within the individual partners or in the relationship.

It is important for couples to recognize the nature of the restlessness that overtakes them approximately ten years into the marriage. If the partners understand that a common crisis of adult development is taking place, the realization can keep them from blaming each other, or sex, for the unhappiness or restlessness they feel.

Indeed, the age-thirty crisis can be looked upon as an opportunity for partners to renew communications that may have dried up. It can actually improve a marriage to talk over negative feelings with one another and modify the relationship in terms of new individual needs. Experts agree that the problems, sexual and otherwise, that typically crop up as individuals move from one period of life to another need not be disastrous. Times of questioning and summing up present opportunities for growth, both for the marriage relationship itself and for the individuals within it.

It is also crucial at this time of life for parents of young children to make time for the husband-wife relationship — and for sex — in the midst of all the career and child-rearing tasks that make this such a busy period of marriage. Weekends away without the children, a lock on the bedroom door, baby-sitters at least once a week so that mother and father can find each other again on "dates," time alone at the end of the day to discuss feelings as well as events — all can help husband and wife keep in touch and preserve a sense of communion and romance that fosters sex even when parenthood seems to demand all their energy and attention.

CHAPTER 5

Stage Four:
Muddling Around in the Middle

WHATEVER PROBLEMS that raising young children presented, they often seem preferable, in retrospect, to what a couple has to face when their children become adolescents. According to a well-known study by Harold Feldman at Cornell University, the teenage years are the pits — the worst time in the entire marriage, as far as parents are concerned. Marital happiness and satisfaction dip to an all-time low.

Husbands and wives at this time, of course, are not only living in a combat zone with their budding teenagers, they are coming to grips with a sense of their own decline as birthdays catapult them into their forties and middle age. Sex is often the victim of the stresses that abound at this time of life. Ellen Frank, Carol Anderson, and Debra Rubinstein found in their study of 100 married couples that lack of desire peaked for husbands and wives when they were in their forties; almost a quarter of the men and one-third of the women suffered from it.

A feeling of just how bad things can get comes from H. J. Eysenck, who, in 1977, reported that the wives in one of his studies placed sex near the very bottom of a list of activities that were a source of pleasure — below, if you'd believe it, snoozing and doing housework. Watching television was also on the wives' list of better alternatives, but this did not come as a surprise: Dr. Harold Lief has identified television viewing as one of the common patterns in modern life that detract from the sexual relationship throughout marriage.

If wives would rather nap or wash a kitchen floor, it may be because many of them are unhappy with the quality of their sex lives in middle age. Researchers in a study published in 1955 reported that women in their forties often complained about the inadequacy of their husbands as sex partners. By inadequate, these women perhaps meant that their husband's technique was faulty; it is possible that more men today engage in lengthy foreplay and know about clitoral orgasms. Nevertheless, even in the 1980s, sex therapists still find many men — and women — who could use a good sex education.

Inadequate could also mean not enough sex. Statistics reveal that by middle age, for the average couple, sex has declined considerably from the early days of marriage. Frequency falls by roughly 50 percent between the ages of twenty and forty — which may say more about the average middle-aged husband than it does about his wife. Even in the liberated 1980s, experts agree that the rate of intercourse in marriage is generally controlled by the husband, the partner who usually initiates sex. Statistics and studies in the past have not told a great deal about women's sexual capacity as they age. According to many sex therapists, however, clinical evidence now suggests that while a husband's interest declines, the contemporary middle-aged woman's may actually increase.

"I find when middle-aged couples come in," says Dr. Lief, "it's often the wife who wants more sex and the husband who wants less. Men get less interested; women get more into it."

"When women are young, they have the lowest orgasm frequencies," explains Dr. Helen Singer Kaplan, "but women in their thirties and forties can attain orgasm with greater ease."

Dr. Raul Schiavi, who heads the sexuality program at Mount Sinai Medical Center in New York, describes the situation between husbands and wives at this stage of life — "women becoming more excited and men feeling less desire" — as "an irony of middle age." Some of the disparity may have biological roots. Data reveal that, on average, men peak sexually around the age of eighteen, whereas women do so in their late thirties or early forties. Women, once they reach their sexual peak, are capable of maintaining it into old age, while men's capacity steadily declines.

Experts maintain, though, that the decrease in sexual activity in men, reflected in marital coital rates, is only partly due to biology and the aging process. "The decrease may derive from many things," say John Gagnon and William Simon, who note in *Sexual Conduct* that middle-class men have more sex in marriage than lower-class ones. They suspect that this is partly due to the lack of prestige marital sex has among males in the lower classes, where "scoring" and extramarital affairs, rather than monogamy, earn a man points among his peers. "But even for the middle-class male," say Gagnon and Simon, "sexual activity declines in amounts that cannot exclusively be accounted for by changes in the organism."

Women are sexual late bloomers because of the way they are socialized in our society. Early pressure to be nonsexual means, say Gagnon and Simon, that they "require longer periods of time to either become de-inhibited or to learn to be sexual — depending on your point of view."

Some of the dissatisfaction in the marriage that comes to a head when there are adolescents at home may have as much to do with women blooming and men declining — the disparity of sexual needs that crop up between some husbands and wives at this time of life — as it does with teenagers who make their parents' lives miserable. This is not to let adolescents off the hook, however. They can create a lot of stress for each parent individually, as well as causing trouble between Mom and Dad. Much of the tension they create is unwitting, simply built into the fact that they are teenagers bursting with new sexuality and fresh, young good looks while their parents are beginning to feel and perhaps look a little shopworn.

A father may be particularly vulnerable to the implicit contrast in sexual capabilities that exists between him and his son. There is the kid, on one hand, with practically a constant erection — the father remembers very well what it was like at his son's age. And there is his father — his erections are much less frequent, his desire for sex with his wife is diminishing, it may take him much longer to get excited, and he has heard about impotence occurring as a man grows older. He wonders whether the day when he will no longer be able to "get it up" is around the corner. His son's bursting sexuality acts as a constant reminder of his own waning virility and may give rise to competitive feelings. Many fathers of teenage sons start affairs at this time of life, unconsciously motivated by the necessity to show that they are not out of the sexual running yet. They may also be fired up by their fantasies of what the son is doing with his cute little girlfriends. The fathers' partners in adultery are frequently much younger women who make them feel young again and who serve as symbols that the men are still attractive and sexy.

Feelings of competition are frequently a source of other kinds of direct trouble between father and son. A father may try to cut his rival-son down by making disparaging remarks. He may be overly critical of him or may clash with him repeatedly in a growing war as he tries to show through harsh displays of authority that he is still the one in charge. The son, of course, resents it and fights back. The war between father and son can grow especially bitter during adolescence, when rivalry is an issue. It may cause great consternation for the mother and, often, dissension between the spouses that results in sexual problems or increasing alienation, sexual and otherwise.

A mother may also feel competitive with her daughter. She might turn away from her mirror, where she has been ruefully observing a new wrinkle and a few more gray hairs, to see her fresh-faced and blooming girl fast turning into an attractive young woman. Her daughter's newly formed breasts are firm. The mother thinks her own are sagging. Mother finds her daughter a daily reminder of her own fading looks. She, too, may embark on an extramarital affair that makes her feel excited, young, and desirable again. "I suddenly had fresh color in my face," one forty-year-old mother reminisced about the start of her affair. "My friends wanted to know if I had a new kind of makeup. I didn't. I just had Frank."

Fathers often have a hard time relating to their teenage daughters because of sexual issues. A father may feel uncomfortable in his daughter's presence because, either consciously or unconsciously, he feels sexually attracted to her now that she is growing into womanhood. Again the antidote may be to act out — to have an affair, generally with a young woman. Sometimes fathers handle their own hidden sexual interest obliquely by jealously guarding a daughter's "virtue." They may become overly strict with their daughter, and closely monitor her leisure activities. They may complain that she wears too much makeup or that she dresses like a tramp. They may insist that she come home early every night, even from all-girl gatherings.

Some fathers, in denying or suppressing their sexual attraction to their daughter, end up denying all of their sexual feelings and lose their libido completely. Occasionally, a father will have a mock love affair with his daughter. He will start paying a great deal of attention to her, and less attention to his wife — which can cause trouble in the marriage.

Many more fathers back off: they stay away from home and have less and less to do with their teenage daughter. Not only does the daughter feel inexplicably rejected at this time, but the wife may feel that way, too. The wife does not understand the dynamics. All she knows is that her husband is not around very much anymore. She may suspect that he is having an affair — as many fathers do — although in reality he may have simply retreated from his sexy-looking daughter into a heavier work load, into hanging out more with male companions, or into a health club where he works out religiously.

Men, in particular, sometimes become fearful of death in middle age and start to monitor their bodies or become hypochondriacs. The specter of a heart attack hangs over them. Some, at the same time that they work out ferociously at the health club or start to play tennis every day to stay fit, stay away from sex as a way of conserving their energies.

Both partners may automatically "give up" when they hit middle age. "They think they are over the hill and act that way," says Dr. Lief. They gain weight, develop potbellies and bulges, and leave sex to the kids. "Lack of sexual desire is a frequent phenomenon of midlife," according to Dr. Lief.

When children reach adolescence, parents may become, in essence, teenagers again themselves. They may act out conflicts left over from their own teenage years — for instance, by rebelling against a spouse that they feel is restricting them in life as a parent once did. Plenty of divorces occur at this stage of life because one partner suddenly feels an urgent need for "freedom." Some middle-aged spouses want to experiment sexually, just as they did at adolescence — which sometimes results in a frantic round of promiscuity, or at least an affair.

Beyond the sexual overtones that emerge during a child's adolescence, parents often have difficulty contending with the behavior of adolescents.

Dr. Lief explains that many parents "feel a kind of helplessness coping with teenagers. Obviously, kids can cause conflict. You see situations where the teenager assumes the power in the house. He becomes the controlling influence and parents give up their parental roles. They want to be buddies with the kids, or they're very inconsistent. One time they are very permissive, the next day very authoritarian," Dr. Lief notes, "so the kids never know what to expect and the parents are fighting constantly about child rearing. The tensions about not knowing how to behave as parents frequently spill over into a couple's sex life."

Even when parenting is not so confusing — when mother and father, relatively united, can steer a calmer, more consistent course through the teenage years — life is rarely easy. The normal teenager partially forges his own identity at the parents' expense, by constantly challenging their authority and values. Adolescents can be surly, noisy, messy, defiant. They at times create, for parents, hassles, anxieties, and anger. If all this doesn't cause trouble in the marriage, it at least makes the home a tension-filled place. Sex often withers amid the storm that surrounds parents who are trying to raise teenagers. Moreover, the knowledge that their teenage children know about sex often inhibits parents from having it, at least when the kids are around.

Yet another factor may enervate the spouses and complicate life in the middle years: aging parents may increasingly require more attention from their adult children. Some couples in this stage of life find themselves caught between demanding or sickly parents and rebelling teenagers — pulled at on all sides. The death of a parent can make middle-aged adults, who are usually all too aware that time is growing short, even more conscious of their own mortality: another generation no longer stands between them and death. For some, however, the parent's death may act as liberation of sorts; they find they suddenly want to kick up their heels — Mom or Dad is not around anymore to disapprove.

A spouse who felt a lingering sense of dependency while the parent was still alive may transfer those dependency feelings onto a spouse once the parent is dead. The new emotional needs foisted upon the spouse may be very upsetting to the relationship if they remain. It is often at this time of life, anyway, that some mates become disgusted because they think that their partner remains immature.

The feeling that time is running out — one of the earmarks of the midlife crisis — causes many men and women to want to make their sex lives better before it is too late. A work-oriented person who kept postponing personal pleasure throughout youth may suddenly rush to fulfill his pleasure quota, including sexual pleasure, before it is too late.

Some middle-aged people feel increasingly dissatisfied with whatever may have been wrong all along. A spouse not being spontaneous or inventive enough, premature ejaculation, the inability to reach orgasm, impotence, infrequent sex, or sex used as reward or punishment may all, at this juncture, cause a crisis in the marriage. Pressure mounts to change things — sometimes with an "or else" tacked on.

Just before his recent death, Dr. Jay Mann, director of the Family Program of the Veterans' Administration Medical Center in Palo Alto, California, talked about experiences in his marital-therapy practice: "People who have been temporizing or settling for something sometimes get some new input somewhere. Their friends talk to them, or they read something, and they decide they want more, maybe more in the narrow sexual sphere. I remember one couple in their late forties. The wife had gone to a lecture on sex. She came to me and said, 'I realize there's a banquet out there, and we're starving.' " Dr. Helen Singer Kaplan says she has many middle-aged patients who feel that the request for sex therapy at this stage can be part of a rejuvenation for a couple. "They want sex to be better. It's part of a very constructive attitude."

Although mounting sexual dissatisfaction may bring couples into therapy in midlife, it can also lead them to have extramarital flings. Sometimes it's the other way around: affairs in some instances are the cause of new or increased sexual dissatisfaction with a partner. For example, a forty-three-year-old manager of a small business brought his wife to a therapist complaining that she was not sexually adventurous enough. He was threatening to leave his wife unless she could become more open and free. He had previously considered their sex life adequate.

Although his wife did not know about it before, in therapy it came out that he was having an affair with a co-worker, a young woman who made him feel young and vibrant again, and who introduced him to new sexual techniques. The affair made him realize what he had been missing and played into his concerns about aging. He did not want to grow old without getting more pleasure out of life. Luckily, the wife in this case was able to forgive her husband, to realize that it was also in her interests to change, and, with the help of a therapist, to give up some of her inhibitions. The couple's sex life improved considerably and the marriage was renewed.

Sometimes the discovery of an affair will bring hidden non-sexual problems into the open and push a couple into therapy, where they are helped. On the other hand, divorce is often thought to be the solution at this stage in the marriage.

In some cases, sexual problems start to surface at this time of life simply because the couple's children are no longer young. "People may marry for reasons other than sex, but later, after the children grow up, sex may become more important and turn into a problem," explains Dr. Roman Anshin.

In general, it is characteristic of the midlife crisis for one or both partners to reassess the marriage and ask, "Is this what I want for the rest of my life?" The answer to this and worries about aging, can, for some, lead to depression and subsequent loss of interest in sex. Dr. Anshin explains that "people are coming to grips with losses in middle age: the loss of omnipotence, giving up youthful fantasies, losses in one's job, losses in one's body — it is not the same body one had at eighteen."

Middle-aged husbands and wives also have to deal with the myth of impotence. Many men are mortally afraid that impotence is inevitable at this stage of life and will spell the end of their sexual career. If the fear is strong enough, it often becomes a self-fulfilling prophecy. One episode of erectile difficulty can be enough to cause such concern and panic that the next time sex is attempted, the tension ensures impotence again, which redoubles the terror, which creates more impotence, and so on.

A forty-four-year-old wife in San Francisco who had heard about men becoming impotent in middle age was sure that this was her husband's problem, and she remained sympathetic when he stopped wanting to have sex with her. She was enraged, however, when she discovered that impotence wasn't the culprit after all: It was another woman. Her husband had been having an affair.

Some men unconsciously use impotence to displace all the other feelings of loss that occur in middle age. One psychiatrist described it as a way to deny aging. The man attributes all his problems at this time of life to impotence and concentrates his efforts into finding a cure for it rather than having to deal with aging and the emotions associated with it. In this way he fails to admit or come to terms with the passage of time.

Sometimes impotence occurs as a man reaches midlife because neither he nor his wife understand the aging process. Many men — and sometimes their wives — have the unrealistic expectation that sexual performance will remain the same throughout married life. They fail to realize that as a man grows older he may need more direct stimulation of the penis to achieve an erection and that more time will be required between erections. Impotence can occur because a husband expects to have an erection merely at the thought of having sex or because he pushes himself to have another erection too soon after climaxing.

A middle-aged man also has a less urgent need to ejaculate than he did when he was younger — a change that many men who have had trouble with premature ejaculation find helpful. In general, men can often be better lovers in middle age because they are more able to take their time without the great urgency to ejaculate. They may be more able, emotionally and physically, to enjoy closeness and the emotional overtones of sex with a well-liked partner. Sex often becomes more of an expression of feelings in middle age, rather than the automatic release it was earlier, and it can be more gratifying for both partners as a result.

If this doesn't happen, the middle-aged wife may feel increasingly unhappy about the fact that she wants to make love, while all her husband seems to want is "sex" without tenderness. Women, through increased trust, self-confidence, or a loss of former inhibitions, are often able to initiate sex now, or to express needs that they formerly kept to themselves. This, too, can improve sex in midlife, unless the husband is threatened by his wife's new assertiveness.

Some couples largely abandon sex in middle age because, for a variety of reasons, outlined in the second part of this book, it has become deadeningly unimaginative, unspontaneous, inhibited, unexciting, monotonous, or boring. The feeling is, why bother? Although this is not true for everybody — and there are notable exceptions to it — some experts maintain that for the majority of husbands and wives in our culture, sex declines in importance at this stage in life.

John Gagnon and William Simon, in *Sexual Conduct,* character-ize the average marriage in the middle years as moving to a "nonsexual basis for stability and continuity." Other things, such as affection, respect, children, comfort, the history of the couple, and a sense of loyalty, replace passion as binding forces. "There are only a few periods in the life cycle at which there are high rates of sexual activity that is complicated by passion and high intensity of affective investment," say Gagnon and Simon. "These are usually adolescence in the male, the early and romantic years of marriage for both men and women, and the highly charged extramarital experiences that can be called affairs. Most of the time, sex is really a relatively docile beast."

CHAPTER 6

Stage Five:
When the Kids Leave Home

WHEN THE CHILDREN are finally grown and gone from the home, a crucial test of the marriage begins. For many couples, the departure of the children signals the happiest time in the marriage since before the first birth. According to various studies, satisfaction with the relationship, which had been in a continuous decline throughout the marriage previously, suddenly takes a swing upward again — and so does sex.

"It is just like a second honeymoon," one woman exclaimed. Her last child had just gone to live in a city on the West Coast. With a blush, some giggling, and a bit of pride, she went on to tell how she and her husband had sex in the afternoon, in different rooms, and much more frequently now.

Her experience is far from unique. Although both parents are often speeding toward fifty or have crossed over the half-decade mark when their offspring first become independent young adults, husband and wife may begin to act and feel like kids again themselves — at least sexually, and at least for a little while. "It was like being let out of prison," said a gray-haired business owner in the Southwest. "I love my kids, but I must admit I love being without them more. And," he added, his blue eyes crinkling as he laughed, "I love being able to love my wife, if you know what I mean."

For couples who are basically compatible, companionship and appreciation of the relationship itself, which possibly deteriorated when there was always a child standing between them, may improve. The spouses have more time for intimate gestures and conversations. Accountable to no one but themselves, they are able to go out together whenever they feel like it without worrying about meals for the kids and the like. Spontaneity in their social life and increased closeness often spill over into the bedroom. An intimate conversation or an enjoyable evening out leads to sex, and it can be at any time — they no longer have to worry about being seen or overheard.

Dr. Edward L. Parsons, clinical assistant professor of psychiatry at New York Hospital–Cornell Medical Center in Manhattan, claims that this stage is the moment of truth for husbands and wives. "You can tell now which are the live marriages and which are the dead ones." For some totally child-oriented couples who had used the kids all through the years to hide their own distance from one another, the masquerade is over. No longer able to focus all their conversation, interaction, and interest on children, the parents have to face the fact that there is nothing between them as man and woman anymore. Instead of the sense of renewal that comes to other couples at this stage of the marriage, what often takes place is divorce.

For spouses who knew they were unhappy all along and vowed they were staying together only for the kids' sake, it is put-up-or-shut-up time. They either have to separate when the last child leaves — which many of them do — or to make accommodations that allow the marriage to continue. One fifty-year-old husband who had been having short affairs throughout most of his marriage and who had kept insisting that he would divorce when his last son was grown, found, finally, that he couldn't make the move. When his son took off for Florida after college, the father stayed put, to everyone's surprise. He had grown accustomed to his own unhappiness, his wife's fearfulness, and her lack of interest in sex.

Many spouses, like this man, would rather stay with things the way they are, no matter how miserable, than change. There are a variety of reasons. Some individuals lack self-confidence: they don't think they can make it on their own. (A good number of unhappy, aging wives fit this mold.) For others, it is basic masochism: they have a need to suffer — happiness would not fit their unconscious psychological agenda. Still others fear change of any kind; inertia is more comfortable than action and they value the known over the unknown. Many are terrified of loneliness.

Another group believes in leading conventional, traditional lives — and "traditional" means, to them, staying married. Sometimes a religion forbids divorce, so the marriage, considered sacred, drags on despite the fact that it is made up of two lonely, incompatible people.

Great numbers of empty, distant, unhappy marriages that survived into early and late middle age are portrayed in the study *Sex and the Significant Americans.* Its authors, John F. Cuber and Peggy B. Harroff, found that these marriages fit into three basic categories. First, there is the conflict-habituated couple who quarrel, criticize, and nag constantly. They turn conflict and tension into a life-style.

Then there is the devitalized couple. They may have been deeply in love during the early years of their relationship but have grown completely apart, so that by their middle years interests and activities are no longer shared and all zest is gone. "There is typically little overt tension or conflict," say Cuber and Harroff, "but the interplay between the couple has become apathetic, lifeless. No serious threat to the continuity of the marriage is generally acknowledged, however. It is intended, usually by both, that it continue indefinitely despite its numbness." The couple are caught in habit and in the expectations of the society around them, which dictate that they will stay together. "Many believe that the devitalized mode is the appropriate mode in which a

man and woman should be content to live in the middle years
and later," conclude Cuber and Harroff.

The third kind of marriage that these researchers found involved couples living in what they call the "passive-congenial"
mode. There is a question whether these marriages would be considered unhappy, at least by the principals; although there is a
basic lack of liveliness and intimacy, the couple often considers
the marriage successful. They are similar to the devitalized couple, but the difference here is that the "spark" was never present,
even in the beginning. "The devitalized have a more exciting set
of memories; the passive-congenials give little evidence that they
had ever hoped for anything different from what they are currently experiencing," explain Cuber and Harroff. Husband and
wife are generally calm and sensible, tolerant of each other's idiosyncrasies. They don't engage in overt conflict, and they often
sweep differences under the rug. Both the devitalized and
passive-congenial couples put the accent on "other things,"
say Cuber and Harroff. Both types emphasize civic and professional responsibilities, the importance of property, children, and
reputation.

Some experts feel that the majority of marriages in our society
fit into the passive-congenial or, after some years, the devitalized
mode. In both cases, coexistence is simply a routine; sexual interaction is generally as lackluster as the relationship and is often,
therefore, minimal.

Clifford H. Swensen, Jr., director of clinical psychology training at Purdue University, has written about "post-parental" couples whom he has studied. He estimates that approximately 40 to
50 percent of them in our culture currently fit into the passive-
congenial mode, while 10 to 20 percent are devitalized relationships.

Couples engaged in more total, vital marriages — also found to
exist (albeit in the minority) by Cuber and Harroff, Swensen, and
others — have generally managed, through all the rigors of raising young children and teenagers, to keep their relationship close

and their enthusiasm for each other intact. Sex is an integral part of their marriages and it has stayed alive, if in somewhat diminished frequency, since the early days. These are the kinds of couples who may experience a renewal of passion once children leave the home. Swensen estimates that only 5 to 10 percent of post-parental couples have such alive and close marriages.

He notes still another kind of marriage, which he figures constitutes 20 to 25 percent of the population. These are the men and women who, although the marital relationship remained central to them emotionally, grew apart during the child-rearing years and developed separate interests, which they pursued. A couple like this would catch up with each other intermittently — for example, on weekends away from the children and during vacations — although they could go for weeks, even months, without intimate discussions. Closer, more constant contact between them is renewed once the children leave home.

Dr. Swensen says that 75 percent of the post-parental couples he has observed, regardless of the kind of relationship they have, have described the time after the children have left as their happiest years together. He adds a significant qualifier to the couples' own assessments, however: "For most older married couples there is a certain amount of poignant yearning. Although most of them stated they were happy, when they were asked what kinds and amounts of love expression they would like to receive in marriage all indicated that they neither gave nor received as much love as they would like. For most," notes Dr. Swensen, "there was less intimacy than they wished. Perhaps the most accurate conclusion is that for most older married couples, marriage is a relative success, but not quite as much of a success as they would like it to be."

Partners whose marriage remains intact, no matter what its emotional state, have to face the facts of aging together by late midlife. First of all, there is the wife's menopause, which, for the average woman, takes place around the age of fifty. Some women find menopause sexually liberating. They no longer have to worry about unwanted pregnancies. Other women, who never saw much to sex anyway, or who feel some antipathy toward their husband, use menopause as an excuse to cut down on or cease marital relations altogether.

Some women lose their libido because they subscribe to the myth that women are no longer interested in sex after menopause and act accordingly. If their religion has taught them that sex is only for procreation, and not for love, fun, or communication, women often lose interest in sex when their days of fertility have passed.

Menopause itself does not directly decrease the sex drive. "From a purely physiological standpoint, libido should theoretically *increase* at menopause," writes Dr. Helen Singer Kaplan, "because the action of the women's androgens, which is not materially affected by menopause, is now unopposed by estrogen. Indeed, some women do seem to behave in this manner, especially if they are not depressed, and can find interested and interesting partners. However," she adds, "if the middle-aged husband is avoiding sex and if the insecure, depressed and angry woman attributes this to her declining physical attractiveness, she too may avoid sexuality in order to spare herself the pain of frustration or rejection."

Although many women experience no discernible physical changes due to estrogen deficiencies that occur normally at menopause, others have problems such as an atrophied vagina and inadequate lubrication that interfere with intercourse. They start to avoid sex to prevent discomfort. Many women, determined to stay sexually alive, use water-soluble vaginal lubrication. Others don't find this adequate and resort to estrogen preparations, either applied topically or taken orally, to alleviate uncomfortable symptoms. They may worry about the link between some forms of cancer and taking estrogen, but they are willing to put up with the risk in order to continue to be sexual.

According to Dr. Kaplan, some wives get obese after menopause, and the new matronly look can be a turn-off to a husband: "The wife is not a sexy woman to him anymore. She's a mother." Some men, who base their sense of masculinity on the ability to impregnate, may also turn off when their wives are no longer capable of conceiving. Others buy the myth that women are no longer interested in sex once they reach menopause. These husbands stop initiating sex out of consideration for their wives. The cessation of sex in cases like this often gets misinterpreted, however. There is a tendency for the wife to feel that her husband is staying away from her because she has aged and he doesn't find her attractive anymore.

A minority of women react to the losses implied by menopause (loss of fertility, loss of youth, loss of youthful attractiveness) with depression, which causes them to lose something else: their libido. Depression, with the loss of sexual interest that generally accompanies it, often also befalls husbands and wives who feel in their fifties that it is too late in life for anything good to happen. They lose hope.

Since the aging process is progressive, there is a further deterioration of physical looks and strength during this stage of life, and both husband and wife have to come to terms with it. Some couples decide at this point that they are part of the older generation, and if they feel that sex is not proper in old age, they give it up. Again, if there has been a great deal of incompatibility, conflict about sex, a lot of inhibition, or lack of sexual gratification, aging will be a welcome excuse to put the whole matter to rest once and for all.

As in the earlier part of middle age, having extramarital affairs to deny the aging process or to prove that one is still desirable are common in this age group, as well. There are many spouses who claim that having an affair at this time of life has helped them keep intact marriages that are incompatible or lifeless. Others resort to affairs as a way of coping with a spouse who is no longer interested in sex, or with whom sex is too infrequent for their own needs.

Physiological sexual changes that may have started in the forties continue or intensify in the fifties. A man may find that it takes him longer to achieve an erection and that he requires more lengthy and direct stimulation from his partner. There may be

less seminal fluid expelled during ejaculation and less force behind the emission. The period necessary between erections increases significantly from earlier years. Masters and Johnson
found that many normal men over fifty need twelve to twenty-
four hours to achieve another erection after emission. Older men,
even if they lose their erections without climaxing, may also need
twelve to twenty-four hours to regain them. During coitus there
may be less of a need to ejaculate. "Perhaps one out of three or
four times that aging men have intercourse they may not experience a specific demand for orgasmic release," according to Masters and Johnson. "It's not that they can't ejaculate if they force
the issue; it's just that on occasion the familiar subjective demand
for tension release is either reduced or absent."

For men, there is often a decline in sexual interest and thoughts
and fantasies in the absence of specific erotic stimulation, according to Dr. Helen Singer Kaplan. "Although there are marked individual differences in this," she writes, "after his fifties a man
may be absorbed in his career for weeks without thoughts of sex
and without having an erection."

A wife, not aware that these symptoms are part of the aging
process, is apt to misinterpret what is happening. "When any
physiological alteration in sexual response becomes obvious in her
male partner, her initial reaction may be to question her own sexuality," say Masters and Johnson. "His obviously slowed erective
response may be interpreted as loss of interest in her. If he doesn't
ejaculate regularly, she may be concerned that he doesn't need
her, or she may fear that he has identified some other sexual interest." Masters and Johnson further report that some aging women
may find that it takes them longer to achieve an orgasm than in
the past, and that when it occurs it is shorter in duration or less
intense.

In the fifties, impotence, which has been looming since the forties in men's psyches, becomes even more of a menace, especially
if a man occasionally finds he can't get an erection and starts the
self-defeating cycle: worry, which ensures failure, which causes
further worry, and so on. Frequently, the normal sexual-slowing-

down process that accompanies aging is misunderstood. Men think it is a harbinger — that impotence is around the corner — and panic sets in. Although, in reality, a man in his fifties has years of satisfying sexuality ahead of him, he often mistakenly feels his sex life is coming to an end. When anxious monitoring of performance ensues, it may create the feared impotence. A younger man may be able to shrug off a random episode of impotence from any cause, but a man in his fifties tends to worry much more and to feel that it is all over for him now, for sure. Most experts agree that, barring illness or medicinal side effects, psychological reasons far outweigh physical ones in cases of chronic impotency.

Some wives at this stage in life become ashamed of their body if it is showing the effects of the aging process and start to avoid sex for this reason. Indeed, men who put a great deal of value on physical good looks may find that their sexual interest suffers as their wife visibly ages. Many others are able to put youthful good looks behind them and enjoy their wife sexually, and otherwise, at any age.

Spouses who have an unconscious need to see their mates as strong protectors often have trouble if the partner falls ill or otherwise shows signs of age-related debility. One man was a dutiful and loving husband until his wife became seriously ill at the age of fifty-five. He was upset by her illness, but he was also as upset by the fact that while she was a patient, her hair, which she had been dyeing, showed itself as gray for the first time. For reasons based in his own early background, he needed to see his wife as someone who was strong and invincible and who would protect him from everything, including aging. He couldn't deal with her new vulnerability. Her aging image reminded him that he was growing old, too. He suddenly found himself feeling discontented with his wife, and shortly after her hospitalization, he started an affair with a younger woman and left home.

Men suffering from impotence with their wives may try sex with someone else to see if they can operate any better with another partner. Sometimes a new body acts like magic, but often enough, a man who is impotent with his wife will be impotent with a mistress. Sometimes the husband's guilt over having an affair can cause impotence with the wife where it hadn't existed before. And some men and women turn off to a spouse as an unconscious excuse: it justifies their desire to have an affair.

As a general rule, notes Dr. Lief, "if a couple does not divorce during the transition period of the forties, it is less likely they will divorce later." But there is also a growing trend for immature men in their fifties, in search of the fountain of youth, to make a last-ditch attempt to deny the aging process by leaving their wives for a much younger woman. Frequently, one of the lures of the young woman is the increased virility the man feels with her. A new body can be a vitalizer at any age, but new bodies don't remain new forever.

Divorces of couples in their fifties are increasing. So is the current phenomenon of men over fifty defying time by having babies and starting new families with young wives. Babies are an option that women in this age group do not have.

Although the empty-nest syndrome is much less common among women than it was once thought to be, some women do become depressed after the children grow up and leave home. These are usually women who based their identities mainly upon the role of mother. With the children gone, they feel useless and don't know quite who they are anymore. These days, however, more women probably feel elated rather than depressed: once the children take off, they start a new, productive life. If they haven't gone back to work in their forties, when the children were teenagers, then now, when the kids are completely gone, they may try to find a job or become more active in community affairs or charitable organizations.

The sense of renewal that women often feel as they become more involved in the outside world may create a marked disparity between spouses if the husband's worldly involvement is winding down. Some men are either forced into or choose early retirement. They may be leaving the work force just as their wives are entering it. Resentments can grow if the husband had counted on the wife being available to him at this time in life and, instead, she is rushing around engrossed in her own business. He may feel abandoned, lonely, and betrayed. Sex often suffers if a struggle over the wife's new role takes place.

Other men this age glory in the fact that they are at the height of their power in the work world. The greatest wealth and power, according to statistics, is in the hands of men in their fifties. The specter of the next stage of life is with them, however. This means handing over the reins of power for some, and plain old retirement for others. Both may cause — depending upon the person — anxiety or anticipation. According to Boyd C. Rollins and Harold Feldman, who did a study of marital satisfaction over the family life-cycle, the thought of imminent retirement creates a temporary setback in marital satisfaction, which may have been increasing after the child-rearing stages. "The most devastating period of marriage for males," they say, "appears to be when they are anticipating retirement."

In their fifties, men find they are more vulnerable sexually to the effects of fatigue, alcohol, or other drugs. Some men start to ration what they feel are limited physical resources. Dr. Alex Finkle, a urologist writing in *Medical Times,* commented that "some men suspect that sexual exertion is unduly fatiguing and therefore choose to expend their limited energies in more enjoyable pursuits." He illustrated his point with an anecdote: "I have one patient who told me bluntly that he preferred golf to coitus and that he would avoid the enervating effect of intercourse in order to improve his golf score!"

Many men in their fifties and older discover that they can function better sexually in the morning than they can at night. They are generally aware of one advantage: they aren't tired. What they usually don't know is that nature is helping them along, as well. The level of the male hormone testosterone is generally higher in the morning, after a night's rest, than it is late in the day. If they want to, it is easier for a couple to shift to sex in the morning rather than at night at this stage of life (an approach that sex therapists often recommend to older couples), because children are no longer around.

Various studies show that for the average married couple, sex continues to decline in frequency in the fifties, even if there is a short upward surge of interest after the children leave home. Masturbation in middle age, at least among women, may increase. And, in the fifties, the sexual shift that started to show itself in the late thirties and forties — when women began to have more interest in sex than their partners — may continue to cause trouble in the marriage.

In any event, the aging couple is moving closer to each other in one important way: the need for more affiliation and expressiveness in men that may have started in the forties continues into the fifties and makes some husbands more similar emotionally to their wives than they were at younger ages. At the same time, women often become more like men as their assertiveness increases and they become more interested in things outside the home. Each partner continues to let loose formerly suppressed parts of their personality. In the process, the couple heads toward what some experts have called the "normal unisex of later life."

HEALTH

As a couple ages, they become more concerned with their bodies. Not only do conversations about health increase, studies show, but actual illnesses that may have important consequences for a couple's sex life begin to occur more frequently, starting in the forties and fifties.

Diabetes, for example, can cause impotence in men, and, indeed, may be the first sign of the disease. Although its effect on women's sexuality is less clear, some researchers say female diabetics have more difficulty in reaching orgasm. While high blood pressure, by itself, has no sexual side effects, antihypertensive medications used to treat it, such as reserpine, clonidine, and methyldopa, do; they are often the culprits behind impotence. It has been estimated that a third of treated male hypertensive patients suffer from potency disturbances.

Unfortunately, doctors frequently fail to talk about sex to their patients, and since patients are usually just as reluctant to discuss their sexual problems, the conspiracy of silence may lead to wrong conclusions. Patients often incorrectly blame the aging process for lack of sexual interest or impotence, when its cause is really medical.

If a patient with erectile difficulties does bring himself to tell his doctor about them, it may be possible to switch medications and thus restore potency. However, serious interruptions in the aging person's sex life, or new, grave anxieties that have set in as a result of sexual malfunctioning, can have consequences that outlive the cause. A fifty-five-year-old college professor in the Southwest developed hypertension and was given medication for it by his doctor. He was not told of possible side effects, however. Soon after starting his medication, he found he was unable to achieve or maintain an erection when trying to make love with his wife. He struggled with the problem for seven months, becoming more and more anxious about his sexual capabilities as he continued to fail. By the time he informed his doctor about what was going on, he had stopped attempting to have intercourse altogether: he was too afraid of not being able to perform.

The doctor put him on another medication, but by then this man was so uptight about the possibility of sexual failure that he found himself unable to resume his sex life despite his doctor's urgings that he try. His wife, who knew her husband to be a sensitive man, did not press him. And she, on her part, had developed her own performance anxieties: she was afraid that after all the months of abstinence she would not be able to respond to her husband and that this would create even more doubt in his mind about his sexual ability. Today, this husband and wife, who are a loving couple in every other respect, have simply abandoned sex as part of their life together — something that probably would not have happened had the medical disruption never occurred.

Gastric troubles and ulcers, which many people in their forties, fifties, and older years are prone to, can also indirectly lead to a sexual crisis. In recent years, some medications widely used to treat ulcers and other gastric ailments have been suspected of causing potency problems. Not knowing this was fatal to one marriage: A fifty-six-year-old southern business executive undergoing a lot of stress in his career and in his marriage was given medication for gastric symptoms he had developed. Soon after starting on the medication, he tried to have intercourse with his wife and failed. He blamed her, saying that it was her fault and that she would make any man impotent. His accusation led to a round of arguments that put a further strain on the marriage. Each time he attempted to have intercourse thereafter, he failed to achieve an erection. Convinced that it was, as he put it, "because my wife was a castrating bitch," he decided to cure his impotence by having sex with someone else. He invited his secretary to accompany him on a business trip. She accepted. The wife got wind of her husband's plans and had a detective photograph the couple. She was now convinced that her husband's impotence was caused by his interest in another woman. She used the photographs as evidence of adultery, and proceeded to sue for divorce. It wasn't until a year after the divorce that the wife was made aware by an article in a newspaper that the medication rather than the other woman may have been the true reason for her ex-husband's impotence.

There may be medical reasons for loss of sexual interest as well as for failure to achieve an erection. A failing libido can be caused by hepatitis or any other generally debilitating illness. Liver diseases and endocrine disorders can decrease libido and impair erections, and vascular disorders may cause impotence. Conditions that cause pain or a great deal of discomfort — for example, arthritis, lower-back problems, extreme obesity, some kinds of hernias — can have a negative effect on sexuality. In addition, some drugs used to treat eye disorders can reduce sexual desire and impair sexual response.

Much more is known about how some illnesses and medications affect men sexually than is known about how they affect women.

For example, although some drugs used to treat high blood pressure cause impotence in many men, there is uncertainty about sexual side effects in women who use the same drugs. Thus far, no concrete evidence exists to show any effect at all.

Dr. Helen Singer Kaplan has pointed out adverse sexual effects of poor hysterectomies done at any age. She also warns both sexes about sedatives: "Their chronic abuse seems to generally diminish sexuality." Drug abusers hooked on substances like heroin are known to have very poor sex lives.

Although middle-aged and older people may be especially vulnerable to the effects of alcohol abuse, it can have serious sexual consequences at any age. "Chronic alcoholism or even habitual heavy alcohol intake frequently seriously impairs the sexual response of both genders, but most especially of men," writes Dr. Kaplan. "Often, the man who complains of erectile difficulties is found to drink three martinis at lunch, a scotch before he gets on the train and three more drinks before dinner. Such alcohol intake may significantly depress his sexual response."

Unfortunately, when alcohol directly affects a heavy drinker's sexual response, the sexual response of the spouse to the mate's drinking is often overlooked. Dr. Jay Mann related a typical case history as an illustration:

A couple came for treatment and the husband stated they were there because his wife was not interested in sex. Over the course of several sessions, my co-therapist and I both had the feeling that there was another big, unspoken problem in the background. We tried hard to find out what it was and even confronted the couple together, but we still couldn't discover what it was. Finally, we decided to split the couple up and talk to them separately. When my co-therapist talked to the wife alone, she finally let it out. This guy had a big drinking problem. The wife wasn't able to address the problem directly, but she had turned off to him sexually as a result.

HEART ATTACKS

The possibility of a heart attack starts to become of particular concern to men in their forties and fifties and stays with them throughout the rest of their lives. Sex problems abound among those who survive the misfortune of actually having a heart attack.

Since heart attacks are such common occurrences as men age (and since increasing proportions of women are experiencing heart disease), they constitute a major problem for sex in marriage for the upper age groups. Study after study has pointed out that sexual activity is greatly reduced after a heart attack and that a substantial loss of sexual interest occurs. For example, in a group of 100 Swiss heart attack victims, sexual activity was reduced by nearly 50 percent. Other studies reveal anywhere from a 30 to a 60 percent reduction in sexual activity among post-coronary patients. In one population of cardiac patients, 60 percent of the men reported erectile difficulties at least half of the time. In another, 65 percent of women with heart trouble were unable to have orgasms, as opposed to 24 percent of women hospitalized for other ailments. Studies also show that a substantial number of people give up sex altogether after having a heart attack. One survey of patients who had undergone coronary bypass surgery found the same kind of sexual deterioration in their postoperative lives.

Since experts agree that heart damage is not the reason for the sexual changes recorded, then what is? First of all, many people who have heart attacks or bypass surgery become depressed and can remain that way up to a year and a half after their hospitalization. Depression is a major cause of loss of sexual interest. In addition, certain medications given to coronary patients are known to have sexual side effects. Frequently, high blood pressure is a complicating factor and heart patients, on the advice of their physicians, start to use antihypertensive drugs such as those mentioned earlier, which can cause sexual problems. If diuretics are prescribed, as is often the case, there can be additional sexual complications. Some studies link such drugs to varying degrees of impotence, and to failure to ejaculate in about one-third of the subjects. There is evidence that some of the new "beta blockers" commonly given to heart patients can cause sexual difficulties, too. In one study of patients using the beta blocker propranolol, 15 percent developed impotence, 28 percent had decreased potency, and 4 percent had decreased libido. The greater the dose, the more severe was the sexual dysfunction.

Of supreme importance are the psychological problems. They probably account for the most severe and widespread sexual difficulties encountered in the heart-disease population. To begin with, there is the matter of ignorance. Although there is usually plenty of worry on the patient's part about sexual activity now that he — or she — has survived a heart attack, it generally isn't aired. The patient doesn't ask the doctor about sex and the cardiologist generally doesn't offer guidance unless asked. "The patient leaves the hospital with concerns that have not been addressed or for which the patient has received only vague information. Thus, often the couple is left with the responsibility of deciding what is correct," according to Michael McLane, Harry Krop, and Jawahar Mehta, the authors of a paper about the adjustment of heart-attack victims that was published in the *Annals of Internal Medicine*.

Often, unfortunately, both spouses — the heart patient and the healthy partner — are inhibited by fear. The victim is worried that sexual activity will bring on another heart attack — possibly a fatal one. Meanwhile, the spouse worries about the same thing. Both partners dodge sex. If they do overcome their reticence and have intercourse, it may turn out to be unsuccessful anyway. "The wife may find she is unable to enjoy sex because of anxiety about her husband's condition, and this may, in turn, produce feelings of sexual inadequacy in the patient, thereby further exacerbating his psychological condition," say McLane, Krop, and Mehta. It is easy to see how a sex life can disintegrate under these circumstances. And yet, were the correct facts communicated routinely by physicians to both heart-attack victims and their spouses, many formerly satisfying sex lives could be saved. (Of course, those whose sex lives were poor, sporadic, or troubled before may use the heart attack as a convenient excuse to stop sex altogether.)

For most coronary patients, sex is not considered to be a dangerous activity. Indeed, some experts feel it can have a salutary effect on convalescence. Tests to determine just how hard the heart beats and how much energy is expended during intercourse have proved that sex is about as taxing as a variety of ordinary occupational pursuits. Doctors say that when a recuperating patient is able to climb two flights of stairs, he or she can have sex with a spouse without undue concern.

Extramarital sex is another matter, however. Although death due to a heart attack during sex is quite rare, most of the few such mortalities that do occur take place during extramarital liaisons — when there is more stress because of unfamiliarity with the partner, when there's more strain to perform well, and when sex is often preceded by overeating or too much alcohol. It is stress rather than sex that can trigger a heart attack.

Sexual counseling by the patient's cardiologist, a psychologist or psychiatrist, or a sex therapist is helpful in preventing sexual deterioration in the marriage of the heart-attack victim. It can also help to resurrect a sex life that has already suffered in the aftermath of cardiac disease. The counseling should include both spouses. It is important that the patient and spouse understand, and believe, that in most cases, conjugal sex does not put excessive strain on the heart. In some instances, doctors prescribe medications known as vasodilators, which widen the patient's blood vessels. They can help overcome fear, since they minimize the possibility of chest pain (angina pectoris) or a heart attack occurring during sex. Some vasodilators, like nitroglycerine, can be taken shortly before having sex.

Many doctors advise heart-attack patients to wait three hours after a large meal or heavy drinking before having sex. Also, some experts recommend masturbation — which is less strenuous and therefore less scary than coitus — for the heart-attack victim trying to ease his or her way back into sex. Sensate focus exercises (discussed on pages 109–110) are often recommended for the couple whose sex life has been impaired by a heart attack. Since they involve no demand for performance and are initially limited to stroking rather than actual intercourse, sensate focus exercises are an unpressured way to reactivate sex.

Reports indicate that there is a bonus in store for some aging couples when they go for sexual counseling after a heart attack: they find themselves finally dealing with — and solving — long-standing sexual problems in their relationship. During a therapeutic interview arranged while he was hospitalized, a fifty-two-year-old salesman was encouraged to bring up any sexual fears connected to his recent heart attack. He started talking about his wife's ongoing inability to reach orgasm and his dissatisfaction with their sex life because of it. He was encouraged to bring her in for counseling, which he did. He found during the joint session that she was eager for help, and the two of them were directed into a sex therapy program. The wife, with her husband's help, learned to achieve orgasm for the first time in her married life. Today this couple has a much better sex life than they did before the husband had his heart attack.

CHAPTER 7

Stage Six: Sex in the Golden Years

WHEN A COUPLE is past the age of sixty, the full flower of prejudice against sex for older people blooms. Although there has been a push in recent times to recognize that sex is, indeed, part of life at any age, the aura of the "dirty" old man or woman still clings to mature people who overtly express an interest in sex — unless the man happens to be wealthy and well preserved; ads for luxury items like expensive furs or fine jewelry are full of distinguished-looking, gray-haired older men consorting with fresh-faced young women. The sexual aura of women is even harder to preserve, past a certain age, than that of men. There are seldom media images of older women with sex appeal.

How is this kind of societal bias reflected in marriage? Many people buy the cultural prejudices. Women are often very concerned about losing their youthful looks and, as they age, are prone to interpret any slowing down of their husband's sexual functioning as proof that they are no longer attractive to him. When they notice a few wrinkles and their skin begins to lose firmness, women may stop thinking of themselves as sexually attractive and act accordingly. Unfortunately, some husbands do, indeed, lose interest in their wife sexually when she begins to look older. Some husbands have affairs with younger women. Some divorce their wife and acquire a younger one. Others accept the loss of interest in their aging spouse as a natural occurrence and settle into an asexual or sexually sparse existence. Still others retreat into a fantasy sex life: they masturbate to centerfold images of young women.

"The idea of beauty needs more sophisticated redefinition so that it includes character, intelligence, expressiveness, knowledge, achievement, disposition, tone of voice and speech patterns, posture and bearing, warmth, personal style, social skills — all those personal traits that make each individual unique and that can be found at any age," say psychiatrist and gerontologist Robert N. Butler and Myrna I. Lewis in their thoughtful book *Sex after Sixty.*

Some grown children apply subtle negative pressure if their parents show erotic interest as they age. Many adults still carry with them the childhood notion that other people may engage in sex, but not *their* parents. It makes them very uncomfortable to think of their parents as fellow adults with sexual needs such as they themselves have. In one sense, they are clinging to the image of themselves as children and locking their mothers and fathers into parental roles — which, in their primitive, childlike view, exclude sex.

RETIREMENT

Retirement is very tricky for both spouses. The retiree — until recently, usually a man in our society — has to adjust to the loss of power and prestige that went with working, or at least to the loss of a regular routine and an outlet for his energies, which, as a man, he was trained to use in the business world from an early age on. If they share new leisure activities with each other, the retired couple can grow closer and have the time of their lives having fun together. "We travel, go to the theater, take long, quiet walks. We feel closer than we ever have," explained one sixty-four-year-old retired executive who moved from his large house near an East Coast metropolis to an apartment in the city soon after he retired. "We have been married close to forty years and sex has become deeper, more personal over the years. In fact, I am almost embarrassed to admit it at our age, but sex has really never been better!"

Closeness can be threatened, however, by the important power shift that occurs in a marriage when one spouse retires. Suppose, as is often the case, that the wife has been the homemaker and her mate the sole wage earner. Upon retiring, the husband loses power and the woman gains it, since he is now in her domain — the home. Some housewives inundate their newly retired husband with myriad requests to fix things around the house or run errands; depending on the man, this may be welcomed or could sit badly. Some men attempt to "take over the reins again" in the relationship by being very critical of the way things are done around the house, which can cause friction that results in sexual impairment. Other men graciously pitch in with the housework — it gives them something to do. Some men help but, if they have very traditional notions of sex roles, find that doing so adds to their unhappiness and confusion. They feel that they are not only out of their life's work, but are being demeaned by doing "woman's work" as well.

For the housewife, a husband's retirement is often a mixed blessing. "I married him for better or worse, but not for lunch" sums it up very well. The woman often has trouble adjusting to having her husband underfoot all day.

In many marriages, both partners have careers. If a wife is younger than her husband and is still working when he retires, the shift in power and the amount of adjustment required may be especially great, since she will be bringing in an income and sticking to a work schedule while he has neither a paycheck nor a regimen. In retirement, money is often tighter than it used to be and this may add stress to the relationship. Just the fact that a major change is occurring may cause disturbing stress in the marriage. In a well-known study by Thomas H. Holmes and Richard Rahe, retirement was ranked tenth in a list of forty-three life events that create stress.

How well all the required adjustments are made will often affect how sex fares during the post-retirement years. But what about aging factors per se and sex? Aging accounts for some physiological changes that mean a sexual slowing down rather than a total fade-out. In the male in his senior years, the need for more direct genital stimulation, a diminishing need to ejaculate during each sexual encounter, slowness in achieving erections, and a need for more time between erections — all of which may have become evident in his forties and fifties — continue. The elderly man may find that he has only partial erections rather than full ones, or that he loses erections and doesn't recover them as easily as in former years. Masters and Johnson report that men past sixty in their sampling were slower to effect intromission.

"Some men," writes Dr. Helen Singer Kaplan, "compensate for their age-related decline in sexuality by seeking out and creating intensely erotic situations, fantasies and partners. They may avail themselves of sexual techniques that rely heavily on intense physical stimulation of genitals and/or erogenous areas. Other men, by contrast, cease having sexual intercourse in their fifties and sixties. This abstinence is, of course, not purely a function of the physical effects of age," she says, "but rather a psychological avoidance of the painful feelings of frustration, anxiety, or depression that may be elicited by confrontation with their declining sexual performance. Impotence is a frequent complaint in this age group." Kinsey reported that 20 percent of men at age sixty were impotent. This increased to 75 percent at age eighty. His sampling, however, is notoriously low in the older age categories.

Impotence may reflect lack of desire (for a variety of reasons) rather than impotence per se — no desire, no erection. It seems that earlier sexual interest determines how much desire will remain in the older years. In one of the reports issued by the Center for the Study of Aging at Duke University, all of the subjects, without exception, rated their sexual urge as lower in old age than in youth. "However," notes the study, "those who rated their sexual urges as strongest in youth tended to rate them as moderate in old age; most persons who described their sexual feelings as weak to moderate in youth described themselves as being without sexual feelings in old age." Masters and Johnson, as well as other experts, have also concluded that individuals who were highly sexual during their younger years are likely to be sexually active when they are elderly.

Dr. Kaplan maintains that "a healthy man . . . is able to enjoy sexual intercourse throughout life. Indeed, freed of the intense need for fast orgastic relief and of the inhibitions of youth, more satisfying and imaginative love play is often enjoyed by the older man and his partner. For the secure man, age need never be a barrier to sexual pleasure providing good health and opportunity exist."

The capacity to be better lovers may involve making quality compensate for quantity. Overall, statistics from many sources show clearly that sexual frequency gradually declines during each decade of a man's adult life, and that by his sixties, it has dropped considerably from earlier levels and will continue to drop. The husband's decline means less sex for the wife whether she wants it that way or not, since, in general, men determine coital rates in marriage. In a study by Eric Pfeiffer, Adriaan Verwoerdt, and Glenn C. Davis published in the *American Journal of Psychiatry,* wives who reported the cessation of intercourse in their marriages blamed it on their husbands — who, for the most part, agreed with them.

No one is sure whether sexual frequency in marriage would be greater in older age groups if women were in control. Research shows, however, that although older men need considerably more time between erections and often don't climax with emissions, women still retain a full capacity for orgasms, including multiple orgasms, into ripe old age. One study of older women gives a clear indication that if the opportunity were there, women might be interested in more sex: women with younger husbands reported more sex in their marriages than those with older mates.

Dr. Kaplan has summed up the fate of the older woman:

"Women of this age group depend for their sexual expression on a dwindling supply of men whose sexual needs have declined markedly. A woman who has regular sexual opportunity tends to maintain her sexual responsiveness; without such opportunity, sexuality declines markedly."

Although older women are able to respond to sexually functional husbands to the point of multiple orgasms, Dr. Kaplan notes that with age there are gradual physical changes in women similar to those that occur in men. The process of vaginal lubrication becomes slower, for example, and contractions during orgasm become less frequent. Five or six contractions occur during an average female orgasm at age thirty, as opposed to only two or three at age seventy. Nevertheless, Dr. Kaplan and other authorities maintain that women's libidos remain more intact and react much less to the physiological aspects of aging than do men's. "Perhaps the physical determinants of sex are relatively more important for male than for female sexuality," she speculates in *The New Sex Therapy*.

Various studies prove that sex and advanced age are not antithetical. At Duke University researchers found that sexual desire continued in 75 percent of men and women in their seventies. Of the married subjects, 54 percent were still sexually active. In a recent study of older Americans — *Love, Sex, and Aging*, done by Edward Brecher for Consumers Union, 80 percent of the wives and 77 percent of the husbands reported themselves to be still sexually active. Researchers have discovered people in their nineties who still enjoy sex.

Nevertheless, although the potential for sex exists in the golden years, it often isn't expressed. In addition to the large number of senior citizens who are ashamed that they still have sexual feelings, others simply cave in under the deadening effects of monotony. Some couples have done nothing new in bed for forty years or more. Masters and Johnson have repeatedly stressed the harmful effects of monotony on sex in older age groups.

Sometimes in old age a feeling of sudden discontent with a mate sets in, accompanied by a distancing of oneself from a partner that includes sexual withdrawal. This often represents, sadly, the opposite of what it seems to: the spouse who pulls back is really very attached to the mate but becomes concerned about separation due to death. The withdrawal is an attempt to diminish the anticipated pain and loneliness by pulling away emotionally before the inevitable happens. Other couples misunderstand the physiological effects of aging and panic themselves into sexual dysfunction or disuse.

Experts quarrel with narrow ways of defining sex. They believe we have to get away from the limiting concept of it as only intromission and orgasm. Seeing sex in such a confining way leads to a sense of failure if either is not accomplished. For any couple, but especially for elderly ones, sex does not always have to end in a climax, nor does it always have to include penetration. Hugging, kissing, touching, petting, and stroking can all be very satisfying forms of sexual contact. The noted psychoanalyst Erik Erikson, a pioneer in the study of the various stages in the life cycle, talks about old age as being a time of "generalized sensuality" as opposed to specifically genital sexuality.

One of the things that impairs the sex lives of older people most is illness. Unfortunately, maladies occur with increasing frequency as the years add up. If illness incapacitates one spouse, the healthy partner may be forced into involuntary sexual abstinence. Noting that serious illness frequently develops in men first, Dr. Robert Butler and Myrna Lewis say that "healthy women — especially those who are significantly younger than their husbands — may spend years in a marital relationship without sex."

Sometimes disfigurements that are caused by illness turn one or both partners away from sex. The sick partner's self-image as a sexual person may be totally destroyed, or he or she may be embarrassed by the new body changes and try to avoid sex as a result. The healthy partner, on the other hand, might find the changes in the mate repugnant. Wives or husbands may feel guilty about turning off in this way, but they cannot will themselves into sexual desire.

One sex therapist told of a man whose wife was severely crippled by arthritis. The husband, although he felt very guilty about his reaction, was unable to feel sexual desire for his wife any longer. He wanted the therapist to help him be attracted to his wife again. The therapist, after investigating the situation, decided that it was an impossible task under the circumstances and instead helped the couple adjust to a life together based on loyalty, many good shared memories and experiences, and affection rather than sex. In contrast, another very sexually motivated couple reported that although the wife has been partially paralyzed since the age of sixty-two, they continue to have sex in positions that make it possible and continue to enjoy sex thoroughly. Whether sex previously was sporadic or ongoing, so-so or enjoyable, ill health, more often than it should, frequently brings the older couple's sex life to an abrupt halt, however.

The noted sex researcher John Gagnon has cautioned that recent efforts to promote sex in older age groups may disturb couples who have put their sex lives behind them and are perfectly content to have it that way. They may interpret the current attempt to create a hospitable climate for sex in the latter years as a mandate. They feel they should have sex in order to be "normal." Erik Erikson tacitly agrees. In an interview in *Psychology Today,* he says that "the old attitude was that sexuality in old age doesn't exist or ought not to be. The new attitude permits choice. Sexuality in old age is a potential to be enjoyed, not an obligation."

It is possible to lead a perfectly happy life without sex, as many older people do. But if older people want to continue an active sex life, they should be encouraged to do so. "For many older people," say Butler and Lewis, "it offers the opportunity to express not only passion, but affection, esteem and loyalty. It provides affirmative evidence that one can count on one's body and its functioning. It allows people to assert themselves positively. It carries with it the possibility of excitement and romance. It expresses delight in being alive. It offers a continuous challenge to grow and change in new directions."

"My sex life with my wife continues to be wonderful," a retired man of sixty-eight reported. "It makes me feel in my retirement that I am not finished as a man."

Experts agree that two conditions have to be present if the potential for sex in the golden years is to be fulfilled: good health and a receptive partner. Unfortunately, the absence of a partner becomes a big problem for older women. More than half of all women over sixty in the United States are widows. In contrast, only about 15 percent of men in this age group are widowers. Most studies show that sexual interaction continues for a good percentage of elderly couples fortunate enough to still be together, but that sexual activity dribbles away to practically nothing for the older man or woman who is single. For example, a Duke University study in which the average age of the subjects was seventy found that while 54 percent of the married couples remained active sexually, only 7 percent of those who were unmarried continued to experience sex. The Consumers Union study reported that elderly single men were much more likely to find sex partners than older single women.

So, at least at older ages, you stand a better chance of still being sexual if you are married than if you are not, especially if you are a woman.

CAN SEXUAL INTEREST BE REVIVED?

Drawing upon his experiences as one of the country's leading sex therapists, Dr. Joshua Golden assures that "change can occur at any age and sexual lives can be revived after any number of years of dormancy." He points out that for some, professional therapy is the ticket because the therapist gives the person what he or she needs psychologically: permission from someone in authority to change.

A sixty-four-year-old woman who lives in the South testifies to the fact that sex can not only persist but get better in later life, even when no formal sex therapy is involved: "I could never get myself to talk about sex when I was younger. I couldn't reach orgasms and couldn't tell my husband what was wrong. Well, finally, I bought myself a book and learned about things that really helped, and at the age of sixty finally was able to bring myself to discuss the matter with my husband. I needed him to stimulate me differently," she explained. "He was more than eager to oblige and, believe it or not, I am enjoying sex more now than I did when I was younger. Finally I am having orgasms all the time!"

Sexual-enhancement programs, generally given under the aegis of sex clinics or clinics for elderly people at large universities and medical centers, have also helped many older people improve their sex lives.

HOW TO BE A SEXY OLDER PERSON

Dr. Eric Pfeiffer of Duke University, in a paper discussing sexuality in the aging person, reviewed all data available on the subject and summed up how a person can best prepare for a happy, sexy older age. "Successful aging persons are those who have made a decision to stay in training in major areas of their lives," he said. "In particular, they have decided to stay in training physically, socially, emotionally and intellectually. We have every reason to believe that staying in training sexually will also help to improve the quality of life in the later years."

The late entertainer Maurice Chevalier, speaking from the vantage point of his later years, gave an indication of what sex can be like if a person stays "in training." With a twinkle in his eye, he explained: "The only difference between a man of forty and a man of seventy is thirty years of experience."

PART TWO

The Hidden Dynamics

CHAPTER 8

Bed and Bored

THE FIRST PART of this book described the normal stress points that occur in any marriage — moments in the natural unfolding of a relationship when sex becomes particularly vulnerable. It gave you an idea of the ups and downs of an average couple's erotic life as they travel through the life cycle together, and allowed you to see how your sex life may have much in common with other married couples'.

Now it is time to turn away from the broad, overall view of marriage and to focus instead on individual matters. The rest of this book will examine the ways in which particular psychological attitudes and the emotional baggage we all carry with us into our relationships can affect sexual desire at any age and at any stage in marriage.

Common as many of them are, most of the psychological issues that reverberate in our sex lives generally remain hidden from conscious awareness. We don't recognize that a problem exists, much less how it may be contributing to our turning on or our turning off to a spouse. Other issues, however, are closer to the surface and more easily recognized. These more obvious, relatively minor problems, which are frequently encountered in modern marriages, will be examined first, in this chapter. The more complex, hidden issues that affect sex in marriage will be explored after that.

WHAT THE EXPERTS HAVE TO SAY ABOUT "BOREDOM"

A man and woman meet and are attracted to each other. After getting over the anxiety or awkwardness that takes place during initial sexual encounters, they adjust to each other and start to have an exciting and satisfying sex life. Lovemaking in the morning is as common as sex at night, and they might play around at midday as well. They try a variety of different positions. They make love on the rug in front of the fire in a cabin they rented for a week. They may even take a book like *The Joy of Sex* with them and try out new and different things.

After a number of months of being in love and meeting each other's family and friends, they decide to marry or move in with one another. It is then that the silent, insidious problem that plagues many marriages begins: Over time, they find that their sex life diminishes in excitement and frequency. They gradually lose interest in each other. Boredom sets in — or does it?

Experts disagree about whether boredom alone can explain marital doldrums and sexual ennui. Many authorities who deal with sex in relationships think that it is much easier for a man or woman to say, "Sex has become boring," than to have to look further and recognize the more complex issues that cause sexual desire to dim and die.

For example, Dr. Otto Kernberg, the prominent psychiatrist who has written extensively on love, says that "a couple with a deep, stable relationship maintains sexual interest. Interest can go up or down according to tensions or irritations between the couple or according to whether one feels closer or more distant to a partner at different times, but the sexual interest never disappears. Boredom sets in when there is a great deal of unconscious hostility," he maintains. "There is boredom when one is trying to avoid awareness that one is very angry or disappointed with the other person. Boredom is a cover-up for feelings that are not recognized or expressed openly."

Dr. Fred Gottlieb, the Los Angeles psychiatrist who is director of the Family Therapy Institute of Southern California, feels very differently. He maintains that boredom is both genuine and common. "Sex diminishes or stops," he says, "when people get bored."

Dr. Harold Lief, professor of psychiatry at the University of Pennsylvania School of Medicine and former director of the Marriage Council of Philadelphia, and Dr. Helen Singer Kaplan, director of the human sexuality program at New York Hospital–Cornell Medical Center, two of America's leading sex therapists, take a middle-of-the-road approach. For the most part they agree with Dr. Kernberg that boredom is generally a cover-up for larger problems in the relationship. But both say that occasionally they do find marriages where the relationship is basically sound but where, for minor reasons, boredom nevertheless has set in.

The less complex problems that can result in what might be called simple boredom follow. Many of you will recognize them.

WHERE HAS ALL THE ROMANCE GONE?

For some couples the problem is romance.

"He used to admire me, tell me how pretty I am, surprise me with gifts, give me flowers, give me unexpected kisses, make me feel special. It was all so romantic. Now he touches me only when he wants to have sex. Well, I'm turned off. I need some buildup to feel sexy." That's the way a lot of women feel.

"I don't feel important anymore. She is so wound up in the children. She used to dress up for me, look her prettiest; now she doesn't care. She slogs around the house in old clothes, never wears makeup except when we go out. She used to come alive when I walked in. Now I practically have to club her to have her pay attention to me when I'm home." That's the way a lot of men feel.

What women and men who feel this way are expressing is their desire for more romance in their lives. They remember the good old days before they lived together, when each evening was a grand event. With nostalgia they secretly recall the early days of their marriage when they would always hold hands as they walked. They would want to do everything together. He would bring a special bottle of wine. She would cook special things.

Now it's no wine and fast cooking. Gourmet food is confined to days when company is expected — never for just the two of them. Each partner feels that he or she is being taken for granted and is no longer considered "special." There is no "charge" felt in just being together anymore as there used to be. Each spouse wonders, with a sigh: "Where has all the romance gone?" The feeling that romance has gone out of their lives haunts them, makes them seem less interesting to each other, makes sex seem like just another ordinary event in a string of ordinary days. Maybe so ordinary, in fact, that sometimes they feel, why bother? Good-bye romance, and, for some, good-bye sex.

A letter to columnist Ann Landers expressed the romance-is-dead theme.

Dear Ann:

I am getting sick and tired of reading letters from men who complain about how lousy their wives are in bed. I would like to ask a few questions that might put the picture into proper perspective:

When was the last time you told your wife she was attractive or sexy and that she turned you on?

How long has it been since you behaved like a lover, kissed her passionately and made an effort to get her in the mood? Or, is your lovemaking routine, matter-of-fact, something you get over in a hurry?

Have you surprised your wife with flowers or a gift lately?

A little thoughtfulness can work wonders in the bedroom.

Do you listen — really listen — when she talks to you and respond in a way that lets her know you are interested in her ideas and her feelings? Communication is the name of the game. Nothing meaningful can happen between two people unless they talk to one another.

I urge you men out there who think your wives are dull or boring to answer the above questions honestly. Then go to work to make things better. You couldn't invest your time and energy more wisely.

— Hope My Husband Sees This

Dr. Harvey Caplan, a psychiatrist who with his ex-wife and co-therapist Rebecca Black helped found the human-sexuality program at the University of California School of Medicine at San Francisco, explains what causes romance to vanish: "Once a couple signs the contract that says, 'You're mine forever,' they feel, 'If you're mine, I don't have to work to win you anymore.' A husband and wife start taking each other for granted. This taking-for-granted business is deadly."

What can you do if this has already happened to you — if romance has disappeared from your relationship and taken your good sex life with it?

You can stop assuming that it is inevitable and, instead, take Dr. Caplan's prescription to heart. "People should treat each other as if they are always in courtship," he says. "They have to win each other every day if they want to keep the excitement going. To use a mundane example: If you want to keep a car running, you have to pay attention to it, keep it tuned, change the oil, the spark plugs. It is very important for people to pay attention to their partners in the same way and to become perpetual courters."

Compliments that are genuine go a long way. Think of something you like about your spouse and communicate your good thoughts. Tell your wife that she looks great — and sexy — in the dress she's wearing; tell your husband that his big, competent hands, or his crinkly blue eyes, have always turned you on. What's wrong with telling your husband that you appreciate how hard he works to support the family, or telling your working wife that you appreciate the extra income she brings in, or that he or she is really a terrific parent? In general, let your partner know that you care — on a regular basis. This is the thing that husbands and wives past the courtship stage tend to forget, and yet it's one of the secret ingredients in keeping a sense of romance alive.

Try simply hugging your partner spontaneously at some time during the day when the gesture is not connected to sex. Women in particular find nonsexual affection a turn-on that reaps its rewards later in the bedroom.

Think of yourself as lovers. Send the kids off to a relative for a visit and pull out the candles, good dishes, and gourmet food for just the two of you. One couple with young children gets a relative or baby-sitter to stay overnight with the kids every now and then while they go off to a country inn, just as they used to before they were married. "The sex on those weekends is great!" they confided.

Dr. Joshua Golden, director of the human-sexuality program at the University of California, Los Angeles, tells of helping to resurrect the love life of an elderly couple by sending them off to a place with a hot tub. The experience was so different from the unromantic routine they had fallen into over their many years together that it worked like a charm, restoring enthusiasm and vitality to their sex life.

Even when you don't go that far, try getting each other into the mood for sex instead of leaping right into it. One man who has been married close to twenty years reports that every Saturday night he and his wife listen to their favorite jazz records and leisurely share a bottle of good wine as a prelude to lovemaking. Loving words are great foreplay. So is aesthetically preparing yourself for making love as you used to do. This means no greasy face creams, no hair up in rollers. No boxer shorts or uninspiring pajamas or nightgowns, and no irritating stubble on your chin.

In starting a program to put romance back into your marriage, naturally there has to be cooperation between the partners. This means that you have to start talking together about what you are feeling. As important as talking about your own emotions is listening with sympathy and receptiveness to your mate's point of view. Honest, open communication between two well-meaning people can rekindle romance as much as hand holding can.

Of course, some men and women make the mistake of thinking that marriage will be *all* romance. When the inevitable problems and disillusionment with a partner crop up as the couple settles into a domestic existence, they may feel that they are falling out of love. "Most people expect to live happily ever after," says Dr. Golden. "When troubles begin to arise in the marriage, they're very disappointed. They don't recognize that the difficulties they are experiencing are part of the natural process of accommodation in marriage." So although it is important to keep a sense of romance from going out of your relationship altogether, don't go to the other extreme and expect marriage to be all high romance either.

THE LIFELESS RELATIONSHIP

For some couples, it isn't only romance that is missing from the marriage — it's life itself. Sex has lost its thrill because vitality has gone out of the relationship.

According to Dr. Gottlieb, it's a problem that affects a large number of the couples he sees. Husband and wife have become involved in other areas of their lives that, over time, have become more exciting and satisfying to them than each other. "Running a big department in a million-dollar corporation can become more exciting than turning on with one's spouse. Pursuing a new career can be much more interesting than paying attention to a humdrum husband," says Dr. Gottlieb. "Or raising children may become more satisfying than relating to a spouse."

If you no longer focus on each other, even though you may not consciously realize it, you will inevitably begin to feel bored in each other's company. And when boredom takes over, sex, too, loses its sparkle and becomes mechanical. Sooner or later the couple in a devitalized relationship begin to avoid the lackluster sex. One partner stays up until the other goes to sleep, or both complain of exhaustion — a signal to forget about sex. A million reasons start to interfere and the couple ends up having sex less and less frequently.

Take Betty and Bob. They married while he was still in medical school, just after she had graduated from college. While Bob finished his training, Betty worked as a secretary to the head of a department at a university. Soon after Bob started practicing medicine they decided to have children, and before long they were the happy parents of a boy and a girl. Betty stayed home with the children while Bob built up his practice. He became a leading doctor in the community.

When the children were both in school, Betty decided to go back to school herself and become a lawyer. She worked hard and managed successfully to juggle her roles as wife, mother, and student. After graduation she started working as an attorney for a large law firm, where she had to work late many nights.

Now both Betty and Bob had demanding careers with long hours. They spent more and more time away from each other. Most of the time they would fall into bed exhausted. Although sex had been good for most of their marriage, it now started to become a rare item. Today, they are lucky if they get together once a month. Betty and Bob still get along when they are together, but they have fewer and fewer interests to share. Their real passion lies in their careers.

Roger, on the other hand, started out working in an ordinary corporate job that allowed him to keep regular hours and gave him plenty of time to be with his young wife, Harriet. Harriet preferred being a housewife to working. Seven years into the marriage, Roger landed a new job with an international cosmetics company. He began to travel all over the world. He dined with famous men and women. He went to glamorous parties. He lived in the best hotels of Paris, Rome, London, and the Far East.

Meanwhile, Harriet stayed home raising the children. When Roger came home, it seemed such a comedown from the exciting existence he had left behind. Life with Harriet lacked the luster he enjoyed on his job. Sex began to fall off until Roger and Harriet almost never slept with each other.

Sometimes the problem is that after you're married, your life together seems less interesting than it did while you were courting. "The context changes," says Dr. Gottlieb. "The couple's current ambience is no match for the more colorful one in which they met, fell in love, courted, and married."

Dr. Gottlieb gives as an example one couple who met at college when they were involved in working for the same cause. "At nineteen they marched and picketed and slept on the floor of the Unitarian Church. Even if sex wasn't so wonderful then, they were caught up in a heady, exciting ambience and they felt excited with one another. That's a very different kind of loving experience for this couple than now," he points out, "when they are in their late thirties, have two kids, dinner gets burned sometimes, and one of the kids is using drugs.

"Couples get drained," says Dr. Gottlieb. "They get drained by the myriad demands of their roles. They have jobs, kids, households, problems with in-laws and dying or senile parents. They get caught up in the humdrum, trivial, involved, everyday events of life and they can't find time to attend to each other or do the things that would re-create that initial, marvelous, exciting sense of being two people with just one skin."

Some couples allow their relationship to lose its zip because they never make time just to have fun together anymore. They went out on "dates" before marriage and as newlyweds, but now they feel they don't have enough time or money for mere frivolity. Or they may go out only with the children in tow so that they never have recreational time alone. Or, after marriage, they may just slip into a deadening routine of dinner, TV, and then, plop, into bed.

Inevitably, sex reflects the lifelessness that has settled in elsewhere and becomes boring, too. Dr. Gottlieb often suggests that bored, devitalized couples embark on a program of surprising each other. The surprise can be anything, just as long as it's unpredictable. It could be a new hairdo, totally different from the one you have been wearing for fifteen years; it could be airline tickets for a mini-vacation over the weekend. The purpose of the surprises is to shake up the relationship. "When you have to devise something new, something that will really surprise your partner," explains Dr. Gottlieb, "you have to begin to think about yourself and who you are, as well as what is expected from you. Then you have to come up with something that will change you in some way — which, in turn, necessitates a change in your partner in response to your innovation." Soon new and interesting things are going on between you and, says Dr. Gottlieb, "the discouraging downward spiral has a chance to become a new upward cycle."

Couples with lifeless relationships also have to begin to set aside blocks of time for just each other — time in which they can shut off jobs, children, worries. Commit yourselves to at least two evenings a week and one weekend a month to be spent as "couple time." It may mean hiring baby-sitters so that you can be undistracted by other demands when you are alone. Don't worry about the kids. Creating a better relationship between you and your spouse is the best thing you can do for them. If you have young children, it may also mean putting a latch or lock on your bedroom door so that your boudoir becomes a private place for just the two of you to enjoy each other sexually again without the fear of intrusion. It may mean deliberately not turning on the television set a couple of nights each week so that you can get to know one another again by talking. Most of all, it means refocusing your sights, giving your relationship priority over jobs, kids, or all the other things that have taken top place in your life. Of course, first you have to agree mutually that you really want to start a program to rescue your devitalized relationship from boredom and restore some of its original pizzazz. This means you will have to bring the problem out in the open and discuss it.

Remember Roger, whose glamorous job made his marriage

seem dull by contrast? Realizing at age forty-eight that his marriage had gone dead, he decided to do something about it. He reestablished his priorities and took a decisive step: he quit his job and bought a large farm, where he and his wife could lead a simple life and rediscover each other. In a matter of months they drew closer together again and found that sex followed. It increased in both frequency and intensity.

You probably don't have to do anything as drastic as quitting a job. You just have to put as much energy into your marriage as you devote to those other parts of your life that are draining you. Sometimes, however, a man and woman are stuck with the fact that they never put much life into the marriage from the outset. Often, they may have approached their union "sensibly" rather than emotionally: perhaps she looked for a husband who would be a good father and a reliable provider; maybe he looked for a woman who would be a good mother and a fine housekeeper. They may have married simply because it was time to do so, or in order to further individual goals in life: she may have been the boss's daughter, which would help his career along; he may have been rich or from a social class she wanted to enter. Whatever the reason, the marriage was not undertaken out of love or excitement, and sex reflects that fact. Unexciting from the start, their sexual relationship became more so over the years — to the point of expiring altogether from ennui.

Marriages like this generally cannot be brought to life, nor can the sex. Dr. Helen Singer Kaplan thinks that there are hopeless cases and that these include spouses who were never attracted to each other from the beginning.

THE PERFECT-SPOUSE SYNDROME

"Boredom" also commonly occurs when the man and wife enter into a conspiracy and decide that they will always be "the perfect couple."

Sometimes when a couple marries, they have already been dubbed "the perfect couple" by those around them. She may have been the most popular girl in her class; he may have been a football star. Or perhaps they were the offspring of two of the most prominent families in town. Maybe he graduated at the head of his class and she ran away with almost all of the other academic honors; or she was very beautiful and he was very handsome; or they both came from religious families active in the church. For whatever reason, to everyone, including themselves, they looked like an ideal match.

Once married, they are determined to keep up this image forever. They decide that they will always be reasonable, thoughtful, and kind. They will never become annoyed or raise their voices to one another. They will never have arguments.

In sex, one will never turn the other down. Neither of them will ever say, "I'm bushed tonight, let's wait until morning," or feel too distracted by a worry, or feel just "not in the mood." And neither will ever hint that he or she might like something different or better in sex.

Sometimes people who fall into the perfect-couple trap had parents who were divorced. Determined not to repeat the mistakes of their parents, they decide they will never argue or do anything else to imperil the marriage.

Perfect couples may spend a lifetime sweeping problems under the rug. A secretly reluctant partner may have sex because the other wants it, or because that's what good couples are supposed to do. They never communicate about anything that is bothering them. As a result, they grow more and more apart from one another emotionally. Things may feel a little empty at home and in bed, but they never admit it to themselves or each other. They have a relationship that is all form and no content. Still, along with their friends, they continue to think of themselves as "the perfect couple."

The late Dr. Jay Mann saw couples like this disturbingly often in therapy. He said that they often start out saying, " 'We were the envy of our friends. We were the perfect campus couple.' But if you look at what was going on with them, they had the name without the game. These couples get along well, they do things together, they share a lot of interests, but you find that they're shoving a lot of stuff away," according to Dr. Mann. "Each one thinks, 'Since we are having such a good relationship, why should I quibble about little inconsequential things? File it away.' They both want to maintain the myth of the perfect marriage but, in the process, what they do is suppress a lot of energy in the relationship. In the process of suppressing other things, they suppress the sexual energy as well."

The desire to maintain a perfect facade may be one-sided. A wife, for example, may decide that she will always be perfect and reasonable even though her husband loses his temper and allows himself to be less than perfect. She always has sex when he wants it, even though she may not.

Jane was like that. She came from a broken home and remembered the arguments that preceded her parents' divorce. She was determined to have a conflict-free marriage, one that would last forever. Jane knew that sex was important to her husband, Ken, but after her three children were born, she was sometimes too exhausted from caring for them to want sex. Nevertheless, she pretended enthusiasm whenever Ken approached her at night. To her consternation, after a while Jane found herself dreading their frequent sexual encounters — although she never let Ken know this. Soon she stopped having orgasms and started to fake them, and then she stopped feeling any desire at all.

The perfect-couple or perfect-spouse syndrome generally leads to less-than-perfect sex. Perfect spouses have to learn to do two things: to establish honest, meaningful communication, which presently does not exist between them; and to start tuning in to their own needs and wishes.

Tomorrow, instead of automatically trying to please your partner when you are together, pull a mental switch. Look inward. Rather than ask yourself, as you usually do, "What does he (or she) want?" ask, "What do I want right now?" It may be difficult for you to get an answer to that right away. You may have trouble locating your own feelings and wishes — after all, you are out of practice. You probably haven't listened to yourself in years. But keep asking yourself, "What do I want?" until you get an answer, then tell your mate what you want.

At first, you may feel selfish trying to insinuate your needs into the relationship. If you believe the adage that it is better to give than to receive, you may also feel guilty. But experts believe that it is healthy to understand your own needs and express them in a relationship, and so should you. Indeed, experts agree that you won't have a real relationship until the two of you can learn to give as well as receive.

You also have to learn not to push your feelings away when you feel annoyed about something. Discuss with your mate what is bothering you, in a nonbelligerent way. Talking about things that are wrong does not ruin a marriage. If done in a nonhostile way, it saves the marriage by bringing the partners closer together.

In sex, too, you have to start tuning in to your own needs and desires, instead of just having sex when your spouse seems to expect it, and in the way he or she wants it.

Theresa, a wife who was trying to shake the perfect-spouse syndrome, learned to do this. "I used to feel myself freeze up when my husband approached me for sex, but I would do it anyway, and then not enjoy it. Now I take time to check myself. I ask myself, 'How do I feel? Do I want sex now?' If the answer is no, I tell him, and if the answer is yes, then I find I don't freeze. Since I want it myself, I feel freer to participate actively and enjoy myself."

"Surprisingly enough," says psychologist and sex therapist Lonnie Barbach in her book *For Yourself*, "most couples' frequency of sexual contact rises rather than declines once the partners feel that they have the freedom to refuse sex if they choose to do so."

If you are both acting like "perfect" spouses, one of the best things you can do is work together on your major problem as a couple: not paying enough attention to your needs as individuals. In sex, a good way to learn about your own likes and dislikes (as well as your partner's) is to use the kind of sensate focus exercises that couples are taught in sex therapy.

SENSATE FOCUS EXERCISES

Set aside a series of approximately ten one-hour sessions with your partner for the purpose of merely exploring yourself and each other. An hour each day or every other day would be a good schedule. Avoid intercourse until the series is completed. Get ready by taking showers, then going to bed without any clothing on. The first five sessions should be devoted to touching and stroking each other all over your bodies, but not in genital areas. These are called pleasuring exercises.

Take turns. First, one of you lies on your stomach while the other caresses, gently and tenderly as possible, the back of the head, ears, neck, down the back and sides, down the buttocks and the inside of the thighs. Now turn over. The partner proceeds to caress the chest, belly, sides, thighs, legs, feet. The penis for men and nipples and vagina for women are temporarily off-bounds.

The person who is being caressed should concentrate only on his or her own feelings and not worry about whether the partner is getting tired. It is important to give feedback. If something feels good, tell your partner; if something doesn't feel good, say so, too. The caressing should continue until the person being stroked feels that he or she has had enough. Then it is the partner's turn. The same exercise is repeated now, with the other spouse being caressed — first all down the back side of the body, then all over the front — and telling the first partner what is pleasing and what isn't. Again, the partner being stroked should concentrate only on personal feelings and should not worry about the other partner. Intercourse is forbidden. These pleasuring exercises, meant to increase sexual communication as well as individual awareness of what feels good and what doesn't, are also devised to create a context devoid of pressure to have intercourse or to please a partner.

After you have finished a series of five touching-and-caressing sessions, with each of you taking turns in all five, you are ready to go on to phase two of sensate focus, which is genital pleasuring. In the next five sessions, the purpose is to give each other genital pleasure. Again, do as much body caressing as you like, putting to use what you have learned from the previous pleasuring exercises to arouse your partner, but this time you can play with each other's genitals and genital areas as well. Continue to be as gentle and sensitive as possible.

Once more, it is essential to concentrate only on your own sensations while being caressed and to tell your partner what feels good and what doesn't. Intercourse is still forbidden. The aim of these genital pleasuring exercises is not orgasm, but simply to learn what turns you on and what turns your partner on.

You may want to use body lotions or oils, which some sex therapists recommend to increase the sensual experience of these exercises. Only after you have gone through the whole cycle of ten sensate focus sessions should intercourse be attempted once more. By this time, you should have learned how to be "selfish" and ask for what you enjoy, as well as how to be giving and please your partner in sex. Pleasuring exercises should also have helped you to communicate better with each other about sex — which, according to Lonnie Barbach, often leads to improved communication about other matters as well.

If you find that you resist doing these exercises or sabotage them, you and your partner may need help from a therapist in sorting out the sexual and emotional problems that have accrued in your relationship.

NO TELL, NO SHOW

Another simple cause of boredom in sex is lack of sexual communication. Sometimes a husband or wife will be afraid to tell a spouse what they really yearn for in sex. She may want more foreplay; he may want fellatio. They both keep silent. Husbands and

wives continue to put up with sex that lacks an essential ingredient or that fails altogether because of their inability to communicate what it is they do or do not want.

Dr. Helen Singer Kaplan gives as an example of this a husband
who had a good relationship with his wife but lost interest in her
sexually because he felt their lovemaking lacked variety. He
wanted to add some new positions to their repertoire, but was
afraid to suggest them to his wife because he felt that she would
then realize he had had better experiences with other women.

Another of Dr. Kaplan's examples: a wife who was satisfied
with her husband in other ways but was turned off sexually because he always touched her in a way she felt to be rough and
clumsy. She kept avoiding sex with her husband but failed to tell
him what the problem was.

One woman interviewed for this book revealed that she had
just gone through menopause and found, to her dismay, that the
same kind of lovemaking that was satisfying to her before menopause now caused her discomfort, even pain. Because her genital
area had become more sensitive, she would have preferred that
her husband touch her lightly rather than in the somewhat more
forceful way that had been effective in the past. But instead of
telling him that a heavier touch now irritated her, she kept quiet
and endured the discomfort. As a result, she began to avoid sex;
she went to bed early, complained of tiredness, purposely failed to
pick up her husband's sexual signals. Though she had enjoyed sex
all of her life, now, in menopause, she found herself turned off —
not because of the change of life, but because she had failed to
communicate her new needs to her husband.

It can also be difficult to tell a partner about simple things like
unpleasant body odors. For example, one woman had found
everything fine before marriage because her husband had always
showered just before coming to meet her. Now, she discovered, he
had a body odor by the time he came to bed at night — he had
not showered since the morning, before going to work. She was
bothered by this, but did she tell her husband about it? No. As a

result, she found herself feeling more and more turned off, even though she had been married less than a year.

You may object to bad breath, to the smell of after-shave or face creams, to the feel of stubble on a man's face. Whatever the cause, if you don't speak up, your feeling of aversion may, eventually, translate into ennui. You will care less and less about having sex with your mate because you couldn't bring yourself to talk about what was troubling you.

If you aren't talking about what's bothering you, it's probably because you are afraid of offending or alienating your partner. What will happen, in reality, if you speak up will have a lot to do with the way you present your complaint. If you phrase it as a command — "You had better do it!" — or a threat — "I'm going to leave you or find someone else unless you change!" — of course you will get a negative reaction. Your mate will feel attacked and called upon to defend himself, perhaps even to counterattack. But if you communicate in a way that makes this seem like an opportunity for growth in the relationship — "There are some changes that could increase our pleasure and make our sex life better" — chances are that your mate will react favorably.

Talking about what is bothering you may create an opportunity for mutual disclosure. Ask questions to find out if your spouse has been hiding anything from you, too: "Is there anything you would like to change? . . . Are there different positions you might want to try? . . . Is there anything that I do that offends or displeases you?" If your mate comes up with something, remember to listen in an open and receptive way — just the way you want to be heard.

You may feel uncomfortable the first time you try to bring up delicate matters. You may even be determined to open up, then find that you stop yourself before what you have to say comes out. Try again soon, and keep trying until you succeed. Your only other choice is to remain quiet and stay dissatisfied, or turned off, for the rest of your sex life. A chance at improving things is certainly better.

THE STATISTICAL APPROACH

Another almost surefire way to turn sexual excitement into boredom is to keep count: You feel that you should have sex two or three times a week, or every other night, or every night. Whatever you decide is your proper statistic, you try, like a good worker, to fulfill your quota. You make love not because you are excited, not because you feel horny, not because you feel close to your partner or she or he looks particularly good or is particularly lovable at that moment, but simply because you know you should to keep up your score, or, even worse, because you want to keep up with or surpass the Joneses.

The statistical approach can ruin sexual enjoyment. Some spouses, according to Dr. Ruth Clifford, a clinical fellow at the Masters and Johnson Institute in Saint Louis, define elaborate, self-defeating goals for themselves. In the journal, *Medical Aspects of Human Sexuality,* she notes that "sex may be planned to match, or better yet surpass, the national average in frequency, duration, and number of orgasms for both sexes." She concludes that for couples like this, "sex is treated as a discipline rather than a spontaneous and natural form of play."

In the statistical approach to sex there is little spark. Excitement is overshadowed by the undercover worry that you won't consider yourself good enough unless you fulfill your quota. This is also true in the hygienic approach to sex. You may have heard that it is necessary to make love a certain number of times a week for good physical or mental health, so you think of sex as a necessary "release" rather than a pleasure in itself. One woman confided that she once read in a magazine that orgasm helps keep a woman looking young. Ever since then she has approached sex as part of her religious program of creams, vitamins, and exercises that she believes will keep age at bay. She insists on sex once a day for beauty's sake.

If the statistical approach is ruining your love life, it's time to restructure your thinking. When you next decide to have sex, ask yourself, "Why now?" Do you really feel sensual? Does your partner really seem appealing to you tonight? Be honest. If the answer is no, then consider the fact that you may be driving yourself to have sex out of worry. Are you feeling horny, or are you really thinking something like this: "Here it is Thursday. The last time I had sex was on Tuesday. If I don't have sex tonight and at least once on the weekend, I won't be a three-time-a-week person anymore, and then I wouldn't be normal or above average." Sex cannot remain fun and pleasurable if you constantly keep score.

SEX AS WORK

Even if you don't keep count, sex can become work. "I am always monitoring what's going on," admitted one man. "I pride myself on being a good lover. I like to do what pleases my partner and bring her to heights of ecstasy, so I try to pick up clues as to what she likes, what is turning her on. If I feel she isn't getting turned on, or she isn't as turned on as she can be, then I begin to worry that I am not good enough."

The man speaking is typical of people who have turned sex into a job. They become a "spectator," self-consciously watching what's going on during their sexual encounters rather than enjoying themselves. "Workers" at sex worry about how they are rated as lovers. They are also goal-oriented: they can't appreciate sex for itself; instead, they have to give their partners an orgasm every time so that they can give themselves an "A" on their own internal report cards.

Another form of sex as work has to do with attitude. Instead of feeling that to bring a partner to orgasm is part of a pleasurable process, some men and women inwardly resent having to "work" on their partners. For example, a man may find it tiresome to engage in lengthy foreplay, or to stimulate a woman's clitoris for the amount of time it may take her to reach orgasm. A woman might wish that she didn't have to spend so much time and effort stimulating her partner's penis either manually or orally. Although each partner may continue to do whatever is necessary, neither enjoys it. Both wish that the "chore" were over with or that they didn't have to do it at all.

Some women start to regard sex as work when they find themselves having to "beat the clock" in order to keep up with their partner. If a woman knows that she takes a long time to reach orgasm, for example, she may try to speed herself up. She will certainly try to hurry if she knows her sexual partner ejaculates prematurely or loses his erection quickly a good deal of the time. One woman was even forced to hurry by her husband, who placed a three-minute egg timer by the bedside and told her that was all the time he was going to allow her. But even without a sandglass, a man who makes his distaste for lengthy foreplay obvious might be making his partner rush.

The search for heightened pleasure can, by itself, turn sex into work. For example, many couples these days buy books and manuals about sex and, like good students, follow all the prescriptions in them. They constantly search for the right formula to produce sexual bliss. They approach ecstasy as a discipline and work methodically to achieve it — and, of course, they fail.

For those who continually monitor themselves during sex, or those who keep wishing they didn't have to do something they find irksome in order to bring a partner to orgasm, or those who otherwise have oriented themselves toward achieving a goal in sex rather than enjoying the act for itself, sex can become as tiring as any kind of hard work.

If you are a spectator, always watching and rating yourself during the sex act, sensate focus exercises such as those described earlier (pages 109–110) can be very helpful. They enable couples to learn to concentrate only on what is pleasurable during sex. By thus structuring sex so that orgasm is not the goal, the performance aspect of the sex act — the obsessive aspect — is banished. You learn to think in terms of "What feels good to me?" rather than "How am I doing?"

If your problem is irritation at having to "work" at sex, such as by engaging in lengthy foreplay, there are some questions you should ask yourself. First, is your feeling that you have to work justified? Does foreplay really last an abnormally long time — an hour, for example — or does it actually take only ten or fifteen minutes? Is the problem your partner's or yours? If it seems that your partner suffers from an orgasmic inhibition that necessitates extraordinarily long foreplay, you can talk about it — non-belligerently and sympathetically, please. Then, together, you can share the responsibility of bringing your partner to an orgasm by sharing the foreplay. You can stimulate your partner's penis or clitoris for some of the time, and your partner can do it the rest of the time. Although, like many people, you may feel there is something wrong with such self-stimulation with a partner present, experts refute this notion. The problem, however, may not be your partner's, but yours. Perhaps you don't like having to engage in foreplay. Or maybe one particular kind of foreplay bothers you. If the latter is the case, ask your partner if another kind of stimulation can be substituted. For example, can you stimulate the penis or clitoris manually rather than orally. If, however, you feel irritated at having to take part in any kind of ordinary foreplay, if you feel it's a drag rather than a pleasure to do whatever is necessary to bring your partner to orgasm, you need to work on your attitude.

There may be something in the relationship that is making you angry, so that you have a begrudging attitude toward your partner. Having to do sexual things for your mate may make you feel controlled. You may like to receive but resent having to give. Husbands may have a hidden underlying macho attitude — "women exist to serve men, in bed or out" — and resent having to "work" for a wife. You may feel that intercourse itself is okay, because it is necessary for procreation, but that other sexual activity is sinful.

If, on your own, you can't restructure your thinking so that foreplay becomes an act of pleasure rather than one of work, you might want to consult a qualified psychotherapist or sex therapist to find out why.

ONLY LATE AT NIGHT

It is easy once you are living with someone to let sex become the P.S. to the day — the last thing you do. For most couples, sex was originally spontaneous. You would come home on a Sunday afternoon, for example, and suddenly decide to make love. Or you would make love practically nonstop for a whole weekend, or you would awaken from sleep and spontaneously your bodies would draw close and a delicious, lazy, half-asleep sexual interlude would take place. Or you would make love on the living room rug, or on the couch.

"Before we were married," one wife remembered fondly, "Mike and I used to meet at my apartment during lunch hours. Instead of eating lunch, we would make love and then go back to work feeling wonderful." Unfortunately, she and Mike have done nothing sexually spontaneous in fifteen years. Like most couples, they make love only late at night, when they have fallen into bed to go to sleep.

Lovemaking only late at night can turn sex into the last effort of an exhausted mind and body. The result? Sex becomes hurried, uninspired, and uninspiring. Eventually, you may begin to equate the exhaustion you bring to your lovemaking with the sex itself. It lacks energy. It becomes less and less appealing. It's boring, so you stop doing it so often or at all.

You could do wonders for your love life by scheduling sex before dinner some evenings, while you are still fresh and perky. Setting your alarm an hour earlier in the morning could change sex from the soggy leftover it has become into a piquant sexual appetizer to your day. Lovemaking on a weekend afternoon could give you a whole new perspective. One couple solves the problem of evening tiredness by setting the alarm, going to sleep for an hour or two, and then waking up and having sex before going back to sleep again. A woman who has had a glorious sex life with her husband for eighteen years revealed that they frequently wake up in the middle of the night, make love spontaneously, and then fall asleep again.

Sometimes the only-late-at-night syndrome is fostered by the presence of children: you feel they might barge in if you "did it" at any other time. Try a latch on your door. It won't make you a bad parent to keep the kids out while you and your husband learn to put a little zip back into your own relationship.

GUILT

It is rarely talked about, but many people continue to masturbate after they are married. This becomes a problem if they feel guilty about it. There are many reasons why married people masturbate. They may, for example, be compensating for problems with the quality of their sex life.

Some husbands, for instance, masturbate because they feel their wives don't really like sex and they don't want to bother them too much. Or a wife may want sex less frequently than her husband and turn him down so often that he resorts to masturbation.

Some women masturbate secretly after sex with their husbands because they feel left up in the air: they experience excitement, but without an orgasm to resolve it. Often this can happen because a wife has failed to tell her partner to do something she needed him to do to help her climax. She may have faked an orgasm or, acknowledging that she didn't have one, covered her dissatisfaction by assuring the man, "It doesn't matter. I'm satisfied just feeling close to you." For physical satisfaction, she secretly turns to her own devices, masturbating in the bathroom, for example, or after her husband has fallen asleep.

On the other hand, many men and women masturbate because they simply like reaching orgasm alone sometimes, with a fantasy in mind. One of the reasons men's magazines sell so well is that many men like looking at a centerfold and masturbating.

Yet, despite the physical pleasure they get from it, many husbands and wives who masturbate feel guilty. They feel that masturbation shouldn't be necessary in marriage, if at all. Sometimes guilt over masturbation invades the couple's sex life together: the guilt over masturbation is so strong they start to lose sexual desire altogether.

Rebecca Black, a San Francisco therapist, believes that such guilt comes not only from the old societal taboo against masturbation but also "from the expectation that if I'm in a relationship, my partner is going to meet all my sexual needs. I think that's as unrealistic as thinking my partner is going to meet every other need I have. If solo sexuality is not okay, then every time I'm feeling horny my husband had better be available."

Dr. Harvey Caplan says that many people when they are feeling sexual "may not really want to go through the whole process of making love. They may choose to masturbate only because it is simpler," he explains. "You don't have to start dovetailing your needs, wants, and timing. Sometimes it is preferable to be alone, to have that release when you don't want the release to be an expression of caring or love or whatever."

It is important for couples to make room for masturbation in their marital life. Dr. Caplan stresses that masturbation is okay and wishes that more of the general public realized this. "If people knew it was okay, I think we would see more people owning up to masturbation within a relationship," he says. Rebecca Black underscores understanding to relieve guilt. "I think it is good for a relationship if both individuals accept that each one masturbates," she says.

Besides masturbation, there is another common phenomenon that creates guilt in marital relationships, for men, in particular: they find other women attractive and have sexual thoughts or fantasies about them. The husband who walks down the street and feels a stirring in his groin as he watches a woman with a nice pair of breasts go by, or who finds himself wondering what it would be like to have sex with an attractive co-worker, may feel that this is not what a good husband should do. If he were a good husband, he might reason, he would not find anyone but his wife a turn-on (even though his desire is confined just to looking or fantasizing). This attitude was made famous by Jimmy Carter's confession in a *Playboy* interview that he felt sinful because he had mentally lusted after women other than his wife, Rosalynn.

In order to correct such a fancied defect or "sin" — that of being attracted to other women — a husband may start to squelch his desires even before they start. Pretty soon he not only feels no desire for strangers, but feels turned off to his wife as well. He has succeeded in cutting himself off from his own sexual impulses out of guilt over a little harmless looking and daydreaming. Just as it is important for husbands and wives to recognize that masturbation is normal if it does not replace intercourse with a spouse, so is it necessary for couples to see that fantasy is normal, too.

"Fantasy, if it isn't excessive, is not only normal, it's healthy," says Dr. Edward L. Parsons. "Fantasy is part of healthy sexuality. There is a very real difference between a fantasy and acting on it, and occasional fantasies about someone other than a spouse need not interfere with a happy, monogamous relationship."

UNREALISTIC EXPECTATIONS

Dr. Harold Lief is but one of the many experts who feel that our country is what he terms "sex obsessed." Sex therapists and other observers of the sexual scene generally agree that, as a result of our national fixation with sex, sexual expectations have risen — for many, to an unrealistic degree. Some men and women feel that every sexual encounter should be a bell-ringing experience; if the expected rockets don't go off, something must be wrong.

In the *New York Times*, Dr. James O'Hagan, a clinical psychologist on the faculty of the American Institute for Psychoanalysis of the Karen Horney Institute in Manhattan, blamed books like Dr. Alex Comfort's *Joy of Sex* for many of the unrealistic expectations people have today: "Unfortunately, as helpful as these books have been to many couples, they can lead to unrealistic expectations. People tend to say, 'Why isn't my sex life this exciting? Why aren't we constantly trying these things?' But I don't know why 'normal couples' think they have to be sexual acrobats if they aren't acrobats in the rest of their lives."

Sometimes the disappointment stems from a failure in togetherness. "Many normal married couples think that good sex means that a husband and wife must always have orgasms together — that's the passing grade. But that is not reality," according to Dr. O'Hagan. "Both partners aren't always ready; anything from touching one another to one partner having an orgasm can be very satisfying."

Unrealistic expectations can damage the relationship of older couples who worry needlessly about the husband's slower sexual response. One husband who showed up at a sex therapy clinic with his wife because of impotence revealed that he thought he should be able to get an erection just by looking at his naked wife. He regained his potency immediately when, upon instruction from his therapist, his wife spent some time stimulating his penis. Other men and women expect their first sexual experiences to be wonderful. They don't account for inexperience and assume that if initial experiences are disappointing, something must be wrong with them, or that sex itself is not what it is cracked up to be. One young college sophomore kept saying that sex was a hell of a lot less exciting than he had expected it to be.

"Most people are disappointed with their initial sexual experiences — at least with intercourse, because it doesn't match their expectations," says Dr. Joshua Golden. "It has been oversold. They expect that it is going to be wonderful, that bells are going to go off."

Sometimes men and women expect too much of themselves under adverse circumstances. For example, many women and some men find it difficult to function well sexually unless they are involved in a caring relationship. Yet, if perchance they sleep with someone on a casual basis and find that they can't perform or that the sex is unexciting, they think that something is wrong with themselves or their partner rather than recognizing that lack of emotional involvement was the culprit.

Unrealistic expectations can ruin what otherwise might be satisfying sex lives for many men and women today. It is important, therefore, to recognize the following limitations to sex:

- Human beings are not machines. Some experiences are going to be better than others, even when you adore and are deeply attracted to the other person. Not every sexual encounter is going to be a mind-blowing experience. Not every sexual experience will end in orgasm for one or both partners.
- Wonderful sex rarely happens during a couple's first sexual encounters — even when you are both sexually experienced. It happens even less to those who are just starting their sex lives. It takes time to learn about your own sexuality, as well as a partner's.
- Good sex depends very much upon our feelings. Trust and caring, the right person, the right place, and the right time are important for many people. To expect sex to be grand if the ingredients are wrong is the same as expecting a cake to be delicious even when you forget to put in some of the ingredients listed in the recipe.
- Our bodies and our sexual responses change as we grow older. To think that at fifty or sixty we can function exactly as we did when we were twenty is like expecting a thirty-year-old car to run the way it did the day we bought it.

MUTUAL INHIBITION

Some couples are able to be spontaneous and free in their sexuality before they marry or live together, but then, slowly, unconsciously, they become more and more inhibited with one another. Spontaneity and freedom gradually die. Before they know it, rigid, dull routines take the place of their former free sexual behavior.

They may have sex only on certain days or only at night. Or they do the same one or two things the same way every time they make love. They might wish for something different, but they never ask for it. Mutual inhibition has set in.

According to Dr. Otto Kernberg, mutual inhibition is very common. "A lot of 'boredom' is really a mutual sexual inhibition," he says. "Husband and wife don't dare to be as free with each other as they were initially. "What impresses me," he continues, "is how often there is a gradual restriction of sexual behavior in marriage. Both are afraid of expressing their needs because each fears the disapproval of the other. They make life mutually impossible for each other without even knowing it."

Why does such mutual inhibition take place? One reason is that no matter how liberal people are while they are single, once married they frequently start to identify with the values they were brought up with, which were often antisexual. Frequently, too, the couple consciously or unconsciously may feel that marriage is a way of becoming "proper," or respectable, and they define respectability as refraining from wild sexual behavior.

A good example of this is one husband who used to have sex in the afternoon with his wife before marriage but no longer does. He explained why: "Sex in the afternoon is for affairs!" His tone of voice expressed indignation that afternoon sex should even be thought of within the context of marriage. This same couple made love spontaneously several times a week, at all hours, while they were having "an affair." Now that they are a respectable married couple, however, sex takes place only on Saturday morning. In this case, the wife does not share her husband's orientation and she is increasingly upset by the restricted quality of her sex life, particularly because it contrasts so sharply with her premarital experiences with her husband.

Another reason for mutual inhibition is that all of us, when we were children, were told what to do and not to do by our parents, who often punished us for wrongdoings. We were generally afraid of displeasing our parents. To us, they seemed very strict, prohibitive, and judgmental, often more so than they were in reality. As adults, we still carry the residue of that childish view of our parents, but now it is inside us, acting as a moral judge, ready to restrict and disapprove. Although they may not be aware of it on the surface, when a couple's sexual behavior becomes rigid and inhibited, it is often because they are seeing each other as restrictive parents from their childhood. "We all have an unconscious morality that is much stricter than our conscious morality," says Dr. Kernberg, "and over time a couple tends to bring out this strict morality in each other. Each becomes the other's conscience, with the result that each inhibits the other psychologically and sexually."

Dr. Roman Anshin takes a very Freudian view. "Inhibitions and rigid sexual behavior that set in after marriage are sometimes due to Oedipal guilt," he says. During the Oedipal stage of development, which generally takes place between the ages of three and six years, a child begins to feel desire for the parent of the opposite sex. At the same time, the child feels guilt about this and fears punishment. Such longing for the parent, though normal at this age, is felt to be wrong and sinful. When a person marries and enters into a domestic situation, the spouse often becomes unconsciously identified with the opposite-sex parent, and sexual feelings and behavior may become increasingly restricted because, according to Dr. Anshin, "sex becomes dirty — sexual feelings for mother or father are dirty."

But Dr. Joshua Golden has a much simpler explanation for restricted sexual behavior that sets in after marriage: "Given the importance of being sexually competent in our culture, people who find ways of 'doing it' successfully tend to stick to those tried and true ways because they are afraid of failing if they try something different," he says. "And that, of course, if not fatal, is certainly a serious blow to sexual interest, because if you don't do anything to experience variety and novelty and don't change or experiment, then sex becomes as boring and uninteresting as anything else. I think that is one of the reasons that there is so much appeal in vicarious and not-so-vicarious sexual activities: going to movies, reading erotic material, being titillated by portrayals in the media, or seeking out affairs with other people."

The simplest answer to why some married couples stick to unsatisfying, unvaried sexual routines came in answer to a questionnaire distributed to physicians by the magazine *Medical Aspects of*

Human Sexuality. Although the majority of those queried picked "fear of rejection" or "being considered abnormal" from a series of possible reasons (which fits in with Dr. Kernberg's idea of spouses viewing each other as restrictive parent figures), 13 percent voted for "lack of imagination" — which, alas, for a number of men and women, may indeed be true.

If mutual inhibition seems to be a problem in your marriage, taking the initiative yourself is the only way to break the sexual deadlock you and your spouse are in. It may take courage, it may make you feel vulnerable, but the end result will be worth the discomfort and sense of risk.

Try making sexual overtures at different times and places. Try different positions. Even if it makes you feel silly, try sex in the living room instead of the bedroom, or on the carpet instead of in your bed. Sexual refreshers can take place on Sunday afternoon, early in the morning, or before dinner at six. If you are always on top, try being on the bottom for once, or vice versa. If you never have done it, try a side-by-side position, or even a sitting position.

Since what may be holding you back is your unconscious view of your spouse as someone who would disapprove of any kind of innovation, apply the scientific method to test out your hypothesis. Scientists test their theories by doing an experiment, then checking the results. You can do the same by trying something new and then checking out your mate's reaction to it. Ask your partner how he or she liked the new twist you have added to your repertoire. Chances are you will not be greeted with the disapproval or rejection you inwardly feared. Your spouse may even be grateful, because finally someone — you — did something to break the boredom that was killing your sex life.

Now that you understand some of the relatively simple problems that can snuff out passion in marriage, let's go on to take a close look at some other, more subtle ones. These more deep-seated issues can also be helped but, unfortunately, generally not through "quick fixes." Some couples find, however, that simply by recognizing the nature of the problem that is interfering with their sex life (which the following pages should help them do), they are able to start on a path toward working out a solution together. Others discover that they need outside help to overcome patterns and hang-ups that are interfering with the full expression of sexuality. The list of sex clinics in appendix B may prove useful if you recognize yourself or your spouse in one of the chapters that follow and think that your marriage would benefit from expert help.

CHAPTER 9

Ghosts from the Past

ONE of the underground issues that affects us all, to some degree, is based on a fact that, at first, may seem shocking: When two people are in bed together, they are not alone. Although the door is shut fast and the blinds pulled tight, a population from the past often manages to get in. Ghosts of mothers, fathers, brothers, sisters can haunt bedrooms. Even our relationship to God, formed in our original families, may, unbeknownst to us, affect our most intimate relationships. One of the most common ways that "ghosts" haunt relationships is built into them from the start.

ATTRACTIONS

Quite often, what appeals to you about your spouse in the beginning is the very thing that has the potential for turning you off later: your mate on a subliminal level reminds you of your mother or father. Your mother was petite, and so you choose a petite woman. Your father was big, so you only find tall men attractive.

People often single out a blond, a brunette, or a redhead as a partner for the same reason — it was the color of a parent's hair.

Sometimes, it is just a subtle odor that reminds you of your parent, or the particular feel of a person's skin. One woman realizes that the size and warmth of her mate's hand when she holds it reminds her of the way her father's hand felt when he walked with her on Sundays. Many other adults find it hard to make the connection. They deny any resemblance between their mate and a parent, protesting, "She doesn't look at all like my mother," or "He's not at all like my father!"

Dr. Berta Anagnoste finds that mates are often similar not to the aging parent of today, however, but to the way the parent looked when younger. When she suspects this is an issue, Dr. Anagnoste often has patients bring in photographs of their mother or father when they were younger and then asks them to compare these pictures with the mate. "It's amazing how often there is a resemblance. Often the patient sees it for the first time in this way."

A partner's hidden resemblance to mother or father can raise the subliminal, antilibidinal specter of incest. The original attraction thus bears the seeds of sexual destruction. It's a catch-22 situation that operates in many people's marriages.

MESSAGES

All of us when we were growing up received messages about sex from our families. If we were lucky, the messages were positive: Sex is fun. Sex is enjoyable. Sex is good.

People who received positive messages generally are able to go on and freely enjoy their sexual relationships as adults. Most of us, however, were not that lucky. We received negative messages about sex: Sex is wrong. Nice girls don't. Nice boys don't do it to nice girls. Masturbation is a sin. Sex will drain your energies. Body odors are disgusting.

"A family silence about sex can also be a powerful message which may translate into: S-e-x is so bad we don't even talk about it," writes Dr. Helen Singer Kaplan. Frequently, religious messages reinforce negative messages from the family. "Our Judeo-Christian heritage has equated sex with sin for two thousand years," writes Dr. Kaplan. "A child in our culture is programmed with this equation. He is lovingly encouraged by his family to develop physically, intellectually, socially and artistically. However, his budding sexual feelings are labeled as bad. Sexual curiosity, play and masturbation are all discouraged. In very religious homes," she notes, "masturbation and erotic fantasies are explicitly strictly forbidden, but in more liberal families, where the antisexual indoctrination is more subtle, children can hardly escape the feeling that sexual pleasure is somehow 'not quite nice.' " The result of the negative messages? According to Dr. Kaplan, "most of us experience a 'guilty conscience' when we violate the old taboos later in life and for some persons the messages are so strong, that they inhibit the natural flow of sexual expression." For example:

- A woman named Tess grew up in a happy, loving, and very religious home where she was warned about "impure" thoughts and told they were a sin. When Tess married, she found that she could not feel any desire for her husband. She still could not allow herself to have impure thoughts.
- Serena was taught by her family and her religion that sex was for procreation, not pleasure. As a result, after the three children that she and her husband wanted were born, Serena lost interest in sex: it was now for fun and no longer for procreation — which made it forbidden.
- Bart came from a family that taught him that sex was a man's responsibility. Consequently, Bart watched himself closely in his sexual relationships to make sure he was managing his responsibility well. Unless he brought his partner to ecstasy and orgasm, he feared that he was not performing well as a man. For Bart, saddled with his family's lingering message, sex is more of a worry than a pleasure.

The strict messages we receive about sex from our families or our religion often result in a very common phenomenon — the

Whore-Madonna syndrome, in which men split women into two categories: good or bad.

Take Joe. He and Alice had an exciting love affair that lasted for five years. Sex was an important part of the relationship. Joe was crazy about Alice in bed. He loved her body, the touch of her skin, the way she smelled and moved. "I never met anyone who turned me on more," he would tell her.

Even so, Joe was hesitant about a lifetime commitment, but Alice kept pressuring him to marry her. Finally, Joe decided to take the plunge. He and Alice were married in the Catholic church they both had attended while they were growing up.

After their wedding, Joe and Alice continued to be happy with one another in every way except one: Joe, to his dismay, found that he wanted to sleep with Alice less and less. He, who had never had enough of her while they were having an affair, was progressively becoming turned off in marriage.

Men like Joe are able to enjoy sex in affairs outside of marriage, in more casual relationships, or with strangers because unconsciously they feel that the woman is "bad" for having sex outside of wedlock. In marriage, however, the wife is elevated to the status of a "good" woman and sex becomes impossible because the man has learned too well the message "You shouldn't have sex with good women."

Frequently, men who suffer from the Whore-Madonna syndrome don't have much sex with their wives, or feel that the sex they do have is colorless and without passion. Many of these men have lots of extramarital sex, however. They recover their passion by philandering with "bad" women. Further complicating the sexual picture in the Whore-Madonna syndrome is the fact that wives, in becoming "good" women in these men's eyes, also become identified with the prototype for a good woman — mother — which is another reason for the turn-off that occurs in marriage.

The female counterpart of the Whore-Madonna syndrome is the Saint-or-Sinner syndrome. A woman may enjoy sex with a man until she marries him and then turn off. She may become a philanderer also — passionate and responsive in affairs and casual sexual relationships with "sinners," but a cold fish with her husband, the "saint."

Sometimes the messages we receive in our early years make us feel unattractive or incompetent, so that sex becomes an anxious experience in which feelings of unattractiveness or incompetence are invoked. And in addition to messages from our families and from religion, there are messages from society that prevent people from leading long, full sex lives: "Sex is only for young people. . . . Sex stops after menopause. . . . A man becomes impotent in old age. . . . A man is always ready for sex. . . . Men need sex more than women. . . . A real man doesn't need much stimulation. . . . Women prefer hugging and kissing to intercourse." These messages are not necessarily true, of course, but if you believe them, consciously or unconsciously, they can affect how you perform.

PROJECTION

On top of the messages we have absorbed, "ghosts" affect our love lives in other ways. Seeing a spouse as a parent can have a devastating effect on sex. A common way that people do this is by projecting onto a partner a fantasy that, in effect, represents their ideas of how a good or bad parent behaves.

Projections generally start early in a relationship. You meet an attractive member of the opposite sex. You like the person and grow close, but before you know it, you aren't looking at this partner realistically anymore: you are approaching your lover through the haze of an idealized fantasy. You think this man or woman is the most wonderful person in the world, but your definition of "wonderful," without your being aware of it, often is based on an ideal: how you think a perfect parent would behave — caring, attentive, protective, cherishing, giving, or what have you. Frequently, at least part of your fantasy is compensatory; it is common to see a lover, in the early stages of a relationship, as possessing virtues that you felt were missing in your real-life parents.

Such projection is generally what people call "falling in love." It is also why people say "love is blind" — because you refuse to see anything in your partner that deviates from your idealized fantasy. Your partner is less of a real person at this stage of the relationship; he or she is simply the bearer of traits that you long for in another.

Michael, for example, felt that his mother was willful, strong, and domineering. As he was growing up, he wished that she were different. He longed for an easygoing, flexible mother who would not insist that she knew what was right all the time. When, at the age of twenty-five, he met Glenda, who was soft-spoken and sweet, he thought she was his ideal woman. He saw her as rather frail, amiable, and compliant. He married her with this image in mind. What happened next in Michael's relationship is what happens to most people.

After the relationship has gone on for some time, especially when you start living with your partner, reality starts to intrude whether you want it to or not. You begin to see things about your partner that deviate from your ideal. After several months of marriage, Michael began to realize that although Glenda was soft-spoken, she was really a very sturdy woman who had strongly held opinions that she felt free to voice to the man she loved.

Many people gradually adjust to reality. The fantasy fades and is replaced by a more realistic view of the partner. Other people, like Michael, however, cannot make the adjustment. Instead, they switch fantasies. They go from an all white picture to a black one. Once the partner fails to live up to the idealized projection, they abandon the "perfect" parent image. Now all they see is the partner acting like their version of a "bad" parent — like the mother, for example, who neglected them, rejected them, punished them, frustrated them, disapproved of them, or made them feel overcontrolled, suffocated, or inadequate. However they felt wronged as a child is generally how they will view their partner now.

The mate is again seen unrealistically — this time through the distortion of a projected fantasy in which the spouse becomes the bearer of traits that enraged, frustrated, frightened, or saddened in the past. In Michael's case, all Glenda was doing, in reality, was being assertive and voicing her opinions. But Michael began to feel that she was trying to dominate him. He saw her as having all of his mother's bad traits. He reacted by feeling anxious, fearful, and resentful toward Glenda — just as he used to feel toward his mother as a child.

In most cases, the negative image that replaces the original idealized one is antilibidinal in nature. Husband or wife is seen as punishing, strict, depriving, disapproving, castrating. And the reactions invoked are old ones — as in Michael's case. You become enraged, frustrated, rebellious, depressed, anxious. The war that was originally fought between parent and child is now reactivated in the marriage, and sex becomes a victim on the field of battle. It becomes something to be avoided, or it is so filled with stress that partners are subject to dysfunctions such as impotence, premature ejaculation, lack of desire, or inability to achieve orgasm.

In some instances, the spouse in the projection is seen as still exciting but dangerous — too uncontrolled or demanding — so that sex becomes intertwined with dread. In other cases, instead of substituting a "bad" fantasized image, a spouse stubbornly clings to the original idealized one of the mate, refusing to see any faults or to admit to those moments of anger, hate, or ambivalence that, as Dr. Kernberg reminds us, are part of any normal relationship.

In denying the existence of negative or mixed feelings about a spouse, some people turn any anger or hate engendered in the relationship upon themselves. Their spouses remain the "good" partner and they become the "bad," unworthy one. To make up for their sense of unworthiness, they may fall into a pattern of always trying to please the idealized mate. They may give constant service, shower the "good" partner with gifts, always defer to the other. They suppress any kind of aggression and in the process often end up suppressing libido as well. Sex, which always has an aggressive component, is seen as a defilement of the idealized mate, or as an attack upon the partner, and is therefore to be avoided.

Often, both spouses project in a relationship. Each expects the other to behave like an ideal parent. When the inevitable disappointment occurs, they then respond to one another as defective parents. They accuse each other of the same sins that their parents were guilty of in their eyes.

Much marital dissension and disappointment has its roots in this kind of projection and subsequent interaction. Couples fight out old wars with parents with each other, hoping for a better outcome this time. Since all of this is unconscious, the battle continues unresolved unless some insight into what is going on is obtained. Each mate is an ongoing source of irritation, frustration, disappointment, anger, and, sometimes, despair.

The sexual problems inherent in marriages in which projection is the basis of much of the interaction stem from three things: (1) a partner being seen as forbidding, stern, punitive — anti-erotic, instead of inviting and sexy; (2) dissension ensuing as old grudges and angers get played out (when the relationship turns bad, so does the sex); and (3) through projecting, a spouse being viewed as a parent, which raises the incest barrier (sex with a mother or father is taboo).

IDENTIFICATION

Another way that "ghosts" may interfere in your marriage is through your identification with a parent. Once married, a man might identify with his father and start acting like him, or a woman might identify with her mother and start acting like her. Generally the person identifies with the parent of the same sex, but there are exceptions, such as the man who identifies with his mother, adopts her characteristics, and acts maternally toward his wife.

Once you have become, in essence, your mother or father, you often expect your mate to respond to you as your father responded to your mother or your mother to your father. For example, you may expect your wife to cater to you the way your mother catered to your father. If she doesn't, you feel cheated and all kinds of trouble ensues in the marriage. When you start to identify your husband with your father or your wife with your mother, the incest taboo can come into play as well, blowing out the fire in your sex life.

It is also common for people to replay significant events from their parents' lives. "Take a man whose parents were divorced when the last child went to college," explained Dr. Jay Mann. "There's a possibility, when this man's last child leaves for college, that his marriage will be at risk, too." Birthdays are important in this respect. A man whose father had a heart attack at age forty-five may worry that sex could tax his heart, and he may suddenly withdraw sexually when his own forty-fifth birthday approaches; in addition, the fear that he will repeat his father's history might create anxiety or depression. The process of identification can also damage your sex life if you adopt your parents' negative attitudes about sex and start to think of it as shameful, as a sin, or as a distasteful duty, the way they did.

Some people engage in a struggle *against* identification. Because you disapprove of the way your parents lived or related, or because you disagree with the things they believed in, you may try hard to avoid being like them. Inevitably, you share many of their characteristics anyhow, but you suppress them in yourself. The very characteristics you try to keep below the surface in your own personality are frequently the ones you end up projecting onto your spouse. He or she then becomes the scapegoat for the things you dislike in yourself. You attack and feel aversion toward your partner instead of yourself, and you identify your spouse with your disliked mother or father. Sex often falls apart in cases like this, because the spouse becomes the embodiment of what you reject in yourself and your parent. Negative and warring emotions effectively short-circuit sexual desire.

INABILITY TO SEPARATE FROM YOUR PARENTS

Sometimes the problem that haunts your adult relationships is your inability to separate from your parents. You have grown up, left their home, and started a family of your own, but emotionally you still remain their child. Although this happens unconsciously, you cannot tolerate a good relationship with a spouse because it threatens your relationship with your mother or father, or both. It means separating from them.

Frequently, those who remain tied to a parent choose a spouse that reminds them of dear old Mom or Dad, physically or emotionally, or both. This can happen in two ways: either you have positive feelings for your mother or father and, consciously or unconsciously, you search for someone just like your parent to marry; or you have extremely ambivalent or negative feelings toward a parent and go out of your way to find someone as different as possible. Either way, you are tied to the parent, since Mom or Dad is your point of reference in choosing a love partner.

Therapists know that the antennae of people who go the negative route are almost always unerring: these people often wind up with the emotional replica of the hated parent anyway, even though the mate appears to be completely different on the surface. For example, Laura abhorred her father, who was weak, incompetent, and chronically unemployed. An alcoholic, he was shored up in life by her mother, who was the stronger of the two parents. Laura was determined to marry someone who was the opposite of her father. She wanted a powerful and competent man — someone she could look up to and lean on in life.

Laura started to work as a secretary for a large television network. On her job she met a leading producer, who was attracted to her good looks and flattered by her obvious admiration. Laura thought she had met the man of her dreams. He seemed big, strong, and competent. He had a powerful position at the network. He was worldly and suave, in contrast to her boorish, unsophisticated father.

She and the producer were married after a two-year courtship. Not long into the marriage, Laura began to realize that what she had believed was merely heavy social drinking, which was common in her husband's crowd, was really alcoholism on his part. And in his relationship with her, she increasingly found that she was the strong one: he depended on her rather than the other way around. Her husband's drinking started interfering with his job, and after many warnings, he was fired. He fell into a depression, was unable to mobilize even to try to find another job, and drank the whole day through. He depended on Laura now for everything — emotionally and financially. Laura had managed to find a man very much like her father, even though he appeared to be just the opposite originally.

Frequently, you force your spouse to act like a parent through an unconscious pattern of rewards and punishments. If your father was passive, for instance, you may react negatively — by complaining or becoming cold and distant — when your husband acts in an aggressive way, and you may show pleasure — perhaps by being affectionate — when he is compliant and docile. You thus condition him to be passive and mold him in your father's image.

Sometimes, when there are positive feelings about the parents, a married person chooses to live nearby or even in the same house with them. Keith was making very little money when he married Kathy. He figured that it would be cheaper if they lived with his parents until he started to earn more. From the day they moved in with Keith's parents, their sex life fell apart. Neither felt free either to initiate sex or respond fully. Both felt the presence of the parents in the bedroom next to theirs, and the lack of privacy acted as a tremendous inhibitor.

This is a common problem when a home is shared, and one that even those who are not overly tied to their parents can appreciate. Many husbands and wives refrain from having sex when they are visiting their parents' home or the folks are staying over. They are afraid of being overheard, and the ghosts of old taboos and ancient injunctions from childhood come back to haunt them.

In general, your parents are always looking over your shoulder if you haven't separated from them, whether they are on the premises or not. Virtually nobody can make love in the same room with Mother or Father.

TOO MUCH STIMULATION

Another kind of problem from the past that can infect a couple's sex life is a family background that included too much sexual stimulation. For example, Hal, who had come into therapy at the insistence of his wife, considered sex a matter of duty. He really didn't enjoy it. He grew up with an extremely exhibitionist sister who went out of her way to dress and undress around him. She kept the bathroom door partially open while she bathed so that Hal was able to see her nude in the bathtub. He remembered being sexually stimulated by his provocative sister, which made him feel both guilty and angry. He finally learned to avoid situations where his sister displayed herself. He also learned to suppress feelings of sexual excitement toward her.

When Hal married, he saw sex as a means to have children and to keep his wife happy, but not as a source of pleasure for himself. Although he was able to function, it was in a purely mechanical way. He waited until his wife had an orgasm and he ejaculated immediately afterward. Although he climaxed, he didn't enjoy it. He was just glad he wouldn't have to have sex with his wife again for a few days.

Hal's early repression of sexually exciting feelings about his sister lingered on in his psyche, as did the hidden fear he had experienced that he would be punished for his sexual feelings. Together these throwbacks ruined his ability to take pleasure in sex with his wife in later life.

Rhoda's problem was her father. He used to walk around the house without any clothing on when she was a child, often pulling her onto his lap while he was nude and hugging her. The situation was a stimulating and troubling one for Rhoda. She was placed in the position of being her mother's rival. This created a crippling conflict for Rhoda, since she needed her mother's love as well as her father's. She feared losing her mother's affection. She also was terrified that she would be punished for her sexual feelings toward her father. As a result, to this day sex and stimulation are too full of warring emotions for Rhoda. Though she is very unhappy about it, she finds herself without desire for her husband. She avoids intercourse through a variety of excuses, even though when she does have sex she is able to have orgasms. Orgasms provide her with neither pleasure nor motivation to have sex.

Denise's mother and father divorced soon after she was born. Her mother remarried when she was five. Her mother was neglectful and inattentive, and while Denise was still a young girl, her stepfather lured her into a sexual relationship, which she accepted. She felt both guilty and angry about it, but her stepfather seemed to care for her, while her mother did not. Later in life, when Denise married, she found herself avoiding sex with her husband. She wanted to keep her marriage intact and enjoyed the caring and security her husband gave her, but sex was too filled with rage, despair, and guilt for her to be able to enjoy it.

On an unconscious level, Denise felt that her husband's "mothering" function of caring for her would be destroyed if she allowed sex, which she associated with negative, destructive forces. She also felt raped and exploited by sex with her husband, and this filled her with rage — a transfer of the feelings she originally had felt toward her stepfather. Only in therapy was she able to deal effectively with the ghosts from the past and create a happier sex life for herself.

Seductive mothers, fathers, and siblings, along with parents, aunts, uncles, and stepparents who engaged in sexual fondling and abuse of children, are often found among the cast of characters in the backgrounds of many husbands and wives who have trouble with sexual desire or sexual performance, or who feel no pleasure even when they are able to have orgasms in marriage.

COMPETITION

Some parents actually feel competitive with their children. An example of this would be a mother who keeps her daughter in childish dresses long past the appropriate time and who does everything to discourage her from growing up because she does not want to face her daughter's rivalry as an attractive woman. The feeling the daughter receives from her mother's attitude is that she *is* in competition with her mother as a woman. This frequently produces intrapsychic conflict that results in some form of stunted sexual growth.

In *The Evaluation of Sexual Disorders,* Dr. Kaplan points out that "many women with orgasm and arousal difficulty have a history of having a covertly competitive relationship with their mother."

The same kind of problem may be foisted on a boy whose father is always putting down his achievements because the father can't stand competition from his son. The boy may inherit a conflicted feeling about his own masculinity, which can express itself, in part, as sexual disorders of one kind or another.

Feelings of competition, of course, can work the other way around as well. A girl may be crazy about her father and feel that her mother stands in the way of capturing his attention and love; or a boy may resent his father, who he sees as an impediment to his relationship with his mother. When such feelings persist into adulthood, they are generally manifestations of unresolved Oedipal conflicts (which are normally resolved at an early stage of childhood). There is an overly strong attachment to the parent of the opposite sex and this can create both sexual and emotional problems in adult relationships.

THE PARENTS' MODEL FOR MARRIAGE

When two people marry, they often assume that their unwritten marriage contract will be like that of their parents. Such unwritten contracts generally have to do with what you expect to get for what you give to the other person and the relationship. If, for example, a wife gives to her spouse in the way she remembers her mother gave to her father, but her husband does not give her, in return, what her father gave her mother, great rage can result.

This was the problem of a woman named Flora who entered therapy because she was puzzled over her lack of desire for her husband Don. Flora was a dedicated housekeeper and excellent cook, as her mother had been, but Don was a poor earner — unlike her father, who provided well for her mother. Flora had to work to augment her husband's salary.

Flora did not think of herself as materialistic, so she was unable to admit to herself that she was disappointed in her husband as a wage earner. She expressed her subliminal anger at his failure to assume the role she expected of him, however — by turning off to him sexually. The terms of Flora's unstated marriage contract were a duplicate of her mother's: If I am a good homemaker, you will be a good wage earner. Although it was completely out of her consciousness, Flora did not want to give her husband pleasure because of her hidden rage at him for violating his part of the contract while she was upholding her end of it.

Martin's problem was just the opposite. He expected on an unconscious level that if he earned a good living, his wife would dote on him unceasingly, just as his mother had catered to his successful father. His wife, however, decided that she wanted a career, and two years after their wedding she went back to work. This meant that meals were often not prepared on time or that they were haphazard affairs, and that his wife had interests that did not center on Martin alone. Although he encouraged his wife's aspirations on the surface, on a subliminal level Martin was boiling. He felt that since he was bringing home such a handsome salary, he was entitled to what his father had received from his mother. He ended up in couple's therapy at the insistence of his wife, who was upset because their sex life had fallen apart. It was then that he came to understand that he was operating on a contractual system that neither he nor his wife was aware of — one based more on the past than on the realities of his present life. He was able to modify his expectations of his wife and his marriage, and sex improved greatly.

THE THINGS THAT TRIGGER OUR GHOSTS

Predictably, there are special moments in relationships when ghosts of relatives — mothers and fathers, in particular — are invoked. Parental projections often start at the beginning of infatuation and gather up negative strength when reality begins to intrude. In addition, one of the most common times that a spouse starts to be identified as a parent is when a commitment to the relationship is made, whether it be by moving in together out-of-wedlock or getting married.

Actually, it is not surprising that parents haunt so many marriages. Marriage is, after all, the closest thing in life to the original parent-child relationship. We live with a mate just as we used to share quarters with Mom and Dad. Most of us are cared for and protected in many ways, just as in the past; we feel love, we feel dependency, we feel ambivalence — all echoes of the past.

Some married people find the domestic setting alone enough to raise the specter of the mother or father with whom they shared their original home. For men, particularly, the nurturing aspects of marriage can be the crux of the problem. To begin with, being nurtured causes them to associate the wife with their mother, the original caretaker. Then, for many men, nurturance also creates uncomfortable, dim, early memories of being a helpless infant totally dependent on mother for sustenance. "Men have a hard time with nurturance," pointed out Dr. Jay Mann. "I hear 'She has become a mother to me' a lot."

Some men react to nurturance by becoming a child again — by lapsing into passivity and expecting their wife to take the lead in their domestic life. Others, haunted by the unconscious specter of becoming a helpless child again, react with a conscious fear that they are becoming too dependent on their wife. Echoes of feelings from infancy are complicated by the notion that their masculinity is imperiled; society has traditionally defined dependency as a feminine trait and independence as a masculine one. The end result for many is emotional or even sexual withdrawal, to create more distance in the relationship. It is unfortunate, but distance is often mistaken for independence by men.

No matter whether the man reacts to the emotional overtones of nurturance by becoming passive or by staying aloof, the wife finds herself in the same bind. Because nurturance spells

"mother" to her husband, she becomes, on some level, Mom —
with whom no sex is possible without dread and fear interfering.
There is a built-in irony in this. Since women are trained to be
nurturers in our society, by merely fulfilling their role in marriage
they may unwittingly be turning themselves into "mothers" to
their husbands, and turning them off sexually in the process.

Of course, some women are more nurturing than others, and
some overdo it. They really do act more like mothers than wives
to their husbands, with the result that their mates lose sexual interest, although their husbands may continue to adore these
women in other ways. The incest taboo effectively cuts off desire.
And when a man adopts a paternal attitude toward his wife, the
same prohibition may occur. You can't have sex with Daddy any
more than you can with Mommy.

Changes in appearance may create an identification of a spouse
with Mother or Father where none existed strongly before. A
woman may gain weight and look more matronly, and suddenly
the man starts seeing her as his mother. Or a man might begin to
have a potbelly or become bald, and his wife suddenly finds herself looking at her father. The aging process — gray hair, wrinkles
in a mate — may trigger parental ghosts for some people.

Sometimes the actions of a spouse raise the incest barrier. A
man who felt neglected by his mother may suddenly find old
hurts and angers resurrected when his wife becomes overly busy
with the children or returns to work and is less available to him.
She becomes a resurrection of his unavailable mother. One man
recalled the fury he felt when his writer wife, trying to meet a
tight deadline on a book, worked around-the-clock for three
months. "I knew on a logical level that she had to do it, but in my
guts I felt rejected and as if she didn't love me anymore." She had
become, to him, his mother, who after her divorce from his father
became so absorbed in her new lover that he felt shut out.

Often, husbands and wives are able to keep a parent separated
mentally from a spouse only until the parent dies. After the fu-
neral, husband becomes father, wife becomes mother. There can
be cross-sex transferences, too. A mother's death may make a

woman transfer childlike dependency needs associated with her mother to her husband, for example.

One of the most common times when the transformation from spouse to parent occurs is after the birth of a child. A woman is suddenly seen in her new role of mother, and she becomes a wife-mother; or a man, now a father, becomes a husband-father. Sex may suffer as a result.

It is important to separate your spouse from members of your original family. "Familial expectations need to be brought out into the open so they can be discarded," writes Dr. Philip M. Feldman. "The uniqueness of the spouse must be appreciated, and the couple must be helped to understand that their marriage is a new ball game, not a replay of an old one."

One way to uncover the fact that your spouse may be a replica of a parent in your mind is to make two lists on a piece of paper. In the first, describe each of your parents in terms of the traits you liked and disliked. In the second, do the same thing for your spouse — write down which characteristics you admire and which you don't like. Now compare the lists.

A study conducted in the 1970s did essentially the same thing. People were asked to describe their parents and their spouses. One of the most remarkable conclusions of this study was that both men and women described their spouses as similar to their mothers. Your lists, if you are being honest while compiling them, could reveal the same thing. Have you turned your partner into a parent? Sex rarely flourishes if you have. It may be time to lose the luggage from the past that is cluttering up your view and look at your spouse as the unique individual he or she is.

CHAPTER 10

Too Close for Comfort

STANLEY had a reasonably good sex life for twenty years of his marriage to Wendy, an efficient, amiable, yet distant woman. Then their daughter was involved in a car accident. She was hospitalized for two years and left permanently disabled. The tragedy brought Stanley and his wife closer together and they were truly intimate emotionally for the first time in their marriage. Interestingly, it was at this point in their wedded life together that sex stopped altogether. To this day, Stanley and his wife still do not have sex, although they remain in a peaceful marriage.

Patrick was crazy about Jessica from the minute he met her at a mutual friend's house. Sex with her was exciting — the best he could remember — until Patrick told Jessica he loved her and asked her to marry him. Jessica said yes; then, suddenly, much to her dismay, Patrick's libido went on a vacation.

Patrick had wanted to make love to Jessica several times a week while they were still uncommitted. Now that they were engaged, he rarely wanted to make love to her at all. Jessica tried wearing provocative nightgowns. She tried seducing Patrick with good food, wine, soft music. She took him to sexy movies. She grabbed him suggestively. Nothing helped. Patrick simply wasn't interested in sex anymore, although he was still crazy about Jessica.

Sanford reflected about what happened to his sex life: "It started on the honeymoon. Sex for the two years I had known Rita before that was terrific. But suddenly, right there in Puerto Rico, I stopped wanting her in the same way. When we returned home, I began to avoid her at bedtime. At the end of just a year of marriage, we were sleeping together just once every three or four weeks. Rita likes sex and she started complaining. She wanted to know what was wrong. I couldn't tell her. I didn't know myself."

For Holly, sex was fine all through her courtship with Al and straight through their honeymoon. But when she returned home with Al as her new husband, she began to feel that sex with him was repulsive. She started rejecting him, preferring to masturbate secretly when she was alone.

What happened to the sex lives of Stanley, Patrick, Sanford, and Holly? Something that happens to a lot of people: they fell victim to the fear of intimacy, which for some individuals starts with commitment in a relationship or with increased closeness.

Fear of intimacy is one of the leading reasons why sex disintegrates in loving relationships. Whether we are aware of it or not, each of us has a "comfort zone" — the amount of "emotional space" we need between us and other people in order to feel at ease. When that space is violated by another person's getting too close, or when someone withdraws from us too much, we manipulate to return the relationship back to the comfort zone again. If we feel we have gotten too close for comfort, we pull back and do things to make the other person move away. If relations have become too cool and there is too much space, we attempt to move closer, or try to draw the other person nearer to us.

Everyone's need for space is different. Some people like a lot of closeness; some, a lot of distance. Although closeness seems to be more desirable than distance, it is terrifying to many people — so terrifying that Dr. Helen Singer Kaplan says, "In our society, people are more afraid of intimacy than sex." But this doesn't mean that people who are afraid of intimacy don't have sex problems. On the contrary: intimacy and sex are like love and marriage — one generally follows after the other — and if there is a problem with intimacy, sex soon becomes a problem, too.

Sex therapists have discovered that sex between two people in a relationship frequently starts out good. Passion can run high in the early stages; but just let the relationship reach a certain level of closeness and commitment and wham! — good-bye sexual interest. The scary moment can begin when you move in with a love partner; or, as in Patrick's case, when you get engaged; or when you get married, as Sanford and Holly found out; or when something creates closeness where it didn't exist before, as in Stanley's case. Sometimes, jitters about being too close to your partner don't surface until pregnancy or the birth of a child.

Sexual indifference is one way people withdraw and create some distance. "Shutting off sexual feelings is a defense against the intimacy they find threatening," says Dr. Kaplan. Typically, people with intimacy problems have trouble feeling sexual in close relationships, although they may operate just fine in more casual affairs. The various approaches taken by people who want more space in a relationship can lead to sexual — and emotional — alienation over the long haul. "They insulate themselves from closeness by being busy, tired, indifferent to a partner's needs," notes Dr. Kaplan — and they bring into play any or all of the avoidance techniques described in chapter 1.

Sometimes anger is used. When things are going along particularly well in a relationship, you may suddenly notice something annoying about your partner and become angry. Although the tension caused by fear of intimacy actually motivates your anger, you rarely recognize this on a conscious level. Instead, you may feel only a vague sense of uneasiness or restlessness before a surge of temper.

One man used anger ahead of time — in anticipation of close-ness — to create distance. He was courting a woman to whom he was deeply attracted. They would spend entire weekends to-gether, and he especially enjoyed those full days living as a cou-ple. But because he unconsciously felt threatened by intimacy, he always managed to pick a fight with his girlfriend on Friday nights. Often the arguments would escalate to the point where he would say, "I can't spend the weekend with you," and he would leave, thus escaping the intimate moments he both anticipated and dreaded. At other times, he would stay but say, "I can't have sex with you." Still other times, the explosion of anger was enough of a release of the tension he felt at the impending intimacy for him to be able to go on and enjoy the rest of the weekend.

It was only after a great deal of therapy that this man was able to recognize the true source of his anger and give up the Friday-night fights. Until that point, he had no notion that he was trying to create distance between himself and his partner. He had felt that the annoyances he was arguing about were real and valid.

Although they may feel a certain "loneliness" in their mar-riages, some couples manage to live if not closely, at least in rela-tive harmony if their needs for "space" are approximately the same. They pursue their own interests as individuals, they avoid discussing their feelings, and they limit talk to practical or imper-sonal matters. They may watch a lot of television in the same room, sitting side by side but not really relating, or they may spend all their leisure time with other couples so they don't have to be alone with each other. Little intimate interaction or com-munication takes place between them, but they operate con-genially with one another. There are countless marriages like this.

Sex in such relationships is often colorless and sparse. Dr. Roman Anshin says that "people who are distant tend to be more compulsive and ritualized about everything," which points to the possibility that sex may suffer from lack of spontaneity and variety.

Some couples make distance a way of life. One young husband

and wife have lived apart, in different cities, for the seven years they have been a couple. They saw each other only on weekends while they were unmarried, and although they recently wed, they continue to live in separate cities and to see each other only on weekends. If they were forced to live together all the time, they would probably not survive as a couple.

"For some couples," Dr. Jay Mann said, "sex is used as a replacement for intimacy. They may get into bed and let sex drown out any other kind of intimacy." He pointed out that this can make their sex life, as well as their entire life together, particularly fragile. "If the only way a husband and wife achieve intimacy is by rubbing their organs together, what happens when, for some reason, they don't have sex frequently enough, is that their only means of intimacy erodes. And if the only way they can communicate or reassure each other, or spend time together, or make any kind of contact, is through sex, it is risky. The sexual function starts to rebel — it is overfreighted. If a couple has other ways of developing intimacy," according to Dr. Mann, "it stands to reason that their sex life would be richer. They would feel safer and more comfortable with each other and there would be less garbage on the line in sex. You can't expect sex to do a whole lot of things in marriage that would be done more efficiently in other ways."

Many husbands and wives genuinely want to be emotionally closer to one another, but they are unable to get there. They approach each other, then back off. They are able to reach a certain level of closeness before their fears take over: at that point, driven by anxiety, they behave in a way that creates more emotional space. For example, when a man reaches his *dis*comfort zone of intimacy, he might start to obsess about his wife's spending too much money and berate her for it; or, at the same emotional juncture for her, his wife might actually spend too much, knowing full well how much this will upset him. The issue splits them apart, but once they achieve distance, the partners begin to feel lonely and crave closeness again. They then draw together once more, until they reach the point of closeness when the cycle starts to repeat itself and they have to move away from each other again. A back-and-forth pattern is characteristic of their life together, and it may create tensions and turbulence. Generally, neither spouse is aware of the dynamics that are operating.

Perhaps the greatest problem in a marriage is created by conflicting needs for intimacy. If one partner longs for closeness and the other fears it, an emotional tug-of-war such as the one described by Dr. Helen Singer Kaplan in *Disorders of Sexual Desire* ensues.

> He tries to bring up emotional issues, share feelings, spend time together. The one who is afraid of intimacy is always ducking. She is on the telephone; she does the housework when he is at home; she will only talk about trivia; she will cook his dinner but she is unresponsive to his feelings. One always tries; the other resists. One always feels rejected, puzzled — What am I doing wrong? He finally gives up, becomes angry, becomes depressed, or has an affair. The other feels invaded, pressed, confused — What does he want? He is a bottomless pit. She withdraws further and becomes angry.

Some couples feel mismated and harbor conscious hostility toward one another. They think that the distance in their marriages exists because they are married to the wrong person. Unbeknownst to them, they both may have chosen their incompatible mate because of an inner need for distance in a relationship: if they were married to someone they really liked, they would have to be intimate and then they would be in worse trouble.

Of course, some people's emotional requirements change over the years. Particularly at midlife, they may develop a need for more intimacy. The same marriage with a lot of space between partners that suited them earlier no longer does. Although they had a hand in creating it, they may feel the loneliness, the distance in their marriage, too acutely and sink into depression or seek more warmth, either in extramarital affairs or by leaving the marriage altogether and going out to look for it elsewhere. Some couples seek therapy at this juncture to try to save the relationship — and many succeed once they learn what has been keeping them apart all along.

INTIMACY AND THE SINGLE PERSON

Although fear of intimacy is more noticeable in marriage because the mate is witness to its repercussions, it exists, in a more hidden way, in single life as well. Here is how it can operate: A man becomes attracted to a woman and starts an affair with her. He is very turned on by her until he begins to feel a certain level of closeness, then suddenly he loses interest or starts to see defects he hadn't noticed before. Or someone else may suddenly catch his interest and he starts to go out with her, so that now he is simultaneously seeing both women. Or he drops the first one for the second.

The same thing happens in every relationship this man has. Time after time, when he reaches the level of intimacy that makes him uncomfortable, he terminates the relationship or dilutes its intensity by taking another lover. Does he recognize intimacy as the love wrecker, however? Nope. He thinks that he just keeps meeting women who are "wrong" for him. Or he feels that his pattern is a matter of choice: "I like to play the field," he says with an impish grin.

Occasionally, a man like this will fall in love and feel that he wants to marry a particular woman. His fear of intimacy has acted like radar, however. She will be attached to another man, whom she will not leave, or it will turn out that she is the one woman in the world who really doesn't want him.

Another familiar example of fear of intimacy at work in the single world is the woman who becomes passionately attached only to men she can't have or men who treat her badly — men with whom no real intimacy is possible. This is true of a woman I will call Martha. Martha is thirty-two, good-looking, and successful. She has no trouble attracting men of all kinds. Since coming to Denver seven years ago, however, Martha has been involved with the following series of lovers: a married man who treated her contemptuously; a divorced man who would only see her once a week at most and was emotionally unavailable to her; a married man who could only see her for two hours on Saturday afternoons; a bachelor who was involved with someone else; and a wealthy man who was a notorious womanizer.

These were the only men Martha responded to with sexual enthusiasm, and they captured her interest to the point of obsession. During the same seven years, every free and emotionally available man she met — and she met many — didn't have the right "chemistry" for her. Unfortunately, the right chemistry for Martha — and others like her — is emotional distance. Often, people with intimacy problems, like Martha, can allow themselves to feel and act sexually free with someone they can't have or whom they regard as unimportant emotionally, but they can't work up much erotic interest in someone if there is potential for closeness.

THE INTIMACY FACTOR
IN EXTRAMARITAL AFFAIRS

Although the straying spouse is rarely aware of it, extramarital sex is frequently a manifestation of intimacy problems. Many married people feel committed to their partner but have an ongoing affair with someone else or series of illicit liaisons. It's the "I-love-my-wife (husband)-and-would-never-leave-her (him)-but-she (he)-doesn't-turn-me-on" syndrome. You are always looking 'outside' the marriage for the passion that is missing at home. The crux of the problem is not that you can't share exciting sexual feelings, but that you can't do so with the person with whom you share the intimacy of daily living.

Some people can't be intimate with anyone, in or out of marriage. Impersonal sex is the name of the game. But other men and women are able to reveal themselves more, to communicate better, and to feel closer to a lover than to a spouse. It's another, deeper layer of the same problem: you can't share intimate feelings *or* sex with the partner who shares your home.

The proof that it is necessary for some adulterous individuals to split off sex from their emotional life can be seen sometimes if, indeed, they break up with their spouse and marry a lover to whom they feel closer. Before long they may start to repeat their old pattern. In their new marriage, they withdraw into their shell or start another affair, cheating now on the same man or woman with whom they were cheating originally. Here is an example:

A man who considers himself to be an eternal romantic became involved in a very passionate affair during his first marriage. He finally left his wife for the woman he loved. He lived happily with his second wife for a few years before becoming attracted to the wife of a friend. He started an affair with her that became very intense — so intense that the woman left her husband and he became increasingly estranged from wife number two, who had found out about the affair.

Today this man, who must separate romantic love and good sex from commitment, has found an ideal solution. He remains married to his second wife, although they are now emotionally distant from one another, and he has built a second life, with "the other woman," where the passion and high romance are kept alive. He divides his time between the two women. His wife has moved to their country house, two hours from the city where he works, so he sees her only on weekends. He spends weekdays with his lover. In this way he is not really committed to either woman, and he can keep love and sex together and alive by keeping it outside of marriage.

There are other variations of the triangle game. Many men and women who are in love with someone else can't leave their spouse for a variety of reasons. They may blame the children: "I have to stay because of the kids." It may be finances: "We can't afford to live apart" . . . "I could not support myself and the kids" . . . "Everything is in her name" . . . "Her father owns the company I work for. What can I do?" It may be a general sense of duty or propriety, or religion: "My church does not recognize divorce" . . . "She is my wife. No matter what, I will stick with her" . . . "My parents would disinherit me if I divorced him." Whatever the reason, the adulterous partner keeps running between spouse and lover, thus avoiding complete commitment to either — a neat device for keeping the terrors of intimacy at bay.

CLUES TO INTIMACY PROBLEMS

Even if affairs or sexual escapades are not involved, it is a danger signal if you stay in a marriage for a long time and continually complain about your mate, or if your marriage is marked by no meaningful communication and little or no sex, or if you and your spouse have fallen into a pattern of basically leading separate lives. Keeping an emotional distance may serve more of a purpose in your life than you realize.

It's a clue to intimacy problems, too, when single people keep looking for, and never finding, a "perfect" mate, or keep going out year after year with someone they feel has too many defects: they don't leave the relationship, but they don't commit to it either.

Another signal that sex and intimacy may be like fire and water for you — the former extinguished by the latter — is if you have a pattern of having sex with people that you don't care about, but you are able to confide in and have more intimate relationships with people of the opposite sex whom you regard as friends and don't think of in sexual terms. In addition, intimacy and sex don't mix for you if most of your companions of the opposite sex are homosexuals, or if you are single and manage to get involved only with married people.

Another sign of a problem is if you feel sexually inhibited in the presence of your partner but horny at other times. "She feels sexy all day long," writes Dr. Helen Singer Kaplan by way of illustration, "but as soon as her husband comes home she becomes cranky or tense or sleepy or enraged with him for trivial reasons."

Dr. Jay Mann pointed out a very common clue: "The person may not want to be alone with the partner, or not want to get into emotional issues. It is distressingly common — the minute the emotional level rises in the relationship, the person rushes out of the room." Feeling uncomfortable and changing the subject when the conversation gets too personal or emotional is another tip-off that intimacy may be a problem, according to Dr. Mann.

A subtle way of evading intimacy is through the habitual use of drugs or alcohol during sex, so that the other person is always at least partially blotted out.

People mistake doing a lot of things together as being intimate, but continual activity without quiet times alone may mask the fact that you are avoiding intimacy. A marvelous example of this is a *New Yorker* cartoon that shows two women talking in the chic home of one of them, who is saying: "We ripped down the old ceiling and exposed the beams. We chipped all the plaster off the walls and treated the bricks. After that, we scraped down and refinished the floors. Then one evening we were just sitting here, when for some reason we let it all hang out and decided to get a divorce."

In a paper about the busy-couple syndrome, Drs. Richard Malen and Richard B. Cornfeld, two Manhattan psychiatrists, point out that frantic work and social schedules keep a couple in a pattern where they can hide inner doubts from one another and cover over perceived weaknesses; as a result, "sexual dysfunctions may appear, or a lack of sexual interest in the spouse."

Some husbands and wives avoid closeness by seeing themselves in the victim role in their marriage. There are the wife who feels that she is putting up with a tyrannical husband; the husband who endures a critical, nagging wife; the spouse of the alcoholic; the woman married to the man who fritters away their money on other women or expensive, flashy things they cannot afford; the woman who heroically endures her husband's chronic impotence; the husband whose wife wants sex only once a year. They all think that the fatal flaw in their spouse is the reason why they can't be close, and why they may turn off sexually. If only the husband would stop tyrannizing, the wife stop nagging, the man start having erections, the woman start to desire sex, the spouse stop drinking, or whatever, they could start feeling close again.

Therapists often find that this is a way people avoid seeing their own need for distance. This becomes evident if the "flawed" spouse starts to get better, through therapy or other means. The drinking stops, the sex improves, the criticizing lets up. Whatever change it was that the "victim" thought he or she wanted begins to occur. But to everyone's surprise, the victim mate is not really happy about this and may, indeed, show it — not overtly, but by doing things to sabotage the mate's better behavior, or by withdrawing emotionally, or by suddenly losing sexual interest in the now sexually functional partner. With no more excuse not to establish greater intimacy, the "victims" feel anxious, threatened, and resistant to the changes. If a therapist is involved, at this point the victim can often be made to see that he or she has been contributing to the lack of closeness that has developed in the relationship.

WHERE DOES FEAR OF INTIMACY COME FROM?

The answer to the above question varies with each individual, and for many people there are a combination of causes. But authorities recognize some common reasons why intimacy becomes filled with discomfort or terror rather than pleasure.

Dependency versus autonomy.   When they become close, many people start to worry about becoming dependent on the person they love. Some dependency is normal in all love relationships, but this is rarely recognized or accepted as a fact. Dependency of any kind is anathema for these people. It carries the risk of placing themselves in another's power, of being controlled and losing their autonomy. As a result, they pull away.

For many males the issue of autonomy is a particularly loaded one that frequently leads to fear of intimacy. In our culture, independence is traditionally defined as one of the leading attributes of masculinity. Dependency of any kind is seen as a female trait, as something that works against true masculinity. As a result, when certain men begin to feel as if they need the woman they love, they feel threatened. They often feel as if their manhood is in peril, and they start to create distance to reassert their autonomy.

For other men and women, the issue of autonomy revolves around a sense of omnipotence: their need to be all-powerful. People like this find it necessary to feel as if they can provide everything for themselves, by themselves. Mutual nurturance is inherent in an intimate relationship, of course, but to gain nurturance from another produces anger or fear in these people. To them it means they are no longer all-powerful, since they are accepting something from someone else. Thus, the person who must be all-powerful begins to feel the person who gives him warmth, love, closeness, and gratifying sex in the relationship as a purveyor of things that are poisonous because they threaten his or her notion of autonomy.

Another way that fear of intimacy is played out around the issue of dependence hinges on the feeling of being trapped. You may love your partner, but he or she has taken away your freedom. In essence, this is often the result of a mental turnaround: you try to deny your own need of the other person by blaming the partner for boxing you in. Extramarital affairs, or hanging out with the boys (or the girls) are often ways of making yourself feel less trapped.

For everyone, dependence is associated to some extent with our very earliest feelings. As infants, we were completely in the power of mother and depended on her for everything. This sense of infantile helplessness is often recalled in a close relationship. For men, in particular, this becomes a big issue. Mother was a woman, and men tend to associate all women to some degree with that early female figure who was seen through the infant's eyes as huge, powerful, and completely in control. Males in intimate couple relationships often fear that they will become as helpless with their woman as they were in their original intimate relationship with Mother. Many men unconsciously see their female partner as more powerful than she is in reality. The wife or girlfriend becomes an echo of the huge, powerful mother as seen in early life. Consequently, on a subterranean level, the woman is feared and avoided or kept at a manageable distance.

Many authorities maintain that male fear of women is common in our culture, and an important reason for it is men's unconscious sense of women as huge, controlling, and able to harm as well as nurture.

Early models. Sometimes the person who must keep a distance in relationships is simply reflecting what has been learned. A man or woman may have come from a home where the parents were emotionally estranged, or where there was constant bickering, or where the parents simply led calm lives together but were not warm or loving with one another. There was no role model for closeness between man and woman.

A thirty-eight-year-old Los Angeles computer programmer was orphaned at an early age and was shifted throughout his childhood from one set of foster parents to another. Just as he was getting fond of a family, he found himself transferred to another home. Closeness is now uncomfortable to this man. He never learned what it was like in his early, formative years, and today, although he can operate quite successfully in casual sexual relationships, he loses sexual interest the minute he starts to feel attached to a woman. He has been married twice, both times after brief courtships. In each marriage sexual interest disappeared soon after the ceremony.

Sometimes the relationship that created a poor model for intimacy was between parent and child. A mother or father or both parents may have been distant and unreachable throughout a person's childhood. One Washington government worker, now forty-three years old, grew up with a cold, aloof mother who also drank too much and would become even more unreachable while she was drinking. His father was a busy professional who spent most of the day and night attending to his career. There was little warmth or closeness in his young life. He tried reaching out to his mother but failed.

This man — a very attractive, personable grown-up — craves

and seeks out intimate relationships, but finds that he can be affectionate and highly sexual only while he is trying to win a woman. Once he is secure in a relationship, he increasingly withdraws into his shell, in effect shutting out his partners. In both of his two marriages, he has become asexual for long periods of time. His last wife, who was always packing up and leaving him, and then returning (before she moved out for good), remembers: "The only time I could get him interested in me sexually after we were married was if I left him. Then he would get turned on. That lasted until I moved back home; then, once again, he didn't want sex. I couldn't spend a lifetime leaving him in order to have a decent sex life, so reluctantly, because I really loved him, I finally decided to get a divorce."

Trust. Unfortunately, some people have never developed the ability to trust others, and as a result, they have trouble with close relationships. Generally, the lack of trust has evolved from negative experiences in early life.

An example of this is one woman who grew up with a mother who ignored her except to make sure that she was always well dressed so that she would be a good reflection on the mother in the eyes of the world. Servants raised the girl. She was also privy to the fact that her mother was unfaithful to her father and had a lover. Her father was a warmer person, but he was away a great deal of time because of the demands of his business, and when he was home, his eyes were on his elusive, attractive wife rather than his yearning daughter. Today, this woman is unable to connect emotionally. Ignored by both her mother and father as a child, as an adult she is suspicious of making herself vulnerable in a relationship. Rather than risk intimacy or love, she attaches herself to men for what they can give her and uses sex as a commodity — to trade or use as a reward rather than for her own pleasure or emotional nourishment.

A man with great intimacy problems in his marriage was brought up by his grandmother after his mother died in an accident. The grandmother was a very strict religious zealot who punished the boy whenever he was having fun, for not being serious enough. As a result, he now deeply mistrusts all women. He was able to have good sexual experiences in casual relationships, but in his marriage he is filled with anxiety about sex and either does not desire it or is impotent.

Erik Erikson maintains that the ability to trust is established in the first year of life by mothering that provides consistency and continuity. If for some reason a mother becomes unavailable to the child, or if she seesaws between nurturing and neglecting the infant, this may result in the child's later inability to trust others in relationships.

Lack of trust may have been created by a role model in childhood. For example, if your father distrusted your mother, and feared being controlled or taken advantage of by her, or if you were raised by someone who taught you that men were not to be trusted, there is a good chance you will echo the feelings and behavior of your early models.

Fear of being overwhelmed or suffocated. John did fine with women until they moved in with him; then he started to feel as if they were taking over his whole life. Although his apartment was spacious, he began to feel edgy and "crowded." He interpreted this as falling out of love. After three such attempts at living with a lover, John has now given up. He keeps his relationships casual and sees several women at once to guard against intimacy, which becomes so uncomfortable for him.

There are a good number of perpetual bachelors — and bachelorettes — who, like John, find close contact suffocating. That is why they remain single.

Although they may use various techniques, people trying to defend their identity against a perceived takeover by a partner often do so by keeping their inner life secret and not revealing feelings to a mate. And for some unfortunate individuals, the subliminal fear of suffocation may make intercourse a panicky experience. In the act of joining sexually, they feel that they have become one with their sexual partner and therefore that they have lost their own identity. Some can't allow themselves to reach orgasm, because by "letting themselves go" they might lose themselves. Others avoid sex altogether.

Fear of abandonment. Some people live with an unconscious fear of being abandoned by those they love and need. One way that they deal with this insecurity may be to rely upon a sort of preventive medicine: they never allow themselves to get close enough to someone to risk being left and hurt. In certain cases, this is accomplished by leaving a partner preemptively, as soon as feelings of closeness arise. Others provide emotional insurance for themselves by always juggling more than one partner at a time. As single people, they simultaneously carry on several dating relationships; as married people, they have lovers in addition to wife or husband. Still others who fear abandonment take steps to create enough distance in the relationship to feel safe.

Fear of abandonment often creates the "can't-live-with-it, can't-live-without-it" syndrome. People who fear abandonment often feel they cannot exist without a close lover. It is as if they will disintegrate if they are on their own. This makes them cling to relationships. But at the same time, because they depend so much on another person for their own sense of identity, they feel that their individuality will be swallowed up. This makes them terrified of the very intimacy that they need to survive.

Poor self-image. Intimacy may be particularly threatening if you feel that you have a lot of defects and want to hide them, or if you feel generally inferior or sexually inadequate. In intimate relationships, you may dread that the close contact will allow your partner to see the real you — that your imperfections and inadequacies will be revealed. Here is how this operated with Howard, a manager in a large corporation in the Midwest:

Howard was a man who had doubts about himself, in general and specifically, sexually. He thought that his penis was too small and that other men were better lovers. He was able to date without too much anxiety as long as he was seeing a lot of women, each on a time-limited basis. When Howard was nearing thirty, he began to feel the pressure to settle down. He worked for a company that preferred its employees to be married. Howard suspected that if he did not marry soon, he would begin to be bypassed for promotions; so when he met Sylvia, an even-tempered, sweet-looking nurse, he decided to take the plunge. After a short courtship, he proposed, and they were married four months after they met.

This was the beginning of trouble for Howard. He became afraid that he could not sustain the sexuality that had been part of their brief premarital affair. He began worrying that Sylvia would soon find him a poorer lover than other men that she had known. Instead of dealing with these fears by sharing them with Sylvia, which might have led to her reassuring him, Howard hid his doubts from his wife and instead started to avoid her sexually. His reasoning, on an unconscious level, was this: The less I sleep with her, the less likely that my sexual inadequacies will be found out.

People with fears of sexual inadequacy, like Howard, as well as those who think that they have other defects that will cause them to be rejected if they are discovered, often try to hide out in marriage. They feel they can accomplish this on some level as long as they don't get too close to their partner either emotionally, sexually, or both.

OPENING UP COMMUNICATIONS

If genuine intimacy is to be established, it is crucial that a couple learn to communicate with one another. In addition to gossiping about friends and neighbors, and talking about the children, home repairs, and world events, partners who want to increase intimacy must speak to each other about their feelings — their fears, hopes, secrets, dreams, vulnerabilities, reactions, joys, irritations, and depressions.

It may not be easy to open up at first if you are not in the habit of doing so, but even if you feel uncomfortable, it is important for your relationship that you keep trying. If your spouse is better at communicating intimate feelings than you are, or even if you are both novices at it, you can arrange to help each other. Give your partner permission to ask you, at times, "How do you feel about that?" or "How are you feeling now?" You can do the same for your spouse. Reach an agreement ahead of time that the answer "I don't know" will not be acceptable. Everybody has feelings, but a lot of us aren't consciously aware of what they are. You may have to dig.

Therapists often recommend the following technique for opening up communications in marriage: The husband and wife are instructed to conduct discussions with each only using sentences beginning with "I." For example, "I want...," "I feel...," and "I need...." Sentences beginning with "You" are forbidden. In this way, each partner is forced to explore his or her own feelings and to express them. By avoiding sentences that start with "You," you are prevented from committing another typical communication sin in marriage: telling your partner how you think he or she feels. Mind reading stands in the way of an honest sharing of feelings.

Attentive listening is an important component of good communication. Not only should you tell your partner your innermost thoughts, but you should welcome his or hers and accept, without judgment, what your spouse is willing to impart to you because he or she trusts you. Trust is what intimacy and open, honest communication are all about; you have to be willing to make yourself vulnerable to your mate — knowing that he or she will never harm you intentionally — before you will be able to talk in very personal ways.

Many couples find that when they draw closer through intimate conversations and mutually enjoyable activities, their sexual desire for each other increases spontaneously. Others may need more help in getting the sexual fires burning again. Try the sensate focus exercises described previously (pages 109–110). It is only fair to warn you, though, that sex therapists find that assigned pleasuring exercises are often sabotaged by one or both partners when they are afraid of intimacy. Even when they are desperate for help, the closeness becomes too uncomfortable or frightening. Professional help is sometimes the only way to deal effectively with sexual problems resulting from intimacy fears, especially when resistance to change becomes evident, despite good intentions.

The following portion of a case history is included by Dr. Helen Singer Kaplan in her book *Disorders of Sexual Desire*. It gives you a good idea of the kind of therapy that is available, as well as the kind of sabotage that often takes place.

> Initially, pleasuring and nondemanding genital stimulation tasks were assigned. These met with success but this lasted for only a brief period of time. With every improvement one or the other became resistant and created obstacles. He was "too busy" . . . to spend the necessary two or three leisurely evenings a week devoted to closeness and sexual pleasure. When they managed to arrange a weekend away, she became preoccupied to the point of obsession with her job. On one occasion, when the couple enjoyed some peace and pleasure, she became obsessed about an insult from a casual acquaintance. Her agitated emotional state naturally precluded sex for that weekend.

At this point in the case, the exercises were interrupted and insight therapy — both in the individual and joint sessions — was substituted. Through the psychotherapy, which lasted for several months, the couple gained enough knowledge of the underlying dynamics operating in the relationship to proceed again with the mutual pleasuring and stimulation of sensate focus exercises. The exercises were especially tailored at this point, though, to decrease the anxiety about intimacy that they invoked. The focus was changed, initially, from pleasuring each other to self-pleasuring (masturbation in each other's presence).

"This enabled them to keep a certain distance," explained Dr. Kaplan, "but provided the opportunity to gradually move closer.

After they could do this comfortably, the shared component of the erotic experiences was gradually increased. Some mild resistances were invoked as the couple became more intimate and close in the sexual situation. These were handled by confrontations together with support in the sessions.

"This case ended successfully," notes Dr. Kaplan. "The couple now have sex together with reasonable frequency. When anxiety about closeness arises, as it still does occasionally, they have the insight and psychic tools to deal with this in a constructive manner."

Another good way to attack intimacy problems is to attend one of the many marriage enrichment programs or marriage encounter groups that are given around the country these days. Many couples testify that have been able to draw closer to one another as a result of these experiences. They are often sponsored by religious groups, so if you are interested, you might ask a religious leader to recommend one in your area.

THE OPPOSITE SIDE OF THE COIN

A caution is in order before leaving the issue of intimacy in marriage: Intimacy is not to be confused with total merging. Some people think that intimacy means fusion — that in a good relationship, two people must become one. Separate interests are regarded as a betrayal of love. One woman, for example, remembered her relationship with her first husband, who would insist that she watch him while he did the carpentry he enjoyed as a hobby. "It bored me silly. I had things of my own to do, but if I left him for too long, he would become upset and angry. I remember once taking a bath in the late afternoon and taking my time in the tub, enjoying the relaxation. I emerged from my bath to find my ex-husband in a fury because I had been away from him for too long."

People who see love as fusion aren't dodging closeness; on the contrary, they need it all the time. They don't feel crowded by intimacy — though their partners often feel suffocated. People like this generally do not have a clear idea of who they are as a separate person apart from a partner. Their relationships, on a psychological level, are an attempt to re-create the lost mother-child symbiosis of early infancy.

Often, men and women with the urge to merge find each other, feel that they are soul mates, and marry. "They long for absolute unity, they must belong completely to each other and share everything in total harmony," says Dr. Jurg Willi, a marriage therapist, in his book *Couples in Collusion*. Interestingly, although they are at opposite poles from couples who are compelled to maintain a distance from one another because of their fear of intimacy, symbiotic couples often run into sexual trouble as well. Dr. Willi warns that couples who have adopted relentless "togetherness" as a way of life not only may find that they suffer from a loss of boundaries — they no longer know where one partner's personality begins and the other's ends — but they also often end up suppressing, in their joined universe, "all aggressive, and often sexual, drives."

"Marriage is not a mindless merger," says Dr. Otto Kernberg.

CHAPTER 11

When Mad Is Bad

GINNY FLACK and her husband Harold went into sex therapy because Ginny was no longer interested in sex. Harold, a successful businessman, was increasingly unhappy. He enjoyed sex and was resentful that the only time his wife would consent to intercourse was when he did something special for her.

At first Ginny refused to say anything more than "I'm just not interested — that's all," but in the course of her sessions she began to open up and reveal the real reason for her lack of desire. She admitted that she felt dissatisfied with her role as wife and mother. Her two young children were troublesome. She often felt overwhelmed by her domestic responsibilities. She envied her husband because she felt that he led a more interesting life than hers, but at the same time, she was resentful over the amount of time he spent at work away from her. Not only was he away too much, but whatever time he spent with her was unsatisfactory. "We never go anywhere anymore," she complained. She felt that Harold did not pay enough attention to her. "I might just as well be another piece of furniture in our house," she said with tears in her eyes.

Ginny had tried various ways to make Harold listen to her. She had screamed and shouted and complained loudly — but all he did was walk away, which infuriated her still more. Finally, Ginny started to use sex as a tactic. She was so enraged by this time that she had lost her own sexual urges; so it was easy for her to refuse sex when she felt that Harold was neglecting her and to grant sex to Harold if he took her out, came home early, or helped with the children or around the house. When she consented to sex, she did so without desire on her part.

In another case, Walter, a man in his midfifties, complained that his beautiful, thirty-five-year-old wife Agnes had become completely uninterested in sex. She avoided it whenever possible, and when she did have intercourse, her lack of response was evident. Agnes had been a public-relations account executive before her marriage. Although she found her career interesting and exciting, her husband had insisted that she drop it for the role of housewife and mother. "I don't want my wife to work," Walter insisted. "And thank God, I make plenty of money, so she doesn't have to." Walter was very generous to his wife in material ways, but this did not make up for the way Agnes was feeling.

When interviewed alone, she revealed that although she enjoyed taking care of her two children, she also felt stifled and trapped in her marriage. "I feel like another one of my husband's possessions," she said. Her husband was a man who jealously guarded his beautiful, much younger wife. He wanted her to go out into the world as little as possible. "He won't even let me take part in church activities," complained Agnes.

Her confined life, coupled with her husband's constant suspicions, made her feel not only bored, but also very angry. But she could not admit this anger to herself. It made her feel too guilty. "He treats me so well. I have everything I could ever want," she kept saying to counteract her complaints. Instead of feeling her underlying fury, she turned off to sex.

Another woman was frantic because her husband, after seven

years of marriage, had lost interest in sex. "I don't understand it," she said. "He used to want it all the time. I have pleaded with him to get some help, but all he keeps saying is, 'I never cared about sex anyway.' I know this isn't true. He used to love sex and we always had a wonderful time in bed."

In-depth interviews with her husband yielded the following revelation:

> I guess I gradually lost interest in sex after three years of brooding. I found out then that my wife had had a brief affair with a man she met at work. She confessed the affair to me and begged for my forgiveness. She said she loved me, and only me. To tell you the truth, I didn't have that much experience with women before we married, so I wasn't so sure how good I was in bed, anyway. My wife seemed satisfied and I thought everything was fine until she had that affair. Then, well, I guess I felt like I wasn't much of a man. Having an affair is wrong, I think, and it upset me a lot. I never mentioned the incident again to her but I have been really boiling inside. You know, I never admitted this to myself before, but I think when I lost interest in sex it was a way to hurt and punish her. I guess I wanted to pay her back.

These three stories illustrate what experts believe to be one of the leading causes of impaired sexual desire in relationships: anger. Dr. Helen Singer Kaplan, who calls anger and love "mutual inhibitants," once made the point that "what patients term boredom may be their way of avoiding coming to grips with longstanding, abiding but hidden angers. The anger precludes any feelings of tenderness or desire, but sexual boredom is not the basic problem — anger is."

Of course, the kind of anger that Dr. Kaplan alludes to is not a flare-up of temper in response to an immediate situation. It is not the occasional squabble, the sudden fiery scene, the slamming-door exit, the exasperated burst of tears, the screaming matches that many normal, well-adjusted couples engage in every now and then when something one partner says or does drives the other berserk. In most cases, minor squabbles can be helpful. They can bring an issue out into the open, where the anger is aired and the problem dealt with. The partners may find a compromise, or reach a better understanding of one another's feelings, so that they are no longer angry; or they may decide that the whole thing is silly and forget it. And, although you may feel as if you would rather die than sleep with your partner while you are still mad, occasional minor arguments don't lead to long-term sexual turn-offs. Tempers cool, a reconciliation takes place, and a normal sex life resumes. Indeed, sex is often the sign of forgiveness, the symbol that peace has returned to the house once more. Sex may be even better than usual at the moment of reconciliation because you are glad to be back in one another's arms and good graces again.

Generally, the kind of anger that leads to a lack of interest in sex involves three "*uns*":

- The anger is *un*stated. You harbor a deep grudge, but you don't talk to your partner about it.
- The anger is *un*acknowledged. You not only don't tell your mate, but, on a conscious level, you yourself may not be aware that you are very angry, or you keep denying it to yourself. For example, one woman who was furious at her husband for continually treating her as an incompetent idiot would not acknowledge her fury. Instead, all she kept saying was, "I'm not angry. I'm just annoyed."
- The issue behind the anger remains *un*resolved. As a result, it continues to sit in the middle of your relationship, silently ticking away like a bomb.

Some people act out their anger indirectly. It is rather common for the husband or wife who bears a grudge to take sexual interest elsewhere. The motivation behind an affair may be conscious, with anger at the spouse recognized, as in the case of a man who recalled how his affair started: "I met her at a party. My wife didn't go with me because she was drunk again. I felt after all those years of putting up with her, I deserved it, so I took this woman home and I saw her for about two years, off and on, after that." Often, however, the straying spouse may be unaware that anger has propelled the affair and instead may believe that he or she was simply attracted to or fell in love with the new sex partner. Another way to act out your anger is to do something that will surely infuriate your spouse. For example, one man bought a large, expensive boat, knowing full well that his wife was terrified of boating.

Anger is often one-sided. A husband may be mad at his wife though she isn't angry at him and doesn't even know about his anger, or vice versa. Anger can be mutual. Some key issue may be making both partners furious at each other. Often, anger is contagious. It may have started with one partner angry at the other, but sooner or later, both end up angry.

The following excerpt from an interview illustrates how anger can spread, ultimately creating two armed camps in a relationship — with sex, among other things, a victim of the war. The woman telling the story is an attractive, redheaded divorcée who lives in a large midwestern city.

I was introduced to Bart by a mutual friend. I liked him right away. He was extremely bright and articulate, and he had a good sense of humor, similar to my own. We were attracted to one another and within six months we were married. I was physically attracted to him, but when we became lovers I felt he was not as good a lover as other men had been in my life. He lacked tenderness and finesse. He loved me, was attracted to me, but he didn't know about being gentle or subtle, so I felt a little disappointed; but his lovemaking was reasonably nice and I had orgasms — not one hundred percent of the time, but enough for it to be normal and happy. Then he started getting annoyed with me because I didn't go right back to work. I had quit my job when we married.

He would say, "Why don't you get a job instead of sitting around?" He carried on about my not working and we had miserable arguments. On top of this, his father became ill and his mother started to call and berate him for marrying a poor girl. She blamed his father's illness on him marrying me. There were lots of arguments and sex started going downhill. It certainly wasn't frequent for a newly married couple. This was in the first year. Within months we had a knock-down-drag-out battle and he walked out of the house.

If I had gone back to work, he would have been happier; but if it hadn't been the job, it would have been something else. He would make a demand on me and I would comply, trying to win his approval, but when I did what he wanted, I found that was not what would win his approval. There was always a reason for him not to sleep with me. He got mad, but it was more complicated than that, because if it happened that he wanted to make love, my responses were bad. He was treating me badly; he was abusive in his manner and contemptuous. I would say yes to him because that's what I thought a good and loving wife did, but by then I didn't get excited by him sexually and I didn't have orgasms. In time, he became unhappy that I wasn't aroused. A lot of avoidance on his part was going on, too. Much of the time he was "tired."

After the knock-down-drag-out fight when he walked out, we reconciled and I thought everything was going to be all right. We decided to have a baby and we were very excited by the pregnancy and the baby. Everything seemed normal. There was still a lot of "I'm tired" and avoidance, but not enough to make things seem abnormal. Sex was twice a week. I wanted him to get into bed and put his arms around me even if he was tired, but he got into bed and went to sleep and that was it.

It was like this until a year or two after the birth of my second child. I kept trying to make him see that I needed some kind of attention from him. I was feeling trapped and he was being demanding and critical. I remember once he got up at his usual time, six o'clock, and flew into a rage. I woke up to him hollering, "I told you I needed brown socks. There are blue socks and black socks, but there are no brown socks." He pulled the dresser drawer out and turned it upside down on me in bed.

He became more and more critical and I didn't know what to do. Each time it happened it would get more extreme and more painful. As the years went by I would get to the point where I would think, "This is it. I can't stand being married to him anymore." But he was intuitive enough to realize when I reached that point and he would try a rapprochement and I would think, "Now he understands," until something else would go wrong and he would go into one of his abusive periods again.

By the time my kids were eight and ten, sex was really infrequent and his attitude toward me was so bad I couldn't feel anything anymore. He got into a period of impotence, which he blamed on me because I was unresponsive, which was his fault because he was abusive and critical, which was my fault because in his eyes I was such an idiot. So what happened was that sex stopped totally. It dribbled out, got more and more infrequent, until finally there was no sex at all.

SOURCES OF ANGER

What causes anger is, of course, variable, but there are certain issues that psychiatrists, psychologists, marriage counselors, and sex therapists frequently find at the heart of problems between angry partners in relationships. One of the most common of these is the emotional devastation that can occur when your hopes, dreams, ideals, or fantasies are shattered.

Disappointed expectations. Spouses sometimes experience a sense of having been cheated or a feeling of having been let down. Perhaps you thought you were getting one thing when you committed yourself to your mate and marriage, but what you got was another. For example, you may have expected your husband to be a big success in his field when you married him. Ten years into the marriage, you see that success does not seem to be in the cards. Your husband has been fired from two jobs and, in his current position, he is being overlooked for promotion. You may not express your sense of disappointment to your husband. Indeed, on the surface you may seem the model of a supportive wife; but underneath, you feel angry that you always have to scrimp, that your friends' husbands keep climbing higher and higher in their careers while your man is stuck. You are really furious that this bright man, who had such promise, somehow has not lived up to his potential.

As you become more and more disappointed in him, your sexual interest drops, although you may not have put the two things together. You may imagine, instead, that it is natural to become less interested in sex as you get older. Or you may feel that you are so busy with the kids that, of course, most of the time you feel too tired for sex. Of, if you go back to work at a boring job to make ends meet, you may think that, of course, you are so exhausted from both working and taking care of your obligations at home that sex seems like too much at the end of the day. You don't realize that you are also in a rage at your husband for putting you into the position of having to work at a job you don't like much.

In the case of one couple, the problem, ironically, was not a husband's failure but his success. In the early years of their marriage, both husband and wife struggled together to make a go of a small business. The business grew and prospered, and as it did, the wife increasingly retreated into her role of housewife and mother while her husband became more and more enmeshed in the running of the growing company. Eventually, each partner felt extreme disappointment in the other. The wife felt that her husband had changed and become materialistic, uncaring, and unloving. The husband, on the other hand, felt that his wife did not appreciate him or what he had done for his family. She had expected the closeness and companionship they had at the beginning of their marriage to continue. He felt that she would continue to be totally supportive. The more each felt betrayed by the other, the more their sex life diminished.

One husband currently feels enraged by his wife's weight gain. He had liked her slim, nicely rounded figure when he married her and expected that she would stay slim and sexy as his wife. He felt outraged when she gained weight and became, in his words, "fat and sloppy." He had started to express his disappointment and anger at his wife openly, but was told by a diet doctor that she was interpreting his anger as a demand, which would drive her to eat still more. So now, when he comes home and finds his wife eating ice cream, he sees red but doesn't say anything. He swallows his anger — and since he started swallowing his anger, sex has become more and more infrequent.

All of us enter a marriage with expectations of the relationship and our partner. Some of these expectations are conscious and known to our mates. For example, we may be aware that we expect a husband or wife to be monogamous, and our mate knows about it. We may be semi-aware of other expectations, or we may be fully aware of them ourselves but not communicate them to a partner. For instance, a husband may expect his wife to cater to him as his mother catered to his father; a wife may expect her husband to make her feel protected. Each partner may be aware of these expectations in a hazy sort of way but never communicate them directly to the mate. In addition, everyone also has completely unconscious expectations of their partner.

Anger can result if any of our expectations — conscious, semi-conscious, or unconscious — are not lived up to; but unconscious expectations can create the strongest reactions and deepest rage if thwarted, because they are often based on our wanting from a mate what we, as infants, expected from our parents.

In her book *Disorders of Sexual Desire,* Dr. Helen Singer Kaplan gives an example of the kind of things that can trigger anger when unconscious infantile expectations are operating: "He is enraged because his wife-mother will not feed him, does not give him enough, and worst of all prefers others, brothers or fathers. She is furious because daddy-husband neglects her for business and is controlling or bossy or threatens her with abandonment." So, such surface issues as a wife feeling neglected because her husband spends too much time at work, or a husband secretly seething because his wife appears to neglect him for the children, are sometimes compounded by echoes from infancy — the feeling that we once had when a parent neglected or frustrated us and as a result invoked our primitive infantile fury. Old, forgotten angers add fuel to the current cause of irritation and disappointment.

The happily-ever-after myth.   Dr. Joshua Golden gives another reason for couples becoming angry and disillusioned:

> We have been led to believe, by all the myths that we're raised with, that if only we find the right person, we're going to live happily ever after. We have no understanding that "infatuation," the initial passion, is over with in a matter of months. Many of us see this as if something is wrong. We become disappointed and feel fearful, because we have no understanding of the natural process. When trouble arises, when we find out that it's not all "happily ever after" and that we have many more problems now than we ever dreamed of, we have the feeling that we've made a mistake. We start to think, "I have chosen the wrong person. I have married a lemon instead of a peach."
>
> I think the happily-ever-after myth is a dreadful misrepresentation of the facts, and it causes a lot of misery. People are disappointed when they needn't be. If they had a more realistic concept of the problems that do arise, they would do better. They think a successful marriage is a marriage where you don't have problems. A successful marriage is one in which you learn to solve the problems which you inevitably have. Problems are inevitable, because you're trying to bring two very different individuals, and sometimes many more, into some kind of intimacy, which means differing values and all kinds of compromises. The test of success is not being

without problems but rather how well you can solve the problems and reconcile the difference. That's true of sexual needs as well as other issues.

Ambivalence. Sometimes ambivalence causes problems. For example, Betty was a very good-looking, decisive woman. Her husband Bernard, a philosophy professor, was happy to let her run the show. Betty went into therapy complaining about her husband's passivity. She wanted him to take a more active role in their relationship.

Bernard went into therapy at the same time with another psychiatrist. In therapy, Bernard started to change and do what Betty ostensibly wanted: he became more assertive. Until this point in the relationship, the couple's sex life had remained good, despite their problems. Suddenly, however, Betty stopped wanting to have intercourse with Bernard.

With her therapist, Betty was forced to face the fact that although, on one level, she wanted Bernard to take more control in the relationship and be less passive, on a deeper level — so hidden that she had not been aware of it — she also feared giving up control. Unconsciously, she was resistant to Bernard's newfound assertiveness because it reminded her of her mother. Betty's mother had been a very dominating woman who caused her to feel overwhelmed and smothered, a reaction she was now having to Bernard when he attempted to take more control.

Ambivalence puts a partner into a bind because he or she gets conflicting messages. Another example of the problem is the man who says he wants his wife to have a career but acts as if he expects her to be totally available to him at all times. He complains when she does not have dinner on the table by the time he gets home at six-thirty, and resents it when she has to get up a half hour earlier than he does in order to get to her job on time. Ambivalence is also at work when a woman insists that she wants her husband to treat her as an equal but also expects him to be a "daddy" — to act protectively and always take care of her.

Both partners generally become angry in situations of extreme ambivalence. If you are the ambivalent one, you feel that you can never get what you want from your partner — which is true, since you have opposing wishes. Your spouse feels he can never satisfy you, no matter what he does, and (accurately) that he is caught in a terrible bind.

Unfulfilled emotional needs.   Anger can grow when we are consistently not getting something we feel we need from our partner. For example, a woman may need to be able to talk about her feelings to her husband but he may not want to listen and might cut her off every time she starts to vent her emotions. Or a man may want some spontaneity in his life, but perhaps his wife is a rigid woman who only feels comfortable sticking with familiar routines and schedules. Or one partner may crave displays of physical affection — some hugging and kissing or hand holding outside of a sexual situation — while the other hates to be touched. Or maybe a woman really wants to go back and finish college or to go back to work, but her husband threatens to leave her if she does.

Sooner or later, when a basic emotional need remains unfulfilled, the problem starts to play itself out in the bedroom. Often, the partner who feels that he or she is being shortchanged emotionally withdraws sexually.

Competitive feelings.   Sally was a gifted photographer. Her husband Frank, a talented painter when they met, had given up art in order to take a steady job to support his wife and children. During the marriage, Sally was able to pursue her photography and had several successful shows at galleries. They led a contented life together, but Frank missed painting and in the sixth year of their marriage started to work at it again. When he had completed a number of good paintings, he proudly told Sally that he was going to take them around to the galleries to see if anyone would mount a public showing of his work. At this point Sally exploded. She told him that it was a ridiculous idea. Now, whenever

Frank starts to work on his paintings, Sally tries to leave the house. He resents this, of course, and there is a great deal of tension between them, with the result that sex has fallen off.

Sally is suffering from a sense of rivalry with her husband. She cannot bear the thought of him being as successful as she is in an artistic field. Many husbands and wives feel like rivals with each other. Generally, this is a replay of sibling rivalry, the childhood feeling that a brother or sister is favored by the parents and is getting more than a fair share of attention, food, love, or other things.

These days rivalry turns up fairly often in dual-career homes. If both partners are ambitious, one may feel anxious or surly if the other seems to be getting ahead faster.

In the case of one couple, both writers, everything was all right as long as both of them were struggling. When the woman had a novel published to much critical acclaim, the man grew increasingly unhappy as phone calls kept coming in from people congratulating her or requesting interviews, and the favorable notices piled up. The more her success became noticeable, the less sex they had, to her consternation.

Different values.   Over the course of a marriage, one or both partners may change in terms of outlook, goals, and maturity. If the spouses don't keep up with each other, disillusionment, anger, and growing alienation can result. A good example of this is a minister's son who expected to follow in his father's footsteps. While in college, he looked for a woman who would make a good minister's wife. At a church dance he met someone who came from a religious family, attended church faithfully, and could think of nothing better than to become the wife of a minister. Upon graduation the couple married and the man entered a theological institute. Just before he was to be ordained, this man suffered a nervous breakdown. In treatment for it, he discovered that he really didn't want to be a minister at all. He was just trying to be a good son and fulfill what he felt were his parents' expectations of him. Upon recovery he went back to graduate school to get a master's degree in business administration, then embarked on an entrepreneurial career. In the process, he left behind most of his interest in religion. He no longer attended church and didn't consider himself to be a religious person.

Although he had changed a great deal, his wife had not. She still attended church regularly and she regretted her husband's decision not to be a minister. She was bewildered by the changes in her husband. Although she continued to try to be a good wife to him, she increasingly felt puzzled about how to do this. Her husband now wanted to do more worldly things, to have the fun he felt he missed growing up in a sober religious home. She had been a serious person without much gaiety when he met her, and she continued to have these traits, but he no longer found them either attractive or desirable. He pressured her to change, to take a drink now and then, to learn to dance to rock-and-roll music. But she refused; she just wasn't interested. Although at the beginning of their marriage the sex had been frequent and good, by now the growing differences between them had created a damper. He felt increasingly turned off by his wife, whom he now considered to be uptight and dull; and she felt his changes had turned him into a stranger. She also felt so angry, bewildered, and betrayed by the fact that the very qualities her husband had desired and chosen her for were no longer acceptable to him, that she was just as happy if he didn't come near her in bed.

Often, particularly in couples who marry young, one partner may grow up while the other does not. In one instance, a man set out to find a bride with whom he could have fun. He liked hanging out in bars, kidding around, talking to people, and drinking for hours on end. He found a woman who enjoyed this, too, and they married. All was well until they had their first child. Then his wife started to change. She enjoyed her home and her child and she wanted to spend more time there. She no longer found hours spent in bars fulfilling. She was growing up but her husband was not. He still wanted to hang out and just have laughs. She wanted to conduct a life with more substance. Her husband kept complaining about her new attitudes and slowly she became more and more angry at him, until one day she found herself completely uninterested in sex. She started to refuse him, which infuriated him and convinced him still more that their problem was that she was no longer a fun person. On the other hand, she didn't connect her lack of sexual interest with her anger. She just felt no desire for sex and didn't wonder why.

Sometimes the problem centers on sex itself. For example, one partner might enjoy sex while the other can take it or leave it; or maybe one spouse likes to experiment, try different positions, and act out fantasies while the other likes to stick to one or two ways of having sex and thinks that anything else is "sick." It may be that one partner wants an open marriage while the other believes in monogamy. Even something as simple as one spouse preferring sex in the morning while the other prefers it at night can cause dissension.

One couple married when they were both twenty years old. He was always interested in sex and she was never able to respond. For thirty years the wife never refused her husband, but he always felt frustrated by her lack of interest and enjoyment. Not long ago, in search of a more fulfilling kind of experience, the man, when out of town on business, had sex with a woman he met at a convention. Despite his sense of frustration over his sex life with his wife, this was the first time that he had been unfaithful, and he felt enormously guilty about it. Eventually, he told his wife about the fling. Instead of her being angry or outraged, she told him that she understood. This didn't make him feel relieved. Instead, it infuriated him. He saw her reaction as approbation, as her way of getting off the hook sexually: if he had sex with others, she wouldn't have to have it with him. This intensified feelings he already had that she endured sex with him rather than wanting it herself. It also highlighted the contrast in how each of them felt about sex. As a result of this new anger on his part, sex deteriorated even further. Despite his frustrations and her reluctance, they previously engaged in sex weekly. Now they are down to once a month or even less.

Whenever spouses are in conflict about values, sexual or otherwise, the result can be a great underlying anger that can wreak havoc in the bedroom.

WAYS OF EXPRESSING ANGER

Everyone handles anger — their own and others' — differently. At one extreme there are the anger lovers: people who consciously or unconsciously enjoy getting mad. Anger may make them feel in control or powerful. Life with them is a series of temper tantrums. At the other end of the spectrum are the peace lovers. They hate displays of wrath and react to anger with tremendous anxiety. Allergic to fights, they try to avoid them in relationships. This doesn't mean that they don't get mad. They do, but they don't express their anger openly and may even deny it to themselves. Although they generally don't realize it, they are often afraid that if they allow themselves to get mad they will go out of control, which is why they contain their anger. Peace lovers are frequently silent grudge holders. Theirs is the anger that generally suffers from the three *uns* mentioned earlier.

There are different styles of showing anger. You can express it loudly and belligerently, and, if you are an anger lover, often. You can become violent. Some use the silent treatment. They stop talking to you, or answer only in chilly monosyllables. Other people dash out of the room or house until they cool off. For some, anger is not expressed directly but rather through devious means. For example, one husband, angry because he felt that he could never live up to his wife's expectations, showed his fury indirectly by acting in the irresponsible, childish way his wife hated. Very few people can deal with anger constructively, by saying that they are angry, explaining why, and then sticking to the point rather than going through a general list of the other person's defects and bringing up a host of past grievances.

How you react to anger and express it may depend on your cultural background. Some ethnic groups tend to express anger freely and loudly; others encourage the suppression of anger.

Some families use angry voices as a matter of course. In other families voices are never raised. If you have grown up in an environment where everyone was comfortable expressing anger, displays of temper won't be as forbidding and upsetting to you as if you grew up in an atmosphere where anger was never allowed to be aired.

Problems often arise between partners who have come from different backgrounds and have dissimilar styles. A dove who hates anger and is uncomfortable with it may react more strongly to her husband's anger than he intended, and may remain angry longer than her husband who easily expresses wrath. Her husband, after he screams and shouts, may be able to fall asleep quickly and sleep soundly, while the dove will toss and turn all night after an argument. She will resent not only the cause of the argument but the expression of anger itself, and although she does not talk about it, she may come to harbor cumulative hidden anger at him for always screaming and shouting. In this way, the less belligerent partner may end up being the more angry of the two. Sometimes the dove, by failing to react outwardly, will frustrate the angry partner, who will then escalate the argument in an attempt to elicit a response.

Doves may unconsciously do things that provoke the hated anger of a partner, and although doves see themselves as peace lovers, they may thus, in actuality, be contributing to the anger in the home. An example of this would be the wife who continues to buy shirts and ties for her husband when she finds them on sale, even though she knows her husband hates for her to pick out his clothes; or the husband who continues to leave the unwashed dishes from his midnight snacks in the sink rather than putting them in the dishwasher — something that always irritates his wife; or the spouse who is always "correcting" her mate in front of company, which she knows makes him feel humiliated.

A common anger-producing tactic in marriage is to promise to do something and then to forget about it. This causes continual reminders, which produce anger in the forgetful spouse because the mate is nagging, as well as anger on the part of the one accused of nagging, who feels that nothing ever gets done without a struggle.

Although couples often do not recognize it, some angry feelings in a relationship are normal. Too often, husbands, wives, or unmarried lovers feel guilty about angry or hostile thoughts, or feel that if they have them, then something is deadly wrong in the relationship. But according to Dr. Otto Kernberg: "Those we love most we also hate most. Though love should predominate, it is normal to feel love and hatred toward the same person." He believes that the ability to see others as having a combination of bad characteristics as well as good ones is a sign of emotional maturity upon which hangs the ability to maintain long-term relationships, as well as sexual interest in a partner over time.

"The more neurotic the person," Dr. Kernberg says, "the more love and hate have to be separate, so that others are seen as either marvelous or horrible" — as all good or all bad, with no gray areas in between. "The capacity to admit shadings establishes the capacity to create relationships in depth. If one accepts hating as well as loving the other person, then one can accept getting infuriated without feeling that the anger necessarily threatens the relationship. This permits a healthy expression of conflict," he explains. "You can fight it out and still maintain a love relation.

"Fights and reconciliations, the ability to go from feelings of disappointment and distance to closeness again are very much part of a normal operation in a relationship," Dr. Kernberg continues. "I am not saying the anger should always be expressed in dramatic ways — that Italians, for example, do better than Swedes. How the anger is expressed is cultural. Some show it very little on the surface, but it is there underneath, recognized and tolerated. To be able to contain mutual aggression, without being afraid of it or letting it get out of hand, is what keeps the interest going in the life of a couple," he adds. "Anger may interfere temporarily with sexual interest, but tension and anger also reactivate sexual interest."

So finally, although long-standing, unresolved anger is anti-sexual in the long run, moments of anger are not. As long as the anger is recognized and acknowledged, as long as the issues behind it are ultimately resolved, getting angry at your partner occasionally is good for the relationship. And, funny as it may seem, being able to tolerate some bad feelings toward a mate can actually help you to maintain a vital sex life in marriage or in other long-term relationships. It is important, therefore, to recognize, first of all, when you are angry, especially if your sex life has been falling apart and you are not sure why.

Dr. Edward L. Parsons suggests that the clues listed below may help you tune in to anger that has built up over time in your relationship — anger that you may be suppressing and not acknowledging either to your partner or yourself.

- You feel flat. You don't feel sad, don't feel glad, don't feel bad, but you also don't feel enthusiasm in the relationship. Your marriage lacks normal highs or lows.
- You may feel more tense than usual and more irritable. Although you keep calm at home, you may blow up more easily in the outside world.
- You may feel moody without being able to say exactly why. One woman who was suppressing anger at her husband found herself crying a lot, in general, about other matters.
- Some people, when they are furious, automatically act in exactly the opposite way: they become more polite toward the partner who has produced the subliminal rage.
- Others express underlying anger in another indirect way: they remove themselves emotionally or physically from the object of their fury. If you find yourself more involved than usual with housework, or more preoccupied with the children, with career matters, or with social activities that exclude your spouse, consider the possibility that you may be angry and not expressing it.
- You find yourself avoiding sex through a variety of tactics —

going to bed later, busying yourself with other things at bedtime, becoming critical, or sabotaging in other ways when
your spouse indicates sexual interest.

Dr. Parsons thinks that it's important to get in touch with your
anger and try to understand it; only then will you be able to do
something about it. If you are experiencing one or more of the
symptoms described above, or if you have other reasons for sus-
pecting that you have stored up anger at your spouse, Dr. Parsons
suggests that you try to flush the anger out of its hiding place by
talking to two or more close friends about your feelings. Tell them
what you think is going on and get their feedback. Just one friend
won't do — you may get a distorted response if that person is also
having personal troubles at that time.

If this approach doesn't produce satisfactory results or you
feel uncomfortable talking to friends about your marriage, then
you might want to consult a clergyman trained in counseling
or a psychotherapist who will help you locate your anger and
handle it.

Dr. Parsons believes that once you know you are angry, it is
crucial that you tell your spouse how you feel. Listed below are
some rules about communicating anger that you might find helpful. These rules will also benefit couples who argue continually
without getting anything resolved.

It is positive — and often important for your sex life — to:

- Tell a spouse — when it occurs — that you disagree with or
  disapprove of something he or she has said or done.
- Follow this with an explanation of your reasons for feeling as
  you do. Discussing grievances as they occur prevents angry
  feelings from building up.
- Stick to the matter at hand.
- Help your mate communicate any reactions to your anger by
  asking how he or she feels about your complaint, especially if
  the mate remains silent at first.

- If your partner responds by voicing disagreement or disapproval of you, ask why he or she feels that way.
- Listen receptively and respectfully to your mate. This is as important as stating your position.

It is not constructive to:

- Rehash old disappointments and drag in everything you think your spouse has done wrong since the day you met.
- Speak sarcastically.
- Use generalized derogatory statements, such as "You really are impossible!" or "That was so typical of you!"
- Label your partner's behavior ("That was such an incredibly dumb thing to do!"; "Only an idiot would say such a thing!").
- Call the other person a name ("You bitch!"; "You rat!").
- Threaten your spouse physically or emotionally, by making statements such as "I am going to divorce you unless . . ."
- Hit, kick, scratch, slap, or push.
- Refuse to listen to or discuss your spouse's complaints or his or her feelings.
- Interrupt the other person.
- Show a lack of caring or respect for your partner's feelings or point of view ("I don't give a damn what you think!"; "I don't care what you say!").
- Reject your partner by leaving the room, or by making statements such as "Leave me alone!" or "Get out of my sight!"
- Attack your mate's complaints verbally in a generalized way rather than listen to them seriously ("Why are you such a grouch?"; "You're always looking for things to complain about!").

Remember that the aim of discussions about anger should be to reach compromises and better understand the other person's point of view. The goal is not to win or to prove that you are always right.

Dr. Harvey Caplan states: "I don't believe that a good marriage is one in which there is no anger. It is important for couples to learn that anger is a very useful tool for calling attention to serious issues — that arguing, debating, fighting, and negotiating can end up with both partners being winners instead of one winner and one loser."

Diets and face-lifts, sexy clothing and seductive behavior will not improve your sex life if you or your spouse are angry. Neither will standard sex-therapy sensate focus exercises, which therapists find often evoke negative feelings in angry partners so that they resist doing them or sabotage the process. "Anger is a 'turn off' that cannot be bypassed with sensate focus," writes Dr. Helen Singer Kaplan in *Disorders of Sexual Desire.* "A couple must 'make up' before they can make love; in the clinical situation, anger must be resolved, at least in part, before desire and erotic feeling can be expected to emerge. If this cannot be accomplished treatment will fail."

An angry person does not *want* to give a mate pleasure. Often, submerged anger outweighs even personal pleasure. Although angry partners who have lost desire may sometimes get inveigled into sex and have orgasms, they don't want to repeat the experience. They remain turned off to the mate who has stirred their anger.

So learn to fight and fight well! And heed the words of Dr. Harvey Caplan, who says, "Don't let problems that upset you go on for too long without attending to them."

CHAPTER 12

Sex under the Gun

STRESS

JOHN received notice that he was fired from the job he had held for twenty-four years at a time when he was becoming eligible for large retirement benefits. It took him six months to land another position. John felt infuriated at his firing, which he considered to be the firm's way of avoiding having to give him the pension that he had worked for hard and long, and he felt humiliated by his new position, which, in his eyes, was not as good as the old one even though he was earning as much as he had before. His wife Sue was upset by something else: John was no longer interested in sex. She could not imagine what was wrong and she started to wonder if John was having an affair.

Bernie's mother had cancer and for two years battled the disease, during which time he looked in on her frequently and found himself in despair at his mother's pain and steady deterioration. Bernie felt helpless in the face of something about which he could do nothing. He made sure that his mother had the best medical help available, but everyone knew that she was fighting a losing battle. In the middle of all of this, Bernie's wife Jenny became furious at him. She felt neglected. Not only did he spend a lot of time after work with his mother, but when he was home he was no longer interested in sex. When she complained, instead of telling her how preoccupied and upset he was, Bernie started brooding silently about how insensitive his wife was. He drew further and further away from her, and as he did so she felt more and more abandoned, hurt, and angry. Soon after Bernie's mother died, he and Jenny were divorced.

Corinne's mother, who suffered from Alzheimer's disease, could no longer live by herself. Corinne was faced with the decision of placing her mother in a nursing home or taking her into her own home. Corinne felt that there was no space for her mother in her home, and that she would not be able to look after her properly because she worked long hours on her job. She felt very conflicted, but finally placed her mother in the nursing home and visited her there five times a week to make sure that she was cared for well. During this period, Corinne found herself uninterested in sex. She told her husband Dan that she just wasn't in the mood, which puzzled him, since Corinne had always liked sex until now.

John, Bernie, and Corinne were all suffering from psychological stress. Dr. Helen Singer Kaplan calls stress one of the major causes of impaired sexual desire and points out that during stressful periods, "even loving, healthy couples may experience a diminished desire to make love." A journalist finishing a book about the Mideast under a tight deadline found the pressure so stressful that he woke up one morning after being totally immersed in his project for months and suddenly remembered that he hadn't had sex in a long time.

"I can predict it," said another man, an accountant who gets frantically busy in the two months just before income tax returns are due. "I just lose all interest in sex during this time. I can barely find time to eat, sleep, or breathe, much less make love."

Of course, reaction to stress varies with the individual. Some people go the opposite way — they want to make love more frequently. For them, sex is an outlet to reduce tension. Occasionally, sex and stress get confused. Two studies found that when people were placed in anxiety-producing situations or watched anxiety-provoking films, they felt more turned on to members of the opposite sex than when they were in calmer states.

Some people thrive on stress and go out of their way to create it. They make a big to-do about everything and envelop every project — even the simplest — in a cloud of anxiety. They create deadlines even when time pressures don't have to exist. Stress is a chronic condition for these people and after a while they need it to function and feel well. Life without tension is flat and dull for them. If things are suddenly calm, they invariably will do something to create a sense of pressure again. Their penchant for creating crises can contaminate their relationships. Stress lovers often react to minor issues as though they are major ones, and turn small matters into large ones. For example, they might interpret a random sexual refusal from a spouse who is exhausted as a sign that their sex life is falling apart forever.

Since they create upheavals and crises in their marriages as they do everywhere else, the anxiety-addicted person often manufactures such marital turmoil that the couple's sex life is indeed disrupted. The stress addict is frequently prone to turning off in reaction to a self-created crisis, though often the crisis mentality creates such negative reactions that the spouse gets turned off instead.

There are other kinds of people who don't create crises but seem to function best when in them. Under great stress they keep cool, get more organized than usual, suddenly are more effective, decisive, know instinctively how to streamline and eliminate what is unnecessary. They take charge rather than fall apart or overtly exhibit tension, as others might, while the stressful situation exists. When the crisis is over, however, they collapse, exhausted. In contrast, there are those who become paralyzed or disorganized under stress. They run around more but accomplish less. As the stress increases, they tend to become more and more ineffective, more and more stupefied, or more and more hysterical — or they collapse altogether.

Although stress is generally considered a psychological state and as such causes loss of libido, evidence suggests that it also creates sex-related physical changes. Prolonged stress can cause a deficiency of the male sex hormone testosterone. "Because the activity of the sex centers depends on testosterone, insufficient levels of this hormone or its physiological unavailability may produce diminution of sexual interest in both males and females," explains Dr. Kaplan. One study indicated that men undergoing stressful conditions such as crowding, threat of combat, and military training showed a drop of approximately 30 percent in testosterone levels. Hormonal levels returned to normal when the stress terminated.

A landmark study of the physical effects of stress was done by Thomas H. Holmes and Minoru Masadu, who correlated major stressful life events with subsequent illness. Since marriage by itself was found to be a major stress producer, it may be that stress is occasionally a contributing factor in greatly diminished sexual interest right after the wedding. Other familiar events that Holmes and Masadu associated with high stress were job troubles, the death of a spouse, pregnancy, changes in financial state, changes in residence, marital separation (as well as marital reconciliation), children leaving home, and divorce.

It may seem simplistic to say that stress can cause lack of interest in sex — who wouldn't know that? But if you start investigating people's experiences with stress, you discover that many don't make the connection. For example, one man had the kind of luck others only dream about having. In his early twenties, he was brought to Los Angeles to become a disc jockey on a leading West Coast radio station. His young wife, who accompanied him from the Midwest, where they both grew up, was as excited as he was by his break. Actually doing the work, however, turned out to be less than a dream. The man soon realized that he was not doing the job well enough. He worried incessantly about whether he would be fired, which he felt would ruin his career forever.

During this time, he did not confide in his wife about his growing self-doubt and constant anxiety. All she was aware of was that suddenly her husband was no longer interested in making love with her. As for the man, he didn't make the connection between his anxiety and inner turmoil and his lack of sexual interest. He just felt that somehow his wife no longer had the same allure she used to have. The couple started quarreling. She accused him of seeing other women now that he was a celebrity of sorts. When he denied that vehemently, she then accused him of being a homosexual. He never forgave her for that. Their quarrels grew more and more frequent and became increasingly bitter, until they finally divorced. To this day, she thinks of her ex-husband as a closet homosexual.

The disc jockey, while his career was still in doubt, explained his continued lack of interest in women by saying that he was so embittered by his experience with his wife that he didn't want to have anything more to do with the opposite sex. Finally, this man saved his career by arranging to have himself transferred to a smaller city. He gradually gained more experience and expertise there and then made his way back to the big league in broadcasting. When his confidence returned and the stress about his job lifted, he became interested in women — and sex — once more, and today he is famous, happily remarried, and functioning well sexually.

An amusing example of someone who did not make the connection between stress and sexual problems is given by Dr. Helen Singer Kaplan in her book *Disorders of Sexual Desire:* "A patient consulted me with an urgent complaint of impotence and lack of desire. At the time of the interview he was in the midst of a bitter marital crisis, his son had been arrested for drug abuse, his business partner had embezzled his life's savings and he was being pursued by the I.R.S. for tax evasion. But he was preoccupied with the fact that he was not very interested in making love to his young mistress." Dr. Kaplan says that patients may displace their anxiety about other matters and become obsessed with their sexual functioning instead.

Although work-related stress is very common in our culture, people rarely realize how much it can dampen their sex lives. A new boss, a promotion, or transfer, job insecurity, or unemployment can all make a person practically oblivious to sex. Less obvious but even more common as a source of stress are the frequent slights, humiliations, or grudges that many people are forced to put up with at work. These day-to-day blows to pride can create ongoing, chronic low-grade stress that can cause low sexual interest. Sometimes the stress that is endured silently in the workplace is expressed noisily in the home. The person who silently operates all day under tension can torture his or her family upon returning home — which creates resentments that can reverberate in the bedroom.

Stress may cause a person to move closer to a partner or to move away, depending on which action provides the most relief. If a move for closeness is uncharacteristic, the partner may feel smothered by the new emotional demands and pull away. This can make the person under stress feel even more anxious. Or, if the reaction to stress is withdrawal, the partner may feel rejected or fear abandonment. "When these anxiety driven patterns are operating between a couple, sexual conflicts are most likely to occur," writes Dr. Edward W. Beal of the Georgetown Medical School.

Every couple should be aware that changes in life situations may cause severe stress at any time and create loss of libido. With this knowledge, if John suddenly loses interest in sex with Mary while he is trying to save his company from bankruptcy, or if Mary loses interest in John because she is worried about passing her bar examination or because her mother was just taken to the hospital, the neglected spouse will be less likely to interpret the partner's loss of libido as a personal rejection.

Being alerted to the sexual side effects of stress may be even more important once the first flush of passion has passed. Dr.

Harvey Caplan points out that "as time goes on, sex is probably even more vulnerable to outside stress than it was earlier. So if you're under stress, you may not feel as sexual as you did in the first year of marriage, for example, under similar circumstances."

Under no circumstances should a partner put sexual pressure on a spouse who is under great stress. Part of a good sex life is understanding when your mate has legitimate reasons for not being in the mood. Wait out the situation with patience and empathy. Generally, in good relationships, where sexual interest flourishes under normal circumstances, libido will return by itself once the stressful situation passes.

Dr. Shirley Zussman, past president of the American Association of Sex Educators, Counselors, and Therapists, points out that when exhaustion from stress is causing lack of libido, sex is often seen as still another chore. To counteract this, she suggests that the couple try touching and caressing each other without feeling the necessity to engage in intercourse. "What couples should understand," says Dr. Zussman, "is that touching can often be as satisfying as intercourse, and, once the pressure's off, intercourse often follows."

Many people find that stress-reduction techniques such as meditation or biofeedback help them cope and lead more normal lives while they are under pressure. If you are going through a particularly stressful time, you might want to try the simple meditation exercise described below. It has worked for many people over the years. Originally developed in 1938, it has since been modified by Dr. Herbert Walker, professor of psychiatry at New York University Medical Center.

Get into a comfortable position and take a deep breath. Let it out slowly. Relax. Then silently count:

One: Roll your eyes up. Keep your eyes up and close your eyelids.

Two: Inhale deeply and hold your breath.

Three: Now, let the breath out. Roll your eyes down, keeping the eyelids closed. Then let the breath out slowly.

Now take three breaths, inhaling and exhaling slowly, and imagine that your body is floating. Imagine yourself lying or floating in a very comfortable position, and begin to relax all of your body. Let your neck and your face relax, then your back muscles, your chest and abdomen, your legs.

Continue to think of the image you have chosen. For thirty seconds to five minutes, remain relaxed and buoyant in your image. Then count yourself out of the meditation:

Three: Roll your eyes up, keeping your eyelids closed.

Two: Take in a deep breath and hold it.

One: Let the breath out slowly, roll your eyes down, and slowly open your eyelids.

You will notice that you feel relaxed, buoyant, and calm. You will be completely alert.

DEPRESSION

Depression is another leading reason why people lose interest in sex. According to Dr. Raul Schiavi, "It is one of the most frequent single psychological factors in decrease of sexual desire, as well as in performance problems."

Although loss of sexual interest, loss of appetite, listlessness, hopeless feelings, insomnia, inability to take pleasure in anything, and even constipation are all known as classic symptoms of depression, Dr. Helen Singer Kaplan says that, in her experience, "losing desire can be one of the first signs of depression. It may appear before the mood itself becomes evident." Depression may also show up as impotence. Dr. Harold Lief explains that although impotence has traditionally been regarded as a classic primary symptom of depression, it is actually secondary: "Depression causes decrease in desire and then impotence may follow if a man tries to have intercourse anyway."

Many of the patients who show up in sex clinics and therapists' offices complaining of lack of desire are not aware that they are in a state of depression. They may realize that they have no interest in sex, or that they suddenly seem to have become impotent or are unable to have orgasms, but what remains hidden from their consciousness is an underlying sense of sadness, futility, or hopelessness that is affecting every area of their life. Frequently, loss of libido is the only symptom that a depressed man or woman notices. The person is walking around with what is called a "masked" or "smiling" depression. Such people may have a vague sense of not feeling up to par, but they do not describe themselves as "depressed." Or they may feel a little sad, but since they can find no justification for the feeling, they try to ignore it and carry on as usual. Because the person continues to operate in what seems to be the usual manner, the partner has no inkling that all is not well. The masked depressive's loss of libido may be particularly puzzling and threatening to the spouse, because there is no clue as to what is really wrong. The spouse of the depressed person thus tends to feel unattractive or to wonder if the mate is having an affair.

TWO TYPES OF BLUES

There are two basic types of depression: exogenous and endogenous. Exogenous depression, also called reactive depression, is caused by a psychological reaction to external stress. It is often triggered by situations that a person feels cannot be changed — job problems, a bad marriage, teenagers who can't be controlled, finances, problems connected with ill health or aging, and so forth.

People suffering from reactive depression frequently feel trapped. They feel that they are unable to improve an impossible situation or escape from it, but they are also unable to modify their behavior to adjust to it. Often the problem that causes this involves a loss of some kind — loss of a loved one, loss due to separation or divorce, loss of a body part through surgery, loss of a job, loss of a home or other material thing, loss of looks or vitality through aging, loss of youth (and youth's illusions) in midlife, or even the loss of status or prestige. One head of a major corporation became catatonic when he was fired from his job. He was found by his wife motionless, staring ahead with unseeing eyes. A psychiatrist was called in and the executive was treated for severe depression, which had literally immobilized him. Sports stars and other public idols frequently slip into depression soon after they are forced to retire and leave behind the adulation of fans.

Sometimes the basic problem behind reactive depression is low self-esteem. A person may feel inadequate, unworthy, undesirable. Such negative feelings are enough to cause depression by themselves, but often they also keep a person in an unhappy situation, such as an unfulfilling or bad marriage.

Take the case of Beth. She lives with a bad-tempered husband who beats her when he drinks. Beth feels totally at her husband's mercy, because she is sure she will not be able to take care of herself if she leaves her husband and is convinced that no other man would be interested in her. So she stays in the marriage, suffering verbal and physical abuse; eating too much out of anxiety, so that she is obese; and feeling depressed all of the time. She tries to comfort herself through her religious belief and regular church attendance, but her basic depression persists. She lost sexual desire for her husband many years ago, but she submits to him anyway because she fears being beaten if she refuses.

Another frequent cause of depression is the inability to assert yourself, so that you always feel put upon or abused by others but are unable to express your feelings or stand up for your rights. Behind many depressions is the feeling of being a failure: you lose hope of ever succeeding in life, either in a career or in interpersonal relationships.

In a good number of cases, a person becomes more and more depressed because reality does not match long-standing fantasies. For instance, a woman who lives in the Midwest showed musical talent early in childhood and took lessons from the best teachers available. From an early age, she entertained a fantasy, fostered by her doting mother, that someday she would be a great concert artist. Later in life, however, she discovered that the world did not accept her as a musical genius. She could not make it as a soloist.

Realizing that she would never achieve the worldwide acclaim she felt was due her, she sank into a deep depression.

A man who grew up in a family with money problems had an image of himself that started as a boy: He dreamed of becoming very successful and tremendously wealthy. He saw himself being able to provide his mother and father with all the things they could not afford. Although he worked long and hard and achieved modest success, he could never become the millionaire he assumed he was destined to become. When tremendous success continued to elude him, he sank into a depression.

Sometimes the illusion is simple. For example, a woman might fantasize that she will marry well and be taken care of in comfort for the rest of her life. If for some reason she doesn't marry at all, or she marries an unsuccessful man, she may feel cheated by life of her rightful destiny and might fall into a depression as she feels it less and less possible for her dream to come true. Often, the unfulfilled fantasies that cause depression were fostered by one or both parents, beginning at an early age.

A major reason for reactive depression is unexpressed anger and suppressed rage that is turned inward. Perhaps you are angry at something, or someone, or a multitude of things, but instead of venting your anger and aiming it at its source, you turn it upon yourself. In effect, you end up silently reproaching or attacking yourself, relentlessly and unconsciously. As a result, you feel miserable without really understanding why. Life becomes muted. You lack energy; you don't enjoy anything anymore. Your appetites for eating, fun, and sex are dulled. You may cry, or feel like crying a lot, and you don't sleep very well, often waking up in the early hours of the morning, unable to get back to sleep.

There are milder and more severe forms of reactive depression, with milder symptoms and more intense ones.

Endogenous depression has physiological causes, although there may be psychological ramifications as well. Experts think that there is a biological and chemical basis for this type of depression, which can hit you out of the blue. It is generally characterized by a vegetative state. You stop functioning. You can't eat, can't sleep. You may not want to get out of bed. You can sit staring out of the window for hours at a time. Your bowel movements even slow down to the point of constipation. Everything seems gray and hopeless. There is frequently a history of depression in the families of those who suffer from endogenous depression.

A common example of depression that has a biological component is postpartum blues, experienced by some women after giving birth. Jenny had her first baby three years after marrying Tim. She and Tim were very compatible. They shared the same sense of humor, loved to talk intimately for hours on end, and enjoyed hiking, swimming, skiing, and other outdoor activities together. Jenny and Tim were ecstatic when she became pregnant, and all through the pregnancy they were happy and eager to be parents. Then, suddenly, eight weeks after their daughter was born, Jenny started feeling depressed. She felt weepy a good deal of the time and listless in general. When Tim asked what was wrong, Jenny could tell him nothing. She didn't know why she felt so sad. She refused to have sex with Tim, telling him she just didn't seem to feel like it. Her state alarmed Tim and he insisted that she see her doctor to find out what was wrong. Her doctor knew what the trouble was right away. He had seen it many times before. He told Jenny that she was suffering from postpartum depression that was the result of the sharp change in hormonal levels that occurs after a woman gives birth.

Although myth has it that postpartum blues occur only immediately or soon after delivery, experts are now coming to recognize that this type of depression doesn't really hit some women until many months afterward. They may have been suffering from underlying depression all along, but they are so caught up in their duties with their infants that they go along oblivious to their own mood. Only when things have simmered down a little do they tune in to their emotional state and allow the depression to surface. Postpartum blues may accompany a woman's second or third pregnancy but not her initial one. Or they may occur at a first birth but never again.

Menopause may also trigger biologically based depression as

women react to the sharp drop in estrogen production that occurs at this time in life. Of course, there may be psychological ramifications to depression during menopause as well. Women often struggle with the sense of loss resulting from the knowledge that they will never again be able to bear children, and they may be upset by obvious body changes and diminution of youthful good looks that may accompany menopause.

The majority of women do not suffer from depression after the birth of children or at menopause, however, so those who do may be genetically susceptible. Some people react strongly to biochemical changes; others hardly feel them at all. In most cases of endogenous depression — in both men and women — the biological event that triggers the condition (like childbirth or menopause) is not readily recognized as the cause. The chemical basis is there, but the depression, with its attendant lack of interest in sex, seems to appear out of nowhere. In general, the people with a biological propensity to endogenous depression tend to become more depressed than others in reaction to external adverse circumstances. They generally come from families with a history of depression.

Many cases of depression are a mixture of the psychological and the chemical. Experts are discovering these days what they call "double depressions": A person becomes deeply depressed in reaction to a life event. When that depression is treated and lifts, however, another, underlying depression is uncovered — one that may be chronic and that has a chemical or biological component. For exogenous, or reactive, depression, the treatment is usually psychotherapy. For endogenous, or chemically caused, depression, doctors can prescribe highly effective drugs that generally alleviate symptoms quickly.

TRYING TO OUTRUN DEPRESSION

Although lack of sexual interest is the more usual response to depression, some depressed men and women use sex as a way of trying to beat the sense of gloom that is dogging them. Instead of turning off, they may suddenly start a frantic period of sexual activity. The spouse may be startled by this sudden sexual insatiability — if exposed to it. Affairs and promiscuity are common.

Bob, at age fifty-two, after twenty-five years of being a faithful husband, began a series of affairs with young women in their twenties. He covered his tracks by telling his wife that he was going on business trips. Since the number of trips he was taking increased dramatically, and since he now went to uncharacteristic places like Palm Springs, Hawaii, and Florida, his wife's suspicions were aroused. One day she called him at the hotel where he was staying and the clerk, not understanding her, wanted to know if she wished to speak to Mr. or Mrs. ———. At that point, she hired a detective, who soon found plenty of evidence of her husband's infidelities. Bob's wife confronted him. At first he denied everything, but when shown the evidence, he confessed. He insisted that he did not want a divorce. He loved his wife, he protested, but he also loved all these young women. She insisted the two of them go into couple's therapy, but he refused. At that point she started to see a psychiatrist by herself. The psychiatrist was recommended by their family doctor, who soon clued the psychiatrist in to the fact that Bob had been seeing him about other minor ailments lately and that he suspected he was basically depressed.

Neither husband nor wife understood that Bob's current round of frenzied sexual activity was his way of trying to shake off his depression. Soon after the family physician prescribed an anti-depressant medication for Bob, he stopped taking planes all over the country to carry on his liaisons, and finally he stopped his affairs altogether. He was now able to talk matters over with his wife and they managed to patch up a marriage that had been happy until his depression disrupted it. He also regained sexual interest in his wife, which had disappeared while he was chasing his young lovers in a frantic effort to make himself feel more alive and happy.

The use of sexual escapades to mask depression has been, up until recently, more common among men than women, particularly during middle age. This kind of self-cure is rarely effective in the long run and often does more harm than good, especially if the marriage breaks up because of the affairs.

Other ways that people try to cheer themselves up and ward off their depression are by drinking, gambling, or buying "fun" luxuries like an expensive car or a big boat. The link between alcoholism and depression has been well documented; many heavy drinkers are actually using alcohol to cope with depression, although they generally aren't aware of it. A person suffering from impotence or from loss of libido can, by drinking to fight off depression, compound the problem. Alcohol has chemical effects that depress the central nervous system, and this has a negative influence on sexual response and performance.

Depression that interferes with sex drive needs to be treated professionally. Psychiatrists can prescribe medications that can be very effective in alleviating depression. Other licensed therapists, such as psychologists and social workers, cannot prescribe such drugs, although they may be able to refer you to someone who can. Many hospitals and large medical centers now have special depression clinics where you can receive excellent care. Sex therapists find that once the depression lifts through medication, libido automatically returns, often without need for further treatment.

CHAPTER 13

Sex and Power

WHO is the boss in your family? Do you and your spouse make most important decisions together or does one of you lead the other? Surprisingly, the answer to these questions may directly affect your love life. Who feels superior, who feels dominated or inferior, and how these factors play themselves out are crucial elements that frequently determine not only how a couple operates together in general, but also how well their sex life is faring.

Sociologists John N. Edwards and Alan Booth discovered, for example, that a lopsided power arrangement in a marriage may influence how often a couple sleeps together. Based on their investigation of factors affecting the sex lives of a representative sampling of couples in Toronto, these researchers, in the *Journal of Marriage and the Family,* noted that "a power structure dominated by one member tends to suppress coital frequency." In another paper, in the *American Journal of Psychiatry,* this same team reported a surprisingly large number of young couples who had little or no sex together for long periods of time. They noted that one important reason behind the lack of sex was "the wife's perception that her husband is dominant in family decision making."

If the wife rules the roost, the same thing may occur. A study of 95 couples in their thirties by David H. Olson and Herbert Laube at the University of Minnesota found that couples who shared leadership in a marriage had the best sex lives while couples in relationships that were clearly dominated by either husband or wife had the most sexual problems.

Power struggles are rampant and can erupt at any stage in a marriage. Most husbands and wives engage in them to some degree, particularly in our culture, at this moment in history. In societies where there is a clear-cut, established, and accepted power structure — where, for example, men's and women's duties are clearly differentiated or where it is an accepted fact that wives obey husbands in all matters (and that if they don't, they get ostracized or killed) — there is little room for struggle; the opportunities for competitiveness are limited or the consequences of a challenge to the system are too deadly. But the United States, with its emphasis on democracy, has always had a looser power structure between the sexes than many countries. De Tocqueville, in *Democracy in America,* commented on the unusual assertiveness of nineteenth-century American women as compared to their European counterparts; and today — when women are as educated as men, when they often have economic power through salaried jobs, and when, encouraged by the women's liberation movement, they are more likely to assert themselves and feel and act more like men's equals — power struggles within marriage and other relationships are much more likely to occur.

RULERS OF THE ROOST

The quest for power in relationships can take many forms, ranging from very overt controlling behavior to subtle games. The most obvious power seekers are bullying husbands or shrewish wives who order their mates around and may criticize, humiliate, or belittle them in order to maintain dominance in the relationship.

Generally, these are people who can only feel safe in intimacy if they can be in unilateral control.

"Every time she opens her mouth, it's to criticize me about something," complained one husband who had endured a domineering wife for fifteen years.

"He makes me feel like I'm not a person," explained the wife of an overbearing doctor. "He knows all the answers and I don't know anything. I feel like a nothing in his eyes."

Another woman, married to a high-powered corporate executive, said: "He treats me like an idiot. He automatically says, 'You're wrong,' every time I have an opinion about anything."

Generally, such obviously controlling types end up with spouses who fairly early in the relationship capitulate and accept a role that is either submissive or passive. Such spouses may, because of their own neurotic needs, actually want to be controlled, or they may give in because they feel they cannot win. Although they seem to surrender in the battle for power, they often harbor hidden resentments, however. One woman, afraid to leave her husband because she feels she won't be able to support herself, confided, "I know it's awful, but sometimes I wish he would die."

A bullying husband may extend his power tactics into the bedroom, using sex to reward a wife when he is pleased with her and withdrawing sex as punishment. Or sex may occur at his insistence, only when he wants it. Perhaps he thinks only about his own desires and does not even consider his wife's mood. He may discourage his wife's taking the initiative in sex by becoming impotent when she does, or by deciding that he isn't in the mood. In one way or another, his wife gets the message that he is running the sexual show; and if she has assumed the role of a submissive wife, she gets used to having sex on demand. As the years go by, because the wife is having sex most of the time to suit her husband rather than herself, she stops tuning in to her own needs and desires. She begins to lose track of her own sexual feelings and ultimately loses interest in sex as a result.

She may also be extremely angry at her bullying husband but not showing it, which may lead to loss of libido. Sexual indifference or aversion, or inability to achieve orgasm, may be an unconscious counterattack on her part as well. Without overtly recognizing it, she may know, on a hidden level, that she has hit on a surefire tactic to undercut her husband's power and to exert control herself. In their book *Mirages of Marriage,* William Lederer and the late marriage therapist Don Jackson describe the way this operates: "Despite arrogant domination and threats, there is no way he can force her to get pleasure from intercourse and when she does not he feels defeated and castrated." The woman, by losing sexual interest, seems to be passive but is "in reality defeating her husband's domination in the most effective way possible," say Lederer and Jackson.

Frequently, however, the dominant husband senses what is happening, becomes increasingly furious or frightened about his loss of control, and attempts to reestablish it in any way that he can. He may try to put one over on his wife by starting an affair. He thus moves his sexual needs elsewhere, in effect taking away her weapon in the subterranean power struggle. He may develop a sexual symptom, such as impotence, himself, which puts him in the driver's seat again since intercourse now also depends on his ability to maintain an erection. Or he may escalate power tactics in other areas of the couple's life to compensate. For example, if he pretty much allowed his wife to run their children's lives before, he may suddenly start to criticize her abilities as a mother or interfere with her approach to discipline — by allowing the children to stay up later than she wants them to, for instance. Or, resorting to a favorite weapon in power wars, he may cut back on the money he gives her.

A henpecked husband who allows his wife to control him in every other way may develop sexual symptoms as well. He may gain control in the bedroom by ejaculating prematurely, which robs his wife of sexual pleasure, or by becoming impotent, so that intercourse becomes subject to his erectile abilities. He may undercut her domination by losing sexual interest altogether, so that their intimate love life comes to a standstill.

The partners of "control freaks" are often afraid to express personal sexual needs or to suggest improvements in the dominant mate's technique, because they realize, on one level or another, that this may be interpreted as a threat. As a result, static or unsatisfactory sexual patterns frequently evolve, and this can eventually lead to loss of sexual interest for one or both partners.

Although the reactions and tactics described above are the more usual ones, occasionally relationships in which one spouse must dominate the other contain the seeds of sadomasochism: sexual interest remains high on the part of the submissive partner, who actually "gets off" on being controlled or even abused. If the dominating spouse, through some miracle, changed and stopped being controlling or abusive, the passive partner would lose sexual interest. When sexual desire and response are present in a relationship, the dominant spouse may use sex even more as a weapon of control — giving it to reward, withdrawing it to punish.

SPARRING RIVALS

An even more common form of power relationship between spouses is one of ongoing competition. In this case, there are constant wrangles over large and small matters, and there is never a definitive winner or loser in the overall game. The power tactics employed are less obvious than when one spouse clearly dominates the other, but they often become one of the most important ingredients of the relationship.

What happens as life together unfolds on a day-to-day basis is predictable. Your partner makes a remark, offers an opinion, tells you how to do something, or makes a unilateral decision that makes you feel that you have to defend or assert yourself. Consciously or unconsciously, according to Lederer and Jackson, your mind plays this message: "My spouse doesn't believe I am as competent or as good or as skilled as he is." Your reaction? "I don't like that. I am an equal." Lederer and Jackson say that this conclusion frequently leads to a postscript: "I am equal — and probably better"; and what happens next is that you have to say or do something that will show how good you are.

In ongoing power struggles, the partners constantly inter-change roles. Sometimes the wife challenges her husband, and he feels called upon to defend himself; the next time he is the challenger and she is at bat for the defense. Marriages like this are punctuated by arguments that go back and forth: You are always interrupting each other to make a point. If your partner seems to be right, you start to worry about being inferior, which means that you must do something to prove you aren't. The issues at hand are not the real cause of your squabbles. All your skirmishes are about the same thing in the end: trying to prove how wise and smart you are and having your superiority accepted by your mate.

Take the case of Jeannie and Eric. Jeannie is a health-food nut; Eric will eat anything that doesn't move. Each knows about the other's habits and preferences — after all, they have been living together for seven years — but they still periodically wrangle over food, each trying to prove how wrong the other's eating habits are.

On a recent Sunday morning, Eric decided to make muffins for his wife, himself, and their five-year-old son. He promised Jeannie that he would make a separate batch for her using no sugar. She was pleased, because this seemed to indicate that he finally respected her eating preferences.

At the breakfast table, Eric mentioned that he had used bran in the muffins, as his mother used to do. Jeannie asked, "What bran did you use?" Eric explained that he had used a commercial all-bran breakfast cereal — one that Jeannie recognized as containing lots of sugar. She said, "Then these muffins have sugar in them," and she stopped eating them.

Eric took this as a rejection of his muffins, his efforts, and his own eating habits, which included a good amount of sugar. He complained that Jeannie was acting as if sugar were poison, and, citing his knowledge as a physician (which was a status ploy on his part), he explained that it was a natural substance found in everyone's bloodstream.

She replied that that didn't make it good to stuff your body with sugar, and, drawing on what she considered her superior knowledge of nutrition, she claimed that doctors don't know anything about nutrition, that nutrition is not taught to them in most medical schools, and that eating sugar is bad for people.

Eric maintained that the bran cereal he used was one of the healthiest cereals around. She responded that the cereal was not healthful. He asked his son to fetch the box. She grabbed it and read the cereal's contents, gasping when she found that it contained corn syrup as well as sugar.

"It not only contains one sweetener but two!" she said.

Eric thought that he detected a triumphant note in her voice. He felt obscurely that somehow she had bested him by reading the ingredients, and he then accused her of being a fanatic.

Jeannie, who felt put down by his accusation, went on to try to equalize her position by attacking Eric's habit of eating bacon, sausage, and other fatty meats, calling it unhealthful and uninformed considering what everyone knows about cholesterol.

Since he was made to feel inferior by her remarks, Eric then attempted to regain status by attacking Jeannie's "neurotic" use of vitamins. "You're as much a pill popper," he said, "as those women who get hooked on Valium."

Jeannie then attacked Eric for smoking despite the common knowledge that smoking caused lung cancer and heart disease.

Eric retaliated by telling her that she was ruining her kidneys by taking so many vitamins.

And so it went. By now the picture should be clear: this couple continually bickered to adjust their respective power positions. Neither Jeannie nor Eric understood this, however. They just reacted instinctively to each other without realizing they were involved in a power war.

The same kind of thing goes on in bigger or lesser ways in millions of relationships. Although some couples manage to contain the war and only battle for power occasionally, for most, once the pattern starts, it escalates. Arguments become more frequent, and more vicious. Collaboration on even the simplest matters becomes practically impossible. Hurts, grudges, and anger pile up.

And sex? Power struggles can be played out in bed as well. For example, when the wife initiates sex, the husband might make sure that in one way or another the act never gets satisfactorily completed. He may find an excuse not to have sex, he may become impotent, he may ejaculate prematurely, he may sabotage by bringing up a subject sure to turn his wife off, or he may do something he knows will annoy her. If she suggests a new love-making position, he will not be able to function well in it; if she wants him to touch her in a certain way, or in a certain place, he will "forget." The same kind of sabotage can be engaged in by the wife. Sometimes couples like this trade sexual problems as part of their ongoing battle: A husband may complain that his wife does not have orgasms; but if she goes to a sex therapist and learns how to, he may then become impotent. Or if a husband stops being impotent, his wife may suddenly lose interest in sex. In general, the anger that can accumulate between such partners may serve to turn off either or both of them, so that sex becomes sporadic, infrequent, or stops altogether.

In marriage, who initiates sex, how, and when, may be an indication of a power setup. If one person always is the sexual aggressor, that partner clearly has the most power in the bedroom, either because he or she insists on it or because the other partner has relinquished power by choosing to react rather than initiate. If one partner wants more variety and indicates this but the other resists, power accrues to the resister. If a spouse wants intercourse more often than you do and you are in the position of frequently refusing sex, power is accruing to you. If you have a sexual dysfunction that is clearly upsetting to your spouse, you have achieved a form of power. If you keep doing something your partner doesn't like, you are exercising power. You are controlling, also, if you insist on sex even though your partner has indicated that he or she isn't in the mood.

Some sexual acts are associated with dominance. For many men fellatio is a way of exerting power — sometimes hostile power — over a woman. In their book *Sexual Conduct,* John Gagnon and William Simon point out that during fellatio common male fantasies involve "images of filling up, choking, dominating, degrading. . . . Even though the female is more physically active and dominating and the male more passive, the act of fellatio is symbolically constructed in terms of male dominance and female submission." Gagnon and Simon go on to explain that the same association applies to cunnilingus: "The male, who often experiences fellatio through the metaphors of dominance, tends to experience cunnilingus through the identical modalities, seeing it as control rather than submission." Men often consider anal intercourse as an act of male dominance as well. On the other hand, some men feel that a woman is dominating them when she is on top of them during the act of sex.

POWER TACTICS

If you withhold sex in retaliation for something your spouse has done, you are using a power tactic. The same is true of withholding affection in general.

Criticizing and complaining about a mate's behavior rather than really trying to change it is another way of exerting power in a relationship. For example, a wife may complain that her husband is unreasonable and intolerant because he can't stand the children's toys lying around the house and screams if he finds any of their things on the floor. Perhaps she repeatedly runs around the house before he gets home sweeping toys away and muttering to herself, rather than discussing the matter with him reasonably and making him understand that she will no longer put up with his tirades about toys. By doing so, she feels like the "good" partner and that he is the "bad" one — which is a power ploy, a way of making herself feel superior to her husband. According to William Lederer and Don Jackson, the "tendency to nag and complain instead of refusing to tolerate unwanted behavior is widespread in marriage in our culture." You may recognize this as being one of your own particular power tactics. If so, one way out of your habit is to convince your mate that you will no longer put up with his or her offending behavior.

Moodiness is often a hidden way to control a person. A pattern of pouting, surliness, or irritability can be a tactic to make your partner dance to your tune. Men and women married to moody spouses often try to do anything not to invoke those moods. Martyrdom is also a way of maintaining control: You do everything for others, nothing for yourself. You put up with all kinds of things without complaining. In doing so, you make those around you feel guilty — and that is how you control them.

Some people don't want to be dominant. In the game of power, what they really want is to be dominated. By acting helpless or incompetent, they force their partners to take control. In a sense, by insisting on being taken care of, they are controlling their spouses.

Illness can be a passive form of control, too. If you are sick, people are often afraid of upsetting you and tend to cater to your wishes or feel that they have to take care of you. Psychosomatic or temporary ailments — allergy attacks, minor headaches or migraines, fainting spells, upset stomachs, ulcers — can be ways of dominating those around you. Chronic physical ailments can be used effectively in the service of power as well. There are tyrants in wheelchairs.

Religion can also be misused in this way. Some people control those around them by holding the threat of hell and damnation over their heads. The position of upholder of the faith can also be a terrific way of inwardly feeling morally superior.

Keeping a mate off balance is another way of maintaining control. You may lose your temper just when your mate was beginning to relax and enjoy the relationship again after a big upset. You can keep saying one thing and doing another. You can refuse to be pinned down about social engagements until the very last minute. You can continually agree to something, then not remember that you did. You can be happy one day about the same thing that makes you unhappy the next. These are all examples of ways to keep a mate hopping.

Some people are masters at the art of spoiling things — a covert way to assert power. For example, a wife may consent, without a murmur, to go to an Indian restaurant when her partner suggests it. This makes her seem agreeable and submissive. But once at the restaurant, she only picks at her food. When her husband asks her, "What's wrong?" she says, "Hot, spicy food always gives me a stomachache."

You can spoil things in lots of other ways. You can finally agree to visit a mate's old friend whom you really don't like, then pick a fight in the car on the way there, or drink too much and throw up in the bathroom during the visit. You can agree to go to the opera because your mate adores it (even though you hate it), then fall asleep during the first aria or fidget throughout the performance. In order to "spoil," you might fall down, fall ill, fall asleep, or fall for that flashy blond who arrived with your brother-in-law. Or you might take a vacation that your husband arranged and complain about the accommodations and the food the entire time.

Another subtle power tactic — a special favorite of husbands who feel dominated by their wives — is to agree to do something and then procrastinate forever before doing it, or to "forget" to do it altogether. A variation is to do the thing but do it wrong. One marvelous example of this: A husband, at his busy wife's insistence, grudgingly went shopping at the supermarket for her. He managed to come home with a large bag of Kitty Litter, even though they didn't own a cat. This is called passive resistance. Spouses who use such means of subversion are usually afraid, on some level, to say no to their mate, so they say yes but never get around to doing what they promised, or they mess it up. It's a way of saying, "See, you can't control me!"

A different way to deal a damaging blow to the power of a dominating mate without appearing to mount a challenge is to undercut and undermine. Parents frequently do this through the children — by contradicting their mate's instructions or allowing the kids to break the other parent's rules, for example. Painting a black picture of the other mate to the kids is another way: making Daddy out to be a terrible old grump whose orders can be ignored when he isn't around, or portraying Mommy as a silly idiot who doesn't know what she is talking about most of the time, or suggesting that Daddy doesn't care for the children very much (at least not the way Mommy does), or hinting that Daddy is the kinder parent since Mom makes all the rules and enforces them.

Using the kids to try to get what you want is a common tactic as well. Say that your husband wants to go on a vacation where he can go deep-sea fishing, but you want to go to visit your mother at her place in New Hampshire. Rather than fight it out with your husband directly, you enlist the kids to harangue Daddy about how much they want to see Grandma and Grandpa. There are infinite variations of this game in which the kids become your mouthpiece, propagandizing for you.

The solution to the power struggle for many men is to choose a much younger woman to marry in the first place. These men rarely recognize it consciously, but one of the great attractions of a much younger woman is the built-in authority their own seniority affords them. They feel that they can control the younger woman better than they could a wife closer to their own age.

Finally, of course, in the contest of power, there is the ultimate weapon: force. Some men feel that a little force — a slap, a blow, now and then — is a good way of "keeping a woman in her place." They may do it as an automatic reminder to show her who the boss is, or they may resort to violence only when they feel that the woman is challenging their authority. Other people use force only when they are feeling extremely vulnerable or weak themselves. For example, a man may be humiliated at work and unable to do anything about it without imperiling his job. But when he gets home, he releases his feelings of helplessness and makes himself feel powerful again by shoving his wife around. People who resort to violence as a power tactic are in serious need of professional help.

A HIDDEN MEANING IN SEX

Sex may have a hidden dimension — a particularly important one in understanding why certain people start to avoid intercourse in their relationship. "There are many women," says Dr.

Harold Lief, "who do not respond sexually out of fear of being in the power of the male."

One thirty-two-year-old woman who doesn't want to sleep with her husband — a nice, kind man who treats her well and whom she really likes — told her therapist, "If I really started desiring him, I am afraid I would become his slave." She and women like her unconsciously withhold sexual desire and pleasure as a way of preserving their autonomy. "In their view," says Dr. Lief, "their partner is giving them the intense pleasure of orgasm. They don't see that they are actually giving it to themselves. To them, abandonment to sexual pleasure represents submission."

Many men make the same kind of unconscious mistake. They have an underlying intense fear of being controlled by women, and although they may feel free, sexually, outside of a committed relationship, once in marriage they feel that sex is expected. Subliminally, having intercourse with their wife then becomes a matter of yielding to her expectations, which makes them feel that they are being controlled. They react with subterranean anger or dread, and this gets converted into lack of desire or aversion to having sex with their wives.

One man finds that he even resents having an erection in response to his wife's presence. "Sometimes we are just lying together in bed and I don't think I am interested in sex, but I feel her body lying next to mine and suddenly I am aware of having an erection. It is like my body has a life of its own. I know it's crazy," he said, "but I feel I am being controlled by her because she makes me have an erection even when I don't think I am in the mood."

Frequently, interpreting sexual contact or pleasure as submission is the result of having been overcontrolled in childhood. Dr. Ronald Serwer Poze, a psychiatrist, and Philippa J. Poze, a nurse practitioner, did a study of seventeen couples who had troubles with sexual avoidance. In most of the cases, the man was identified as the partner no longer interested in sex, and these researchers found that many of these males had childhood memories of feeling trapped and controlled by one or more adult women. According to the Pozes, these men were able to retain "a loving, affectionate relationship with their wives as long as they did not feel obligated to be sexually involved."

Sometimes the issue of dependency is behind very controlling behavior. Men who feel very dependent on their mate may interpret these feelings as a sign of weakness or a lack of masculinity. Often, they cover up their dependency feelings by trying to be domineering. Although inwardly they feel that their wife is in control, they feel compelled to act as if they are. Insecurity is also a prime reason for marital power struggles of one kind or another. A partner who feels less attractive or talented or sexually capable than other people is more apt to insist on being in charge than the person with good self-esteem, who doesn't have to use power to prove something.

TRADITIONAL SEX ROLES

People bound by very traditional concepts of the roles of men and women are almost always involved in power issues with their mate. The very macho man expects a woman to be submissive, and if she isn't, he feels that his masculinity is threatened. If he feels that his partner is being assertive or does not live up to his view of women as soft, yielding, and passive, sexual dysfunction can result. He may become impotent, be unable to reach a climax, or simply stop feeling any "chemistry."

Such a man may react the same way to a woman who does not assume a traditional role. A housewife or a secretary is okay, but a woman as a lawyer, a doctor, or a boss is not. If he doesn't feel turned off by an assertive woman or one in a position of authority, he may, instead, feel perversely turned on. Some men feel that sex is an aggressive act and the penis becomes a weapon to "get" or "get back" at women. They use their sexual organ to show who is really the boss. Men who equate sex with domination and aggression sometimes feel bored by passive, compliant, or submissive wives (although they always seem to choose them, stay with them, or return to them). Men like this may have affairs with more dominant women, who seem more exciting initially because they are turned on by the thought of conquering or subduing these women in bed.

Another frequently encountered problem in men who regard sex as conquest is loss of sexual interest when a woman becomes totally available to them. For many men, the "charge" disappears in marriage because they no longer have to pursue and conquer their wives.

Sometimes, according to Dr. George Ginsberg of the New York University Medical School, a wife's passivity can be interpreted in such a way that sex remains exciting. "Men whose sexual functioning is based largely on unaware aggression toward the woman," he states in one article, "will have no trouble performing as long as they can interpret their wife's passivity as her disinterest in sex, and therefore that they are doing something to her which she doesn't want." Should the wife start to show a more aggressive interest in sex, "the male may have moderate to severe sexual performance problems," says Dr. Ginsberg. These could include impotence, premature ejaculation, retarded ejaculation, or a desire to avoid sex altogether.

Women with very traditional notions of females as weak and needing men's protection are apt to feel unhappy with a husband who does not want to take charge or who, for some reason, is unable to be a good provider economically. Frequently, with a husband who fails in these respects, women like this stop feeling sexual attraction or become unable to have orgasms.

Many women buy the traditional notion of masculinity — a man should be tough, hard, independent — and they do not respond sexually to men who are more sensitive, emotionally needy, or expressive, even though on an intellectual level they may protest that they want a man to have these characteristics. Very often women with traditional concepts mistakenly see dominating tyrants as "really masculine" men and as a result find themselves in relationships in which they are bullied.

Men and women are often ambivalent about sex roles these days. For example, a man may think he wants a more aggressive, achieving, "modern" woman but in bed fail sexually with one be-cause he also feels threatened by her. Or a woman may be at-tracted to a sweet, caring man on an emotional level but feel like a pal toward him — and there is no sexual "chemistry" because he isn't tough or dominant.

People who have hidebound notions of masculinity or femi-ninity may carry their rigidity into bed, causing sex to become dull. The macho man may feel that it is his role as a man always to be the initiator: He doesn't like it when his wife takes the lead in sex. He feels uncomfortable or angry if she tells him what she would like him to do to excite her. One man recounted becoming very irritable and turned off, without knowing exactly why, when his partner suggested that he cut his overgrown fingernails, which were hurting her during sex. Some men even react negatively if a woman is too active during the sex act. One man confessed that he had trouble maintaining an erection when his partner, as he termed it, "jumped around too much."

Because of he-man notions that rule out emotional expression, a very macho man often does not express tenderness or touch his wife at any time other than during sex. This can lead to resent-ment on the wife's part. She may feel turned off because there is no romantic buildup. "He comes home and after dinner starts right away working on some papers from the office," complained the wife of an industrial consultant. "He puts them down and ex-pects to get into bed and have sex, just like that. I feel I am there to service him. He can't understand why I don't want to."

The notion of masculinity as strong and silent may keep men from being able to communicate with their wife about problems and feelings. Marriage therapist Jurg Willi, in his book *Couples in Collusion,* says that such emotional withholding may imply a deep distrust of women. Such men "are afraid that if they show stress they will be lost forever, because the partner may misuse their weakness and take advantage of a chance to destroy them."

The wife of a very traditional man who never talks to her about anything may keep after him to communicate. This often makes him feel as if she is trying to control him, however, so he resists talking even more. Frequently the result is increasing tension and unhappiness between the two. But even if the wife suffers her frustration silently, the spouses may grow more and more apart emotionally because there is no significant communication between them. Either way, diminution of sexual interest is frequently a symptom of the deterioration in the relationship.

A very traditional woman may continually try to please her husband and not pay enough attention to her own needs in the marriage bed. She may avoid telling her husband that she needs more or different kinds of stimulation because she is afraid of asserting herself, even though he might welcome the information. Or she may never initiate sex, even though her husband might like her to sometimes. All of this can lead to unsatisfying sex — to rigid, unimaginative patterns that become very boring as they continue over the years.

WORKING WIVES

More than half of the wives in the United States work, and there is almost always a shift in power — and the possibility of an ensuing marital power struggle, with sexual consequences — when a woman returns to work.

After studying new two-career families, Drs. Frank Johnson, Eugene A. Kaplan, and Donald J. Tusel concluded that the changes in status of the partners that took place when the woman returned to work seemed to aggravate sexual dysfunction. These three psychiatrists say that

> for some couples, power shifts following the wife's employment seemed to accentuate differences in sexual appetite, a problem which might have been glossed over or rationalized in more complementary marriages. Many wives seemed less likely to accept blame for unsatisfactory sexual performance. A number of wives had become more "objective" about sex and were seen by their husbands as sexually assertive and demanding. Some women attempted to get their husbands

to read sex manuals or were more vocal about the staleness of their sexual relationship.

Certain experts suggest that although there are some men who are very competitive and will see a woman as a rival when she earns more than they do, other men are just frightened. They have been brought up to feel that if a man earns less than his wife he is worthless. They secretly worry that their more successful wife may no longer want them. Instead of talking about their uneasiness or terror, however, they "act up" and become difficult to deal with, or they try to belittle the wife's achievements.

Unfortunately, sometimes the working wife sets up the situation. If a wife remains supportive of her husband's achievements in life and treats him with respect, the marriage may not suffer undue strain; but if a wife who is suddenly more successful than her husband starts to rub his nose in the fact, reminds him regularly of her successes and his failures, and generally treats him as an inferior rather than an equal, she is apt to have an enraged or depressed spouse on her hands before she knows it.

Usually, if the wife was already the more successful partner when the couple married, few problems occur after the wedding. On the other hand, emotional turmoil often ensues if the situation changes and the wife who previously acted in a secondary role in the relationship suddenly becomes the greater success. Experts agree that sexual difficulties are apt to arise at this point not because the wife has become more successful per se, but because her change in status has created a crisis in the marriage and sexual problems often arise during crises.

MEN, SUCCESS, POWER, AND SEX

For some men, power actually replaces sex. Their real passion lies in their work, and success, not women, is what lights their fires. At best, wives, and sometimes children, too, are peripheral.

"In this town," explained an attractive woman who lives in the midst of the kings of the movie industry in Los Angeles, "there is much less sex than people would imagine. Hollywood has the reputation of being a very sexy place, but the men in the movie industry spend all their energy on making deals. That is what they really get off on. They can have their pick of the most gorgeous, talented, bright women in the world," she observes, "but they can't make real attachments to them. Their commitment is to their work, to making themselves a success and then hanging on to their success once they have it. I can't tell you how many beautiful, charming women sit home here alone night after night, whether they are married or not."

Two studies of the marriages of successful men confirm the devaluation of sex in their lives. In *Sex and the Significant Americans*, John Cuber and Peggy Harroff sum up their findings about the sexual behavior of the affluent in the following way: "Many remain clearly ascetic where sex is concerned. Others are simply asexual. For still others, sex is overlaid with such strong hostility that an anti-sexual orientation is clear." Cuber and Harroff also quote one of their subjects, a prominent psychiatrist, as saying that by age forty the majority of men among the superachievers are "washed up" sexually. These authors say that his view is confirmed by the information given to them in their interviews.

Frances Bremer and Emily Vogl, who surveyed a large sampling of wives of successful men for their book *Coping with His Success*, found that although one-third of the wives reported satisfactory sex lives, the whopping majority — 67 percent — said the opposite was true. According to these authors, the wives of achieving men "maintained that a demanding work schedule often left their husband too tired for sex even when he wasn't traveling. Many men were so exhausted that they simply collapsed after a hard day at work. Others were too preoccupied to be interested. Still others seemed to either have a naturally low sex drive or to have diverted their sexual energy into professional achievement."

Complaints from wives of success-oriented men were concerned not only with sexual quantity but also with quality. "When my husband makes love he does it so mechanically," explained one woman. "He is like a machine. He goes through all the motions, but it is as though he is rushing to get it out of the way. There is no affection, no emotion. It's almost as if he isn't there." According to Dr. Harold Lief, "There are men who are so distracted and anxious about work concerns that they can't even perform sexually. If they do, it's in a mechanical fashion without much feeling."

Many men resent demands for affection or sex because they think of them as antithetical to work. One man quoted in *Sex and the Significant Americans* described this attitude succinctly. He said that he liked all the travel connected to his job because it enabled him to avoid "too much time with my wife. She's that oppressive kind of woman; she always wants to hang around and is always looking for a smooch. It's too distracting."

A sad tale told in *Coping with His Success* is recounted by a woman who had been married to two enormously successful men. This woman divorced her first husband because he in effect abandoned his relationship with her in favor of his work interests. After the divorce, she started an affair with another man at the top who felt that he had made the same mistake as her husband in his own first marriage and was determined not to repeat it. The two had an idyllic romance. They communicated constantly. They made love incessantly. She married this second man, sure that this time things were going to be entirely different. She tells what happened:

> The wedding was wonderful. Our closest friends, my three children, his two. We left for a month's honeymoon in Europe. When we didn't wear each other out talking we wore each other out in bed. I never dreamed life could be so wonderful. . . . As we sat on the plane on the way back to the States from our honeymoon, my new husband said, "Now that the wedding is over our life can get back to normal." *Get back to normal!* What did he mean? I was soon to find out.
>
> If he made love to me more than once a month I had to seduce him. Then it was less than exciting. He brought home

work and when he didn't he was mentally a thousand miles away or he fell asleep in front of the TV.

He didn't have time for romantic lunchtime picnics. He had clients to entertain. What was my problem? Didn't I understand? He had a career. When I tried to talk to him, remind him he was doing the same thing that smothered his first marriage, that I felt lonely and missed what we had before, he was less than kind. He said, "I can't do my job and pay attention to you, too. I lost a lot of ground with my career when I was putting so much energy into our relationship. I have a lot to make up for. Good grief, find something to keep yourself busy. Go to the club. Play bridge, do something, and get off my back!"

The problems connected to sex and men's search for power are probably not confined only to those at the top. In our society, males have traditionally been trained to identify themselves by their jobs. Career success and masculinity are so intertwined in the male psyche that they feel: "If I am successful at work, I am a successful male; if I am not a success at work, I am a failure as a man." Nowhere in the traditional definition of masculinity is there anything that tells a male that it is important for him to be successful in his personal relationships. What happens, therefore, is that men come to value what they do at work too much and what they do in their private lives too little.

It is ultimately the failure in their emotional relationships that causes, for the majority of success- and power-oriented men, the bad sex lives reported by Cuber and Harroff and by Bremer and Vogl. Even if they started out with vital, romantic marriages, as is often the case, sooner or later they abandon passion in their private world for the almost erotic pleasures of power in the outer world. They slip into what Cuber and Harroff describe as Utilitarian Marriages — marriages that are held together by convention or habit but in which sex and love got lost along the way. Cuber and Harroff agree that such marriages span all classes and are not representative of only the affluent. Utilitarian Marriages, they say, "probably express the world of man and woman for the clear majority of middle-aged couples, irrespective of education, income, religion, or other class-related differences."

Women have contributed to male overevaluation of worldly success by responding sexually to power. Henry Kissinger was not wrong in saying, "Power is the ultimate aphrodisiac." It is ironic, however, that male success — the thing that sets the female's juices flowing — is the very thing that also ensures, in so many cases, that women will have little sex as wives. As long as women regard the big successes among men as prizes, and as long as males are taught to pin their masculinity and identity on success and power alone, men will continue to sacrifice love and companionship for careers, and marital sex will suffer.

With women themselves tuning in to the lure of power and making success in the work world a new female goal, one wonders if the same problems won't start to plague achievement-oriented women. Will love and sex take a backseat to the woman's career climb, or will society continue to influence women to give personal relationships a top priority, making the climb up the work ladder less lonely and more sexy for women than it has been for men?

BREAKING OUT OF THE POWER GAME

The most important ingredient in ending power struggles between partners is a conscious recognition of what is going on in the relationship. If you recognize in your own marriage some of the power tactics described earlier in this chapter, then it is time to do something about the situation — particularly if your sexual relationship has eroded as a result. Some therapists feel that sensate focus exercises (described on pages 109–110) are helpful since in doing them both partners learn to give to get. Family therapists also often try to ameliorate power struggles by having couples agree on clearly demarcated areas of responsibility. They ask husband and wife to make a list together of all family tasks and functions and then to divide them up fairly. Division of tasks should take into account what each partner is naturally best at; if, for example, a husband is better at helping the kids with math homework, it would be foolish to assign this task to the wife. Recreational choices — where to have dinner out, which movie or TV show to watch, and so on — should be alternated: husband picks one time, wife another. In this way couples learn to cooperate and respect each other's areas of competence instead of maintaining a life-style based on an imbalance of power or a struggle for superiority.

If you find that the sensate focus exercises are being sabotaged by one or both of you, or if you can't agree on how to split up responsibilities, a therapist may be needed to help you break the power deadlock in your relationship.

CHAPTER 14

The Price of Success

MISSION ACCOMPLISHED

BERNIE met Pamela at a cocktail party. He noticed her first across the room. She was pretty, with her blond, curly hair and her tilted blue eyes, but the thing that really attracted him to her was her throaty laugh. She was full of fun and sexy at the same time, thought Bernie.

Bernie walked over to the group that included Pamela and joined in the conversation. Soon he had managed to corner Pamela in order to talk to her alone. He found her funny and intelligent, and he responded to her seductive manner. Bernie was beguiled. He asked Pamela to join him for dinner after the party and Pamela eagerly accepted. Over dinner, Bernie and Pamela got to know more about one another. They flirted with each other outrageously. Bernie invited Pamela to his apartment for a drink before going home. Pamela never made it back to her own apartment that night. To Bernie's delight, Pamela turned out to be a wonderful sexual partner.

Bernie and Pamela started seeing one another regularly. Bernie, much in love, asked Pamela to marry him a year later.

Pamela, also in love, of course said yes. They both looked forward to a continuation of the good sex they enjoyed together, to raising a family, to a lifetime as a well-matched couple.

It is now six and a half years later. Pamela and Bernie have two children — a boy, three, and a girl, six months old. Bernie is doing well at his job; Pamela works part-time and has a house-keeper to help with the children. On the surface, all looks well, but Bernie knows it isn't. Soon after the birth of their second child, Pamela started regularly to refuse to have sex with him. He wanted to know what was wrong. "Nothing is wrong," Pamela insisted, "I just don't feel in the mood." Bernie could understand her not being in the mood sometimes, but now Pamela will only have sex with him once every two weeks at most, and even then he feels as if she is doing him a favor rather than enjoying herself. Bernie is very puzzled. Pamela had enjoyed sex all the time he had known her until now. She not only used to respond with verve when he instigated it but would often take the lead herself. What has gone wrong? he keeps wondering. Why has she changed so much?

What has gone wrong is that Pamela has accomplished what she believed to be her mission as a woman: she has married and had the two children she desired. There are a whole group of women who, like Pamela, can be very sexy as long as they feel that they are pursuing their dreams. Once they have accom-plished their mission by becoming wives and mothers, however, their sexual interest disintegrates. "These are women with lifelong sexual inhibition who often overlooked it," according to Dr. Harold Lief. "They acted and even felt sexual because it was one way of getting a man, but after getting a man (or child) the job was done."

Wives like this are different from women who feign a fervor for sex (and who fake having orgasms) in order to keep the interest of the men in their lives. Women like Pamela are not faking. They really enjoy sex, in a genuine way, but only as long as their sexual-ity is in the service of getting them the husbands or children they need to complete their roles as women. Of course, there is a whole other group of women who find sex ungratifying or distasteful all along. They don't fake pleasure but put up with what they consider to be an unpleasurable experience because they want to get married or because they want to have children; once their goal is accomplished, however, they more or less "close the bedroom door."

For men, the mission-accomplished syndrome might take the form of enjoying sex only until marriage or fatherhood is achieved. A man may feel that becoming a husband or siring children is necessary to prove that he is a respectable or "normal" male, or that being a "family man" is one of the tickets to advancement in his career. But once he has attained his goals, the man's sexual interest diminishes or disappears. Of course, some men with low libido or a dislike of sex with women have a homosexual orientation. They may muster up enough interest or force themselves to perform in order to marry or have children. Once this mission is accomplished, though, they lose their sexual interest and stop performing — at least with women.

People who suffer from the mission-accomplished syndrome seldom understand what is taking place. They don't say to themselves, "Now that my mission is accomplished, I don't have to worry about sex anymore." Often, they don't grapple with the problem at all on a conscious level. They simply feel uncomfortable with the idea of sex and respond by avoiding intercourse as much as possible, without understanding why; or they employ rationalizations: "With two children [or a young baby], of course I am too tired for sex. I don't know why he can't understand that" . . . "I am working myself to the bone to make a success of my career, and I am doing it for her and the children. Of course, I am knocked out most of the time. Why can't she understand that?" . . . "It's natural not to want sex so much anymore. The novelty has worn off" . . . "I am getting older. Of course sexual desire decreases" . . . "We're mature people now; only teenagers want sex all the time."

You may feel a rush of negative thoughts about your partner when the possibility of sex arises — a person whose mission is accomplished can be adept at finding a suitable reason not to desire sex. Unfortunately, unless the lack of interest in sex is shared by both partners, the mission-accomplished syndrome is quickly complicated by other emotions. The spouse whose libido remains alive either keeps after the one who has turned off and becomes more and more frustrated and angry at being turned down, or, not understanding what has occurred, starts a cycle of self-blame and worry about no longer being attractive, which can lead to ongoing anxiety or depression, or a need to prove desirability or virility with other partners.

The partner who has turned off because the mission has been accomplished often becomes angry at the still desirous partner for not being more understanding, for being insensitive or immature, for being "a typical male who always wants sex no matter what," or for being "a castrating female." They may feel under constant attack and react with anger, or they may become suspicious or jealous of the spouse if they fear that sexual needs will be taken elsewhere.

For some couples, the sense of a mission accomplished is a folie à deux. They may both feel that parenthood, for example, is the holy grail, and that once they have brought forth children their earthly purpose has been achieved. For both husband and wife, sex then becomes a fond memory rather than a current reality. As long as neither continues to be interested in sex, couples like this may continue to coexist in relative harmony. As with all of the syndromes outlined in this book, it is only when the couple is out of kilter and one partner wants sex more than the other that trouble brews.

WHAT SHOULD YOU DO?

A hint that you recognize yourself among the mission-accomplished folk (or, for that matter, in any other portion of this book) is that you felt a little uncomfortable or upset while reading the above section. Dr. Lief has pointed out that people who have turned off once their goals have been achieved suffer from a deep, lifelong sexual inhibition. The roots of such an inhibition are difficult to get at on your own. The best thing you can do for yourself is to consult a reputable psychotherapist or sex therapist and get expert help in tracking down what it is that is preventing you from leading a full and enjoyable sex life.

There is one last, somewhat different manifestation of the mission-accomplished attitude in sex that should be mentioned because it is so common. John Gagnon talks about it in *Human Sexualities:*

> For many of us the important game is over when we get married. What made most of us attractive before we got married is not what we work at after we get married. Thus a young woman and a young man may keep themselves attractive while they are in the marriage market. Finally they get somebody. After the honeymoon she starts gaining weight or wearing curlers, he starts to get a paunch. They were on the hunt, but once the hunt is complete, they do not have to put up a front anymore. They do not have to keep in shape; they feel they do not have to make any sexual presentations of self.

The result of such neglect, of no longer trying to appear sexually attractive, is often a marked slackening of sexual interest in the marriage. If husbands and wives continued to try to make themselves as appetizing to the opposite sex as they did while they were still "on the hunt," there might be a lot more sex in a lot more marriages.

SUCCESS VERSUS SEX

An even more frequent reason why desire fails than the mission-accomplished syndrome is the fear of success that messes up the lives of a good number of people. For some, according to Dr. Helen Singer Kaplan, "it's a trade-off. If they get a promotion, get into Harvard, or whatever — something has to go wrong."

An example of this is Martin, a young tycoon at the age of

forty. Martin was a psychology major at college, but decided upon graduation that he was more interested in business, so he went on to graduate school to get an M.B.A. degree. In his final semester he met a young woman whom he wooed and married. When his schooling ended, Martin went to work for a large corporation. He worked his way up to a middle-management position. In the intervening years, he and his wife also had two children.

One day, while on vacation with his family, Martin met a man with money who offered to back him if he wanted to start a business of his own. Martin leaped at the chance and left his job to start this business. It was more of a success than he had ever imagined it could be, and by the age of thirty-five, Martin was a millionaire.

Martin and his wife had gotten along beautifully while he was still struggling to make his mark, but now, all of a sudden, their sex life suddenly fell apart. Martin was no longer very interested in making love. When his wife complained, Martin, defensive, explained that he had no energy left — it was all going into his new business. His wife, however, could not accept this excuse and could not gracefully accept the fact that she and Martin now had intercourse only once a month or less. She insisted that Martin enter therapy with her. In the therapy that ensued, Martin's fear of success surfaced. He could only allow himself to enjoy his success in the business world by wrecking his private world — in this case, by turning off sexually.

There are many men and women who, like Martin, can't be a winner in their careers and a winner in love at the same time; they trade off one for the other. For some, this means having a good and satisfying love relationship but always losing jobs, never getting promotions, always being in debt, feeling that they are incompetent at their work. They are the mirror image to Martin and his ilk. Since they have success in their private lives, they have to mess up their careers.

A woman on the West Coast recently came to a therapist because she had developed a great deal of almost uncontrollable panic about her job. She felt she couldn't handle it. In giving her history, she remarked: "Just a couple of weeks ago I was thinking how happy I am in my marriage, and how good things were going for me." This woman had been married for four months. Her job, which was a very good one with a large corporation, had never worried her before. But her feeling of success in her private life made her suddenly feel overwhelmed at work and so incompetent that she was thinking of quitting. Her therapist was able to keep her from throwing over the job and creating a serious setback in her career. Meanwhile, he went to work on her underlying inability to fuse pleasure in love and success at work and tried to help her enjoy herself in all areas of her life at once.

People who fear success act as if there are jealous gods watching who will destroy them if they gain too much pleasure or happiness. They generally make an unconscious deal: they offer up one area of their lives as a sacrifice to keep from being totally destroyed for having some measure of success elsewhere. Of course, some people can't even manage a trade-off and are totally unable to allow themselves pleasure for long. They sabotage themselves in every sector of their lives — their jobs, their investments, their affairs, their marriages.

The point at which fear of success starts to go into operation varies with the person. Each individual has a personal boundary that cannot be crossed without invoking malaise. Some can allow themselves moderate success; their psyche starts to balk only when big success becomes a likelihood. Others cannot even let themselves have minor successes. None of this is conscious, however. On the surface, the individual feels as if he or she really wants to be a winner and is fully trying to reach his or her goals. Often the person can be effectual and reach some measure of success, as long as that invisible boundary line where comfort ends and anxiety begins is not violated. If it is, self-sabotage starts and previous successful efforts are stopped dead.

In another typical pattern, some individuals actually achieve their goals but then must do something to ruin their enjoyment — like break a leg. A person who has landed a long-sought-after job may worry continually about failing at it or losing it to a rival. Other people destroy their pleasure by concentrating only on the negative aspects of their work and not on the positive things. According to Dr. Berta Anagnoste, many women who are successful in their careers do this when they are married to men who are having career difficulties or are not as successful as they are; they feel that their success is a threat to the relationship and so they diminish it in their own and their husband's eyes.

Generally, after the sabotage has created enough failure to allow retreat behind the invisible boundary line into the comfort zone again, the person will be able to step up efforts to get ahead once more. So what you see in the life of these people is a stop-and-start pattern that repeats itself over and over again.

Although a whole variety of other ploys can be employed to stop Lady Luck in her tracks, sexual short-circuits are common. They range from impotence and inability to reach orgasm to avoiding sex and losing desire. For some, the sexual manifestation of fear of success takes the form of depression after orgasm. "There are many people who have been raised so that they feel guilty if they experience pleasure," says Dr. Lief. "The inner message is that I don't deserve to have such a good time. So they have to pay the price for it by being depressed after pleasurable sex."

When sexual sabotage is the modus operandi, the individual is rarely aware that he or she is going to do something to wreck intercourse. Nor is the fear of success recognized consciously as figuring in the picture. What happens, instead, is a translation: the subterranean emerging fear turns itself into an immediate anxious or upsetting thought. A man may think about his wife doing something he can't stand, so he feels totally turned off; or a woman may feel resentment because her husband is always finding fault with her, so she can't feel sexy.

According to Dr. Kaplan, loss of desire for a partner is a sign of the deepest kinds of problems associated with success, while impotence is a sign of moderate fears, and orgasm disturbances are the more mild manifestations of this problem.

WHERE DOES FEAR OF SUCCESS COME FROM?

Men and women who suffer from fear of success have frequently
received negative messages about winning early in life. The son of
a famous painter grew up in a home where his temperamental father insisted on always being the center of attention. The father
became jealous when his wife would pay attention to the children
rather than to him. He also could not tolerate any kind of noise or
assertiveness from the children, and he would do something such
as throw a tantrum to redirect the spotlight to him if attention
strayed to the kids. The children in this household were expected
by both parents always to be perfect ladies and gentlemen, always
to obey, be quiet, and use good manners. Afraid of losing her husband — who had a roving eye, and plenty of admirers — this
man's mother catered to the father in every way. The children felt
completely inhibited in their father's presence and blocked by
him in gaining their mother's attention. The messages received by
this man were "Be invisible" and "Do nothing that might com-
pete with Father."

When he grew up, this man, who had considerable artistic inclinations himself, could never allow himself the full expression of
his talents. He wanted to paint and had a few nice canvases to
display, but when a gallery owner expressed interest in having a
show of his works, he never managed to complete enough paintings to mount a show of his own. He worked in the art department of several large advertising agencies but always managed to
get into personality clashes that ended in him being fired. He
married while still in college and soon found that his bride was an
alcoholic. Although the marriage was marked by continual strife,
he stayed in his unhappy relationship. After many years of marriage, he had an affair in which sexual attraction was strong, and
he wondered why he had never felt that kind of intense desire for
his wife. Success evaded him in every area of his life.

If, like this man's, a child's mother or father acted competi-
tively and frowned on the child's being center stage, in later life

he or she may resort to sabotage at the brink of success, insuring the continuation of the second-fiddle, or second-rate, role learned in the early years. This is the only role that feels comfortable.

Another man grew up in a family of radicals who regarded rich people as evil and the common man as good. Although he went to law school to become a labor lawyer, once in school, he decided to change his specialty and to become an entertainment lawyer instead. He was introduced to someone at a big talent agency and went to work there after graduation. In a few years, he became an agent to famous stars, and was soon very successful in this role. He left the company with some stellar clients and formed a company of his own. Once on his own, however, for inexplicable reasons, he became very careless in some of the deals he made. One by one, he lost his most important clients, along with his reputation in the field. Although he was not consciously aware of it, some ancient feelings had come to the fore. He had remembered the lessons from his early life and began to feel evil because he was on the verge of great wealth, and so he did enough destructive things to ensure that he would not become rich after all. The message this man acted on was "If you become rich, you become evil."

In some milieus, sensual pleasure is painted as evil or sinful. A thirty-two-year-old Pennsylvania woman grew up in a small community where religion played a big role. Her parents and the other adults around were very prudish and puritanical. Pleasure was not considered a worthy goal. This woman found that she enjoyed sex when she married, but she also felt guilty about her pleasure. As a result she avoided sex as much as possible, even though she had orgasms each and every time she would allow intercourse to take place. Her pleasure was not enough to overcome the negative feelings about sex that she had absorbed while growing up.

Sometimes sabotaging success is a tactic used by a person who unconsciously wants to remain a dependent. If you aren't successful and can't earn a living, then someone else will have to take care of you. Women often have great conflicts about success based on the issue of dependence versus independence. If they have been brought up, as the majority of women have, to believe that a man will support them, personal financial success is then seen as a threat to their role as women. On another level — and this applies to both men and women — by maintaining the position of dependent, you stay Momma's boy or girl, or Daddy's boy or girl. Fear of success can be a manifestation of the fear of separating emotionally from parents, or the fear of growing up and assuming adult responsibilities.

Other psychoanalytic explanations for why fear of success or fear of pleasure develop involve unresolved Oedipal problems and sibling rivalry. During the Oedipal period of childhood, you felt in competition with a parent for the love of the opposite-sexed parent. Guilt was engendered by feeling Father or Mother as a rival whom you wished would disappear. There was also fear that your secret wishes would become known and that you would be punished for them. If you are successful in love as an adult, you unconsciously feel that you have successfully defeated the parent whom you felt was a rival. This produces both enormous guilt and fear — the reason success becomes something to be dreaded and avoided, if possible. "Winning in love means having Momma," says Dr. Kaplan.

If the issue is a feeling of rivalry with brothers and sisters, when you win in love, according to Dr. Kaplan, it means that "you have more than a brother or sister" — something that is forbidden and filled with guilt and dread. It means that you have bested or destroyed your siblings and can lead to the feeling of being evil and the fear of retribution.

Finally, fear of success can be explained as resulting from poor self-esteem. You may feel that you don't deserve good things. When success rears its head, whether in love or business or even in tennis or golf, you may suddenly remember, unconsciously, that you don't deserve good fortune — and so you destroy your chances of winning, or the fruits of success, in one way or another.

The kind of help available to someone whose sex life is being destroyed by an underlying fear of success is illustrated by the following case history. It comes from the files of Dr. Helen Singer

Kaplan, one of America's leading sex therapists, who reported on it in her book *The Evaluation of Sexual Disorders*.

Peter, a 37-year-old physician who had been married 11 years, complained of increasingly severe impotence over the past year. He was not a seriously disturbed person, but he did have a history of "ups and downs" in his career that is typical of patients that are governed by unconscious neurotic ambivalence about success. In his first year of medical school, he earned top grades, only to be placed on probation in his second year. He managed to graduate and his considerable charm and social skills got him a placement in a first-rate surgical residency program. However, he was asked to leave after his second year because he behaved provocatively with his attendings (staff physicians) and was unreliable about his clinical responsibilities. He finished training at a less prestigious institution and then started a private practice in plastic surgery. After a very rocky beginning, his practice became successful and exceedingly profitable.

About this time his tennis game (of which he was very proud — he was a ranked amateur player) deteriorated and he also began to experience erectile problems. . . .

The analysis of the couple's current behavior indicated that on an *immediate and current level* Peter's erectile difficulty was being caused by his critical thoughts about his wife which emerged whenever lovemaking was contemplated: "She is too anxious, she is too clumsy, she is too flatchested." These negative mental processes effectively interfered with the generation of erotic feeling. He then complicated the problem by compulsively trying to "perform" without being fully excited and obsessively worrying about his sexual performance. His critical attitude together with his increasing performance difficulties made his wife, Perl, who was already unsure of herself, increasingly apprehensive and "turned off"; this became another factor in the escalating cycle of Peter's impotence.

On a psychodynamic level it could be speculated that Peter was "trading off" career success for sexual failure. . . .

The *deeper roots* of Peter's ambivalence about being "a winner" could be traced to his family background. He was raised in a warm cohesive family which was dominated by a highly ambitious and competitive mother. Peter's father, a sweet gentle man, was not very successful in material terms, much to his wife's frustration and despair. Peter's mother was warm and supportive to the children, but exceedingly envious of her two sisters, who had married hard-driving, competitive men, who were much more successful than Peter's father. Maybe she didn't win the "family Olympics," but her sons would. Her approval of the boys was conditional on their excellence and outstanding performance. She was like a coach, drilling them for achievement. When they "failed" they were "out." When they succeeded they were "in." Peter, the brighter of the two boys, was her favorite. He was (unconsciously) torn between wishing to please his mother by "winning" and his guilt about besting his gentle father and his less gifted brother. . . .

The couple [Peter and Perl] was accepted for sex therapy, with the awareness that this would *not* be a simple case and that the behavioral measures would probably have to be buttressed by insight-fostering techniques.

Their response to the treatment confirmed this hypothesis. The behavioral aspect of therapy was designed to reduce Peter's performance fears and his obsessive critical thoughts. The exercises consisted of non-demanding erotic stimulation, first of the non-genital parts of the body, then of the genitals. Peter was also encouraged to make liberal use of fantasy to distract him from his obsessive performance concerns. At the same time Perl was helped with her fears of pleasure and feelings of sexual inadequacy. She became a better and more exciting sexual partner, and no longer allowed Peter to "set her up" when she became anxious.

In the initial stages of treatment, Peter was ambivalent

about and resisted doing the assigned tasks and undermined his wife's emerging sexual self-confidence. His success anxiety could not be bypassed so easily. Some measure of insight into and resolution of his ambivalence were necessary for treatment to move forward.

Peter was confronted with his success anxiety and its dynamic connection with his sexual symptom. He came to recognize his tendency to become anxious when he was successful and to sabotage his victories. Further, he gained insight into the early genesis of his neurotic fears of success. The psychotherapeutic work was done during the office sessions with Peter alone. He progressed rapidly and began to function better in his work. Sex therapy proceeded more smoothly to a successful conclusion. As a bonus, his tennis game improved!

When fears of romantic success are creating sexual problems you have to gain insight, first, into the unconscious fear operating, as Peter did, and learn to stop equating sexual pleasure with winning a fantasy competition that is often part of the problem.

The well-known therapist Nathaniel Branden, in his recent book *Honoring the Self*, recommends paying attention to "the moments and situations in which apprehension related to happiness or success" arises and then studying the way we self-sabotage. "If possible," he says, "this is information to communicate to our partner. One of the very best things we can do when we are feeling happiness anxiety or success anxiety is to talk about it. To describe the experience is to begin to drain it of its power."

Once you are consciously aware that fear of success is operating in your sex life, and once you know how it is affecting you, then sensate focus exercises (see pages 109–110) can help acclimate you to higher levels of sexual pleasure. Dr. Kaplan stresses that the behavior modification of the sensate focus exercises often will not work unless the patient can also modify negative self-concepts, something a therapist frequently helps with by giving the patient positive, reinforcing messages. You have to start to feel that you have a right to pleasure. Very often, success-fearing people have strong, punitive consciences; they have to learn to go easier on themselves and not berate themselves, for example, for simply having problems.

Your inner self may be saying to you, "Be a loser," but once you learn to accept and like yourself better, you can drown out this negative, self-defeating message. If you can learn to say to yourself, with conviction, "I'm a winner," you can be one in sex, and everything else!

AFTERWORD

MANY READERS will have recognized themselves somewhere in these pages. I know I did. At one point, while
writing the chapter on sex and power, I suddenly realized that
some of the behavior I was describing pertained to my fiancé and
me: we were engaging in an ongoing power struggle. I showed the
finished chapter to my fiancé. As he started to read it, his head
began to nod slowly in affirmation — he recognized us, too. Since
that day, power has ceased to be a big issue hindering our relationship. We are now happily married, and each time a discussion
begins to escalate into a power struggle, either we both are able to
recognize the symptoms of what is occurring or one of us points it
out to the other. That stops the coming collision dead in its tracks.

Often, as in our case, simply recognizing a problem is a big step
toward solving it. I wrote this book with that in mind. My hope
was that by describing some very common behavior that gets in
the way of sex and fulfillment in relationships, readers would be
able to see, perhaps for the first time, things about themselves or
their spouses that acted to sabotage their marriage.

Does this mean that if you recognized things about yourself in this book you should consider yourself "sick"? Certainly not. As the saying goes, nobody's perfect — and no one is perfectly "normal" either. Everyone is a combination of healthy and neurotic tendencies. To recognize some of your hang-ups, big or small, along with your healthy traits is simply to recognize your full humanity.

But knowing this, what if you are still troubled about finding yourself in these pages? Does that mean you should immediately rush off to find professional help? Not necessarily. It depends upon the degree of the problem and how much it is interfering with your relationship. For example, perhaps fear of intimacy, a prevalent hang-up in our society, is creating continual fighting and turmoil — a way that some partners increase "space" between themselves — and this is making you feel unhappy in your marriage. Or maybe you don't fight, but because you fear real closeness you can't sustain sexual interest and emotional intimacy at the same time. In either case, you may need outside aid to help your marriage survive on better terms. But if you and your partner share the same need for emotional space, or if your mutual fear of intimacy has not created such turmoil or distance that you have become emotional or sexual strangers to one another, then you may not need any help at all: the problem isn't large enough within the context of your particular relationship to create big trouble. In the end, you, along with your partner, have to be the judge of whether a problem is creating enough discontent in the relationship to warrant professional attention.

In our complex, often confusing world, people divorce in ever increasing numbers, for vague reasons that they lump under the term "unhappiness." Unfortunately, they generally blame all of their unhappiness on their spouse. Understanding the thrust of this book — that sometimes we unconsciously contribute to our own unhappiness in a relationship — is very important, and accepting this may, indeed, save many marriages.

I hope that this book saves many marriages, and for those that don't need saving, creates more understanding so that the relationship becomes even better. I hope, too, that couples who are not yet married, or who are newly married, will let it serve as a lovers' guide — a way to avoid some common pitfalls — so that sex and love can continue to flourish in enduring relationships.

Appendixes
Selected Bibliography
Index

APPENDIX A

Twenty-three Ways to Make Sex Good (and Keep It That Way) in Marriage and Other Long-Term Relationships

HERE is a summary of advice from experts about how to keep sex exciting and fun throughout a couple's life together:

1. Pay attention to your sex life. Too many couples assume that their sex life will take care of itself. Actually, sex has to be guarded and nourished throughout a couple's life together, and particularly after the "honeymoon" stage of the relationship is over. There is nothing wrong with a husband and wife periodically conducting a sexual "checkup." Ask yourself and your partner the following kinds of questions:

- Is there anything that could be better?
- Is there anything wrong?
- What is good about what we are doing — and should we be doing that more often?
- Am I really enjoying myself?
- Has the fun gone out of sex — are we enjoying ourselves together?

- Do I feel unfulfilled emotionally even though I have had an orgasm?
- Do we need professional help with sexual-performance problems or to make sex more rewarding?

This does not mean that you should scrutinize yourself or your partner during the actual sexual experience. Rather, periodically, at a nonsexual time, make an overall review of the state of your sexual life.

2. Make time for sex. Part of paying attention to your sex life is making sure that you give it a top priority in your life. Don't let sex become something that you squeeze in, if you can, *after* everything else — household chores, duties with the children, work activities, sports, gardening, or whatever. At any age, you should regularly set aside prime time — time when you aren't exhausted or drained — for erotic enjoyment. You should allot sufficient time for it, so that lovemaking isn't hurried. Sex is just as important as watching TV, cooking a fancy dinner, fixing a leaky faucet, or taking the kids to a movie — maybe more so: it helps to keep a couple in contact, and serves as a source of ongoing pleasure and renewal in the relationship.

3. Continue to court each other. "After marriage couples no longer woo or seduce each other," says Dr. Harvey Caplan, the well-known San Francisco psychiatrist and sex therapist. He suggests that one of the best things you can do for your sex life is to continue the courtship after you have "landed" your mate — even after many years together. To keep the vital signs alive and the sexual juices flowing in a marriage, you have to let your partner know that you still think he or she is valuable and special. You can do this by trying to look nice for your mate; by expressing your appreciation of your partner in words every so often; by saying "I love you" unexpectedly; by giving signs of affection such as hugs and kisses apart from sexual situations; by concocting little surprises, like a small present or an unexpected set of tickets to a show — anything that says, "I was thinking of you."

Once the early, romantic stage is over, many wives complain that the only time their husband touches them is when he wants sex. Once children arrive, many husbands complain that they become low man on their wife's totem pole. Resentments like this, which turn mates off to one another, could be prevented if men and women remembered throughout their marriages to keep wooing each other and never to take each other for granted.

Dr. Helen Singer Kaplan, the noted sex therapist, who is studying happy long-term relationships, says that the mates in these marriages never stop considering their relationship the most important thing in their lives. She has noted that the eyes of her subjects seem to light up every time their partner enters the room. "A woman like this will meet her mate and she knows she is giving him a present by being there. He knows he is giving her a present by being there." When was the last time your eyes lit up for your spouse?

4. Communicate about sex to your partner. This is crucial. Some couples, of course, don't communicate in any area of their life. Others, who can talk intimately about everything else, simply do not talk about sex. Communication often can spell the difference between a satisfying or disappointing love life.

Good communication includes telling your partner what you want or need, and being specific and explicit when you do. "Touch me down there" isn't good enough. You should tell your partner exactly where you want to be touched. Or you can use another form of sexual communication: you can *show* what you want by taking your mate's hand in yours and leading it to the right place. Some people find it easier to show than tell, which is all right as long as the message is given and received correctly. Showing by guiding your partner's hand is often the best way to communicate the exact pressure you enjoy or the rhythm of stimulation that you respond to best.

Telling your partner what you don't like is as necessary as communicating what you want, but it is important to try to offer a positive alternative along with the negative message. For example, if you don't like your breasts squeezed a certain way, let your partner know — verbally, or by demonstrating — how you do like your breasts to be touched.

Be wary of trying to communicate by doing to your partner what you want done to you. It may not work. One therapist tells of a couple who got caught in an impossible pattern in just this way. The wife wanted to be touched in a more gentle manner and she thought that she was showing her husband this by touching him very lightly. He liked to be touched very firmly, however, so he responded to her lightness by touching her more heavily. He thought that he was showing her, in this way, what he wanted. It was only when this couple finally started talking to one another, under the therapist's guidance, that they were able to deliver their messages correctly and understand one another. Now they both get what they want from each other, and a bad sex life has turned into a good one.

If your partner forgets a request you have made, don't be shy about repeating yourself.

Another part of good sexual communication is telling your partner when there is something that you think would be fun to try. If you hate doing something that your partner has suggested, you must talk that over, too. One wife had a good sex life with her husband for fifteen years until he announced one day that he would like to try oral sex. The wife agreed but found it totally repugnant. Instead of telling her husband this, though, she started to avoid sex with him. She was afraid that he would want more oral sex. Sex, which had been frequent until this point, started to dwindle because of lack of communication.

Sometimes partners can negotiate and find acceptable alternatives when sexual tastes are different — if they bring their likes and dislikes into the open. For example, the woman just described might have suggested to her husband that she bring him to climax manually instead of orally, or, since he seemed to be in search of variety, that they try different sexual positions.

One subject that couples rarely discuss is frequency of sex. Various studies have shown that dissatisfaction with sexual frequency is often a silent problem in marriage: one partner may want more sex, the other less, but neither is willing to talk about it. Experts find that mutually acceptable compromises can often be worked out — three times a week instead of five, or twice a week instead of once, for example — but only if the matter is discussed.

Another part of good sexual communication is telling your partner when you are uncomfortable or in pain. It is easy to lose your zest for sex if you continue to endure silently a position that is physically uncomfortable, a cramp, the breath being squeezed out of you by a partner who weighs too much, thrusting that causes pain, or too vigorous stimulation that causes painful friction. Tell your partner, and change positions or alter the technique so that sex becomes enjoyable instead of uncomfortable.

Unfortunately, some marriage partners, because of their own psychological problems, respond to even the gentlest request for change in sex as "control." People like this may resist being "controlled" by constantly forgetting your requests, no matter how many times you express them, or even by losing sexual desire when you make suggestions. Unless you get help from a therapist, it is difficult to establish open and honest sexual communication with a partner who responds to suggestions as though they were demands and resists change because it means being "controlled." (A list of reputable sex clinics can be found in appendix B.)

5. Give positive feedback.   Part of being a good sex partner means letting your mate know when you are enjoying yourself. You can say, for example, "I like that," or "Keep doing that, it really turns me on," or you can express your delight by making pleasurable sounds instead of using words. Partners learn about each other's preferences in this way and have their own security boosted in the bargain: they know they are doing the right thing. Positive feedback also means letting your mate know that you feel turned on when he or she looks or acts a certain way. It means telling your wife that you think she is sexy or letting your husband know he is a good lover. Positive feedback in the rest of the relationship also nurtures good sex. Too many spouses only criticize each other.

They forget to let a partner know about the things they approve of or admire. I am talking about genuine positive reactions to your partner, in or out of bed, not false compliments or feigned ecstasy — which leads to the next rule for good sex.

6. *Never fake orgasms.* Faking orgasms is primarily a female problem, although — and this may come as a surprise — some men pretend to climax as well. Most people who moan and groan in phony ecstasy are afraid to be considered an inferior sex partner, want to save face, are trying to cover up a sexual dysfunction, or think that they might be rejected by a mate if the truth gets out. Many women feel that they are protecting their partner's ego by pretending to have orgasms. Some people fake orgasms all the time; others, occasionally.

A pattern of faking is destructive. Covering up — keeping a sexual secret — is not part of good, honest, open sexual communication. It does not help your partner, because he or she never learns about your needs, or that you might prefer a different technique. Your mate is misled into thinking that you both are doing just fine. It doesn't help you, because you are cheating yourself out of the genuine sexual pleasure that might come about if you owned up to not being able to reach orgasm and if you explored and experimented together to find out what kind of stimulation or technique would excite you enough to have a real climax. If you fake all the time because you have never had an orgasm with anyone and don't know what to do to have one, it is time you stopped faking and took care of the problem in a constructive way. Go to a reputable sex therapist. Professionals have had great success in teaching women how to reach orgasm; on the average, such therapy takes approximately fourteen sessions.

7. *Use positive reinforcement.* If you are consistently turned off by something your partner does — for example, by your husband failing to shave or your wife wearing hair curlers to bed — besides communicating this fact, you can try a positive approach to effect change. When your husband is clean-shaven, or when your wife doesn't put in curlers, act sexy and affectionate and attempt to

seduce your mate. If you do this often enough, your spouse may be able to make the connection and begin to realize that certain kinds of behavior or appearance lead to a reward: you respond sexually. If your partner values sexuality, he or she may be motivated to repeat the desired behavior — and you'll both win out in bed.

8. Tune in to your own sexuality.   Many people have never tried to explore their own sexuality independent of a partner. This is particularly true of women, who generally have been more repressed sexually than men in our society. And yet, unless you understand how you tick sexually, you can never be a really good sex partner. You have to know what you need or want before you can communicate it to someone else.

Although it may seem shocking, most sex therapists believe that masturbation is an excellent way to get acquainted with yourself as a sexual human being — even when you are married. You can learn what excites you, what you don't respond to, and what fantasies give you an erotic charge. You do this alone, without the presence of someone else, who may inhibit or distract you from thinking — and learning — about yourself. In sex therapy, many wives have learned to experience orgasm for the first time through masturbation. They can then use what they have learned about what they respond to, during intercourse with their husband.

Another way to understand yourself better sexually is to pay more attention in general to the sensual part of your personality. Watch for erotic or sensual responses as you go through your day-to-day life. What kind of music makes you feel romantic or sexual? What kind of setting? Do you find yourself daydreaming about making love in a certain place — by the ocean, for example, or in front of a fire, underwater in a pool, or in a field of flowers? Do you think someone you pass on the street looks sexy? Does feeling the fabric in your silk dress or your leather jacket rubbing against your skin make you feel sensual?

Dr. Harold Lief often recommends keeping a daily journal of sexual thoughts, feelings, and fantasies. If you start to tune in to erotic responses that you may have shut out before, you will be cultivating the sexual side of yourself, as well as learning things about yourself that you could put into play with your partner. The music that makes you feel romantic or sexy can be used as background to intercourse with your mate. You can drape yourself in the silky cloth that you discovered feels so soft against your skin, and let your partner slowly peel it away. At those times when you are slow in responding to your mate, you can summon up the fantasy that excited you during masturbation. You can ask your partner to touch you as you touch yourself to come to orgasm. People often think that masturbation takes away from sex with a mate, but incredible as it may seem, sexual self-exploration can enrich your marital sex life.

9. Realize that sex is not divorced from the rest of your life.   Our sexual selves are part of our entire selves. This means that psychological problems that we bring with us into our relationships, such as a fear of getting really close to someone, or an inability to tolerate much pleasure, or an early antisexual orientation, or an unconscious desire to see a spouse as a parent, as well as others, can get in the way of full erotic enjoyment.

Sex is also part of our entire relationship, which means that negative or angry feelings from other areas in the marriage can spill over into the bedroom. Hostile or angry feelings toward a mate have to be brought into the open and resolved generally, before sex can be expected to improve.

10. Discuss ahead of time the possibility of sexual refusals and how you will handle them.   In all marriages, situations will arise when one or both partners will not want to have sex. Partners may get angry at one another temporarily; there may be trouble with jobs or children; a person can be unusually fatigued, or may not feel well, or, for one reason or another, simply might not be in the mood. Experts advise couples to be straight with each other — to say, "I don't feel like it tonight," followed by a simple, honest explanation of why, so that the partner does not feel personally rejected. Unfortunately, most people use devious tactics to avoid sex — such as staying up later than their mate, working on a home-repair project, or even starting an argument. Instead of saying, "I'm not in the mood," they make up excuses, such as "I'm tired," or "I have a stomachache." Behind lies and evasions is the feeling that somehow it isn't ever right to refuse sex in marriage and that your mate will get angry at you if you do.

Respect each other's right to occasionally not feel like making love and make a pact ahead of time that you will not be afraid to tell one another the truth. Agree to try to avoid evasions or excuses, which often create hurt feelings or misunderstandings (such as "He doesn't think I'm attractive anymore," or "I must have done something wrong," or "She must be mad at me").

11. Realize the danger of sexual "signals." Most couples use indirect ways to indicate that they are or are not ready for sex. Some are unspoken signals. For one couple, the signal that the husband wants sex is that he closes the bedroom door. If the wife goes to the door and locks it, that means she wants sex, too. If she leaves it unlocked, it means "Not tonight, dear."

Sometimes the signals are phrases. In his book *Human Sexualities,* John Gagnon, the noted sex researcher, takes a look at the kind of talk that occurs in most households. "What usually happens is that the husband may say, 'I think I'll take a shower.' What that really says is, 'I am going to be clean for you.' . . . The wife then says, 'I will be upstairs in a few minutes.' That is a 'Yes.' Or she says, 'I am too tired today; I have a headache; I have been to the hairdresser; the kids might wake up.' Those are all 'No.'"

Couples have all sorts of private signals — ranging from one of them deciding to go to bed early (which is an invitation) to saying, "I feel like staying up late" (which is a way of saying, "No sex tonight"). Frequently, when a man starts to complain that he's tired or that he has to get up early in the morning, it is a signal not to expect sex.

There are some intrinsic problems in using sexual signals. For one thing, according to John Gagnon, sexual signals become a form of negotiation between husband and wife — which is one reason why sexual frequency declines with age. "As we get older such negotiation gets more tiring," he explains. "The immediacy of our interest in sexual gratification is reduced, and we say to ourselves, 'Well, maybe tomorrow' (even though we have fewer tomorrows)." Gagnon points out still another danger: "Finding that negotiations are difficult to manage, we may ritualize sex. . . . Thursday night becomes the night. Knowing that it is going to happen on Thursday night makes it okay. A lot of effort is not required. But feeling amorous on Wednesday night starts negotiation all over again."

The final danger of sexual signals is that they may not be clearly understood by both partners because they have never been discussed and agreed upon. One therapist tells of a wife who thought she was giving her husband a sexual signal by staying longer than usual in the bathroom while she prepared herself. The husband interpreted this as stalling, however. He thought that she was evading him by staying so long in the bathroom. So if you are going to use sexual signals, at least make sure you both know what you are *not* talking about, by discussing your signals ahead of time.

12. Respect your partner's aesthetic sensibilities. If your partner really doesn't find overweight people appealing, or is bothered by the smell of perspiration, or does not like the smell of a particular face cream, or can't stand ragged, unclipped fingernails, show some courtesy by respecting such personal tastes and trying to ameliorate the thing that offends.

Conflict over aesthetic preferences occurs outside of the bedroom, too, and unless resolved, it can create anger that may interfere with sex. "Let's say a man's aesthetic preference is that peanut butter lids have to be put back on jars, and his wife's is that he doesn't leave his socks on the floor," says Dr. Fred Gottlieb, the psychiatrist who is director of the Family Therapy Institute of Southern California in Los Angeles. "These kind of aesthetic preferences are trivial, but if spouses pay attention to them, they speak for a kind of sensitivity about the other, a willingness to do trivial things to communicate to the other: 'I respect your aesthetics — and you.' "

Dr. Jay Mann, a psychologist who, before his recent untimely death, treated couples in Palo Alto, pointed out that some people's sexual responses are more stimulus-bound than others. To some, looks don't matter; to others, appearance is an important ingredient to feeling sexually interested. In the same way, smells don't bother some people sexually but turn others off.

If your partner's sexual response seems to be tied in to personal aesthetics, it is particularly important not to ignore or denigrate the stated preferences but to cater to them as much as possible. You, of course, should expect the same in return.

13. Create privacy. The Study Group of New York recently published a book called *Children and Sex,* the results of a survey of 225 parents. They discovered that the parents' bedroom was often used by the children as the TV room, a reading room, and a gym, with the bed used as a trampoline; it was also where group discussions and cuddling sessions took place. Children were free to come and go in the bedroom as they pleased. The Study Group of New York concluded that parents felt that the needs of their children came before their own privacy. Parents like this, who probably constitute the majority of mothers and fathers in the United States, are putting the whammy on their own sex lives. No wonder that surveys show that couples' sex lives deteriorate markedly once children are around!

In order for their sex life to flourish, a couple has to create an atmosphere in which they will not be afraid of being interrupted — one where they can concentrate on enjoying each other and put everything else out of their minds for the moment. Installing a lock on the bedroom door and teaching the kids that they must knock before entering is one answer. So is putting the TV in another room and encouraging the children to get in the habit of reading and doing gymnastics elsewhere.

14. Guard against falling into rigid or boring routines.   A typical rut is
the only-on-Wednesday-and-Saturday-night routines — or only
on Sunday mornings, or only at night before going to sleep, or
only doing it in the same one or two ways each and every time.
Although some couples thrive on complete predictability, most
find fixed schedules and doing the same things over and over
again boring or uninspiring at best, especially as the marriage
goes on in years. Variety and spontaneity to spice things up is important to keep sex interesting and to stop it from dwindling. This
doesn't mean that you have to hang from chandeliers, but it does
mean that you dare to be a little creative. Even if it makes you feel
silly or embarrassed initially, experiment. Try different positions,
different times of the day, different lighting, even different places
to have sex besides your bedroom every now and then. Take
weekend or one-day mini-vacations; it is well documented that
sexual interest and frequency increases for couples during holi-
days. If you have difficulty thinking of something new to do in
bed, buy a book like Alex Comfort's *Joy of Sex,* which has plenty of
suggestions.

Dullness in the rest of your relationship often reflects itself in
the bedroom, so, on a regular basis, try to inject new life into your
marriage as well. Therapists often recommend to couples that
they create things to look forward to: plan a party or a trip, take a
series of dance lessons together — anything that will be exciting
and fun to contemplate doing as a couple.

15. Think of sex as a loving experience.   Too many people consider
sex just an act; to them, it is primarily genital, and relief of sexual
tension is its goal. Sex in marriage should have a dual role. One is
physical "release"; the other is the expression of affection, tenderness, and caring. You can emphasize sex as an experience rather
than sex as an act, by occasionally caressing and fondling each
other while refraining from intercourse. This helps a couple relate
to each other in an affectionate rather than a purely sexual way.
Remember, too, that sex begins long before you reach the bedroom. A little affection at nonsexual times can reap its rewards

sexually later on. If you really believe that sex is a loving experience, you also won't be tempted to use in it nonloving ways — to reward or punish a partner for other things.

16. Make use of fantasies and other aids to enhance interest and excitement. The majority of experts encourage the use of fantasies in a couple's sex life. Fantasies can be used in many ways. New excitement can be injected into tired sex lives if couples learn to reveal their sexual fantasies and sometimes act them out together. Shared fantasies can also be used as prevention — to keep sex lives from going stale in the first place.

You can use fantasies solo, as well — by dreaming up something that turns you on while you are making love to your spouse. Although you may want to, you do not necessarily have to tell your mate about your private fantasies. Fantasies, and acting them out, may be particularly beneficial to couples past the rush of early passion, or as they age.

Many people feel that it is wrong to think of someone besides their partner during a sexual fantasy, to think of something they regard as perverted, or to play out kinky stuff from their fantasies. The consensus of opinion among sex authorities, however, is that to do all of these things is normal, common, and often beneficial. The well-known marriage therapist Dr. Clifford Sager has written that "playing out romantic or sex-in-danger-of-being-caught situations, mild sadomasochistic play, master-slave fantasies, call girl fantasies, Don Juan, gay, or troilism fantasies are included in the repertoire of many married couples."

The ability to act out fantasies in sex may even be more of a sign that an individual is mature than is a rigid refusal to do so. The eminent psychiatrist Dr. Otto Kernberg feels that genuinely mature people — as opposed to people who confuse sober, very conventional behavior with maturity — are able to be playful and childlike at times, and that a rich sex life depends, in part, on accepting childish aspects, as well as the mature ones, of yourself and your partner. "Everybody has polymorphous, infantile trends — which means exhibitionistic, voyeuristic, sadistic, masochistic, and homosexual tendencies," he explains. "The acceptance of these partial drives means that one can tolerate having sadistic fantasies, for example, and tolerate acting on them in a playful way. What books like *The Joy of Sex* have done is reeducate everybody to those aspects of one's own needs that may go underground. These aspects should normally be integrated into the sex relationship. It creates intensity and adds variety to sexuality."

Fantasies can be used in still another way: to bypass anxiety or other emotions that may be interfering with a person's ability to function well sexually. In the case of a man who suffers from performance anxiety, for example, and is impotent because he worries too much about being a good sex partner, a sex therapist might encourage the man to concentrate on a fantasy. In this way the patient forgets to conjure up the anxiety-making thoughts that are causing his sexual failure.

In addition to fantasy, many experts feel that sexual interest can be maintained or a flagging libido revived by the use, sometimes, of titillating literature, erotic motion pictures, sexy talk, body oils, vibrators, or the wearing of clothing that either partner feels is exciting — providing that these aids don't go against a couple's values and they find them sexually stimulating.

17. Take responsibility for your own pleasure. Especially if you are a woman, you may think that it is up to your partner to make you enjoy sex. It isn't. It is up to you. This means, first of all, giving yourself permission to enjoy sex. A surprisingly large number of men and women have strong punitive consciences that act as censors, telling them not to take pleasure in sex. Think about whether this is one of your problems. Sometimes the censoring attitude is applied to a mate as well; you might think that your partner should not enjoy sexual freedom either, or you may think your mate would disapprove if you really let yourself go sexually.

In addition, taking responsibility for your own pleasure means communicating well about your sexual needs to your partner, instead of hoping that he or she will read your mind, stumble onto what you want, or divine your needs miraculously. Taking responsibility also means being active during sex: initiating sex when you feel "horny," instead of always waiting for your partner to start things; changing to positions you enjoy, instead of only going along with your mate's activities; and making suggestions, instead of having no ideas of your own about lovemaking. It may also mean educating yourself more about sex. There are plenty of good books on the subject to help you widen your horizons.

Taking responsibility for your own sex life means breaking sexual deadlocks, too. If sex is dull, don't wait for your partner to wake up suddenly and do something new or lively in lovemaking. Initiate changes yourself. If you or your mate are no longer interested in sex, if either of you has a sexual dysfunction that persists, if something in the relationship has poisoned sex, do something about it! Instead of feeling sorry for yourself or resentful toward your mate, instead of heroically enduring a sexual problem or waiting for your partner to say or do something, take matters into your own hands. Go to a sex clinic, a qualified marriage counselor, or a psychotherapist and see what can be done to make things better. And start talking to your mate about the problem (*talking* — not blaming) instead of remaining silent.

18. Learn that you turn yourself off.   Husbands and wives who have lost sexual interest generally blame their partner ("She doesn't turn me on anymore"; "He turns me off"), but Dr. Helen Singer Kaplan offers a different perspective. "People have much more control over whether they are turned on or not than they realize," she says. "People who say, 'I am turned off,' are usually turning themselves off without realizing it. Something about the other person evokes this wish not to have sex and then they turn themselves off. It is involuntary and unconscious, but one can learn conscious control over it."

Here is the way this generally works: You are angry at your partner and have no desire to give your spouse pleasure, or, for hidden psychological reasons, you are inhibited about receiving sexual pleasure so you wish to avoid intercourse. As a result, when sex is in the air or your partner approaches you, you automatically summon up negative thoughts without realizing what you are doing. You may think about something that riles you about your partner; you may concentrate on your mate's most unattractive features; when you are in the bathroom washing up, you may notice a few strands of your wife's hair on the sink and wonder, "Why is she such a slob?"; or as you are getting into bed you may see your husband's socks on the floor and think to yourself, "He is so inconsiderate. I have asked him a million times to put his socks in the hamper." *Your* negative thoughts are what kill off sexual desire, not the other person per se.

In sex therapy, the partner who feels turned off is taught to recognize that he or she always manages to have negative thoughts when sex is imminent. Armed with this knowledge, the patient is taught to banish or ignore antierotic thoughts when they occur and to let sexual feelings flow instead. You can do the same thing. If you feel turned off, start to examine your thoughts just before sex. Discover what negative notion is floating through your head, then send it packing. You can think, for example, about your mate's attractive qualities instead of the drawbacks, or you can just concentrate on the pleasure of the sexual experience.

19. Don't expect sex to be great all the time. Not every sexual experience can be fantastic. Even when two partners are sexually compatible, it is normal for sex sometimes to be good, sometimes so-so, sometimes disappointing — and, with luck, sometimes wonderful. Sexual appetites fluctuate as well. Our hormone levels go up or down; our state of physical or mental well-being changes. These things, as well as events in our lives, can affect our libido. To expect your sex life always to operate at a peak level is to set yourself up for feeling disappointed when normal highs and lows occur. You are not a machine. Don't have unrealistic expectations of yourself as a human being.

20. Don't turn sex into hard work. If you try too hard, sex backfires. Performance anxiety — always worrying whether you are a good or perfect sex partner — is rampant in our society, say the sex experts. It makes people work too hard at sex and turns each experience into a test. You should, of course, take into consideration your partner's needs, but to be really good at sex, you also have to learn to be a little selfish. You have to concentrate on your own sexual pleasure rather than worry about pleasing a partner, as so many spouses do.

21. Remember that the foundation of good sex in a committed relationship is trust and respect for your partner. Dr. Fred Gottlieb maintains that the single most significant factor in staying turned on to a mate is respect — the ability to take a long view of your partner and continue to feel proud and pleased to be part of his or her environment. The implications of respect, he says, "are that you are both equals. Neither is in the judgmental role of feeling superior or is caught in a scramble based on feeling inferior and wanting to catch up. The couple thinks of themselves as a pair sharing an essential humanity." You can see from this definition how ongoing power struggles (which create anger and can infect sex) are minimal when there is such essential respect between partners.

Dr. Edward L. Parsons, a psychiatrist who practices in Manhattan and in Westfield, New Jersey, says that trust means "not only feeling secure with your partner knowing he [or she] will protect and support you, but that you know your mate is also interested in your growth as an alive human being." This means that there is room for both partners to change over the years. "Trust, essentially, is knowing that your mate has your best interests at heart and can consider them as well as his own," says Dr. Parsons. "He wants you to be the best possible person you are capable of becoming."

If for some reason respect is not present or trust is broken, the sexual relationship is often contaminated, and — as marriage therapists and sex therapists know all too well — unless respect or trust can be created or restored, it is difficult to help a troubled sex life.

22. Don't let a problem go on too long before attending to it. You wouldn't neglect a physical ailment that lingered on and on. You would see a doctor. You should adopt the same attitude toward sexual functioning. Don't ignore a sexual problem because you are embarrassed or fearful to discuss the matter with your spouse. Sometimes just by talking together about a minor problem you can solve it before it gets out of hand. If, however, you can't solve it by yourselves, see an expert. (A list of reputable sex clinics is in appendix B.)

In the case of a sexual dysfunction like lack of desire, says Dr. Helen Singer Kaplan, "the faster you recognize it, the better chance you have of curing it. If someone says to me, 'Everything was fine until a year and a half ago,' that has a terrific prognosis [compared to someone who turned off to sex fifteen years ago, for whom successful treatment might be more difficult]. Length of time is important," warns Dr. Kaplan. "Don't neglect lack of interest in sex."

This doesn't mean that you should give up hope, however, if you have had problems in your sex life for many years. Sex lives can be helped at any age, or at any stage in a relationship, provided that both partners are mutually determined to do so and are firmly committed to each other.

23. Pay special attention to sex as you age. Too many couples, starting in their forties and fifties, begin to let their sex lives evaporate. It is important for men and women to understand that sexual responses may slow down due to the aging process — but they don't disappear altogether. Couples should talk to each other about their changing sexual needs as they age, and be willing to experiment together to find out how they can accommodate to new needs as they arise. More direct stimulation of the genital area, the use of additional lubrication, gratifying each other sexually through means other than actual intercourse, a change to positions that might make sex more comfortable for an ill or incapacitated person, and the attitude that successful sex can be stroking and holding without copulation are all possible accommodations that an older couple might make. With an attitude of flexibility and the feeling that sex does not end with old age, couples can go on giving each other pleasure for the rest of their lives.

Dr. Helen Singer Kaplan tells of a happy couple in their eighties married sixty years. Although Dr. Kaplan was reticent to ask them about sex because of their age and dignity, she finally broached the subject when she was alone with the woman. "Well," said the octogenarian, "since Jake had his pacemaker put in, we have to keep it down to once a week."

Is there sex after marriage? You bet!

APPENDIX B

Directory of Sex Clinics

THE FOLLOWING LIST contains sex clinics in the United States connected to leading hospitals and medical schools. It is arranged alphabetically by state and city. Although there are many well-known, highly qualified independent therapists with excellent reputations — such as Dr. Harold Lief (700 Spruce Street, Suite 503, Philadelphia, PA 19106; 215-829-5640) and Dr. Harvey Caplan (1968 Green Street, San Francisco, CA 94123; 415-931-0225), both of whom were consulted for this book — this list is limited to clinics with hospital and medical-school affiliations (which is one way of assuring that the clinics are reputable). Unfortunately, at the present time, there are no accrediting organizations for sexual-dysfunction clinics to help weed out the many questionable clinics that have proliferated in recent years. This compilation is meant as a guide rather than as a list of personal recommendations, as the author has not visited or investigated all the clinics personally.

ALABAMA

Birmingham

University of Alabama in Birmingham
Marital Health Studies
Department of Psychiatry
Birmingham, AL 35294
205-934-2350

Codirectors: Robert P. Tavris, Ph.D.;
  Patricia Y. Tavris, M.A.
Patients treated: Couples, singles

ARIZONA

Tucson

University of Arizona College of
  Medicine
Sexual Problem Evaluation and
  Treatment Clinic
1501 North Campbell Avenue
Tucson, AZ 85724
602-626-6323

Codirectors: Diane S. Fordney, M.D.,
  M.S.; Peter Attarian, Ph.D.
Patients treated: Couples, singles, groups,
  children, adolescents

ARKANSAS

Little Rock

University of Arkansas for Medical
  Sciences
Human Sexuality Clinic
4301 West Markham
Little Rock, AR 72205
501-661-5900

Director: Robert Matthews, M.D.
Patients treated: Couples, singles

CALIFORNIA

Anaheim

Humana Hospital West Anaheim
Urological Clinic for Male Sexual
  Dysfunction
515 South Beach Boulevard
Anaheim, CA 92804
714-827-1232

Codirectors: Daniel M. Riesenberg,
  M.D.; Robert S. Stevenson, M.D.
Patients treated: Men only

CALIFORNIA *(continued)*

Long Beach

Center for Marital and Sexual Studies
5199 East Pacific Coast Highway
Long Beach, CA 90804
213-597-4425

Codirectors: William E. Hartman, Ph.D.;
  Marilyn A. Fithian, B.A.
Patients treated: Couples, singles

Los Angeles

Cedars-Sinai Medical Center
Southern California Sexual Function
  Center
8635 West Third Street, Suite 1065
  West
Los Angeles, CA 90048
213-659-5443

Codirectors: Harold G. Kudish, M.D.;
  Stephen A. Sacks, M.D.
Patients treated: Men only

University of California Los Angeles
  Center for Health Sciences
Human Sexuality Program
760 Westwood Plaza
P.O. Box 4
Los Angeles, CA 90024
213-825-0243

Director: Joshua Golden, M.D.
Patients treated: Couples, singles

University of Southern California
  Medical Center
Sexual Therapy and Marital
  Counseling Clinic
LAC-USC Medical Center
1937 Hospital Place
Los Angeles, CA 90033
213-226-5329

Director: Dennis J. Munjack, M.D.
Patients treated: Couples, singles

Pomona

Casa Colina Hospital for
  Rehabilitative Medicine
Sexuality Clinic
255 East Bonita Avenue
Pomona, CA 91767
714-593-7521

Director: Julie G. Botvin Madorsky,
  M.D.
Patients treated: Couples, singles, groups

CALIFORNIA *(continued)*

San Francisco

University of California School of Medicine at San Francisco
Urology/Sexuality Clinic
400 Parnassus Avenue
San Francisco, CA 94143
415-666-1146, 661-1950

Director: Alex L. Finkle, M.D., Ph.D.
Patients treated: Psychogenically impotent men of any age, couples seen when warranted

University of California School of Medicine at San Francisco
Department of Psychiatry
Human Sexuality Program
Langley Porter Building
401 Parnassus Avenue
San Francisco, CA 94143
415-666-4787, 666-4623

Director: Evelyn S. Gendel, M.D.
Patients treated: Couples, singles, groups

Stanford

Stanford University Medical Center
Department of Psychiatry and Behavioral Sciences
Behavioral Medicine Clinics
Palo Alto, CA 94305
415-497-5868

Director: John Bachman, Ph.D.
Patients treated: Adults

COLORADO

Denver

University of Colorado School of Medicine
Human Sexuality Clinic
4200 East Ninth Avenue
Denver, CO 80262
303-394-7482

Director: Carol L. Lassen, Ph.D.
Patients treated: Couples, singles

CONNECTICUT

Farmington

University of Connecticut Health Center
Department of Psychiatry
Sexual Education and Treatment Service
263 Farmington Avenue
Farmington, CT 06032
203-674-2285

Director: Paul D. Reid, A.C.S.W.
Patients treated: Couples, singles

Hartford

Hartford Hospital
Sex Therapy Program
80 Seymour Street
Hartford, CT 06115
203-524-2396

Director: Alan J. Wabrek, M.D.
Director of Sexual Counseling: Carolyn Wabrek, M.Ed.
Patients treated: Couples, singles

Stamford

Stamford Hospital Sexual Therapy Clinic
Department of Obstetrics and Gynecology
Stamford Center of Human Sexuality
Shelbourne Road and West Broad Street
Stamford, CT 06904
203-325-7020

Codirectors: Joseph D. Waxberg, M.D.; Stella Mostel, M.S.
Patients treated: Couples, singles

GEORGIA

Atlanta

Emory University School of Medicine
Department of Obstetrics and Gynecology
Emory University Clinic
1365 Clifton Road
Atlanta, GA 30322
404-321-0111, ext. 3400; 588-4063

Director: Malcolm G. Freeman, M.D.
Patients treated: Couples, singles

ILLINOIS

Chicago

Cook County Hospital
Social Evaluation Clinic
1825 West Harrison Street
Chicago, IL 60612
312-633-7749, 633-7750

Director: Wanda Sadoughi, Ph.D.
Patients treated: Couples, singles

University of Chicago Hospitals and
  Clinics
Sexual Dysfunctions Clinic
41 South Maryland
Chicago, IL 60637
312-962-6185

Director: Robert T. Segraves, M.D.
Patients treated: Couples, singles

Maywood

Loyola University of Chicago
Sexual Dysfunction Clinic
2160 South First Avenue
Maywood, IL 60153
312-531-3752

Director: Domeena C. Renshaw, M.D.
Patients treated: Married couples, singles

Springfield

Southern Illinois University School of
  Medicine
Department of Obstetrics and
  Gynecology
P.O. Box 3926
Springfield, IL 62708
217-782-5880

Director: Robert P. Johnson, M.D.
Patients treated: Couples, singles,
  adolescents

IOWA

Iowa City

University of Iowa College of Medicine
Family Stress Clinic
Department of Family Practice
2033 Steindler Building
Iowa City, IA 52242
319-356-4402

Director: Georgianna S. Hoffman, R.N.,
  M.A., C.S., AASECT-Certified Sex
  Therapist
Patients treated: Couples, singles

LOUISIANA

New Orleans

Louisiana State University Medical
  Center
Sex and Marital Health Clinic
Department of Urology
1542 Tulane Avenue
New Orleans, LA 70112
504-568-4890

Director: David M. Schnarch, Ph.D.
Patients treated: Couples, singles

MARYLAND

Baltimore

Johns Hopkins University School of
  Medicine
Sexual Behavior Consultation Unit
600 North Wolfe Street
Baltimore, MD 21205
301-955-3246, 955-6318

Director: Jon K. Meyer, M.D.
Patients treated: Couples, singles,
  children, adolescents, elderly

College Park

Human Behavior Foundation, Ltd.
University Professional Center
4700 Berwyn House Road, Suite 201
College Park, MD 20740
301-345-2323

Codirectors: H. L. P. Resnik, M.D.;
  Audrey F. Resnik, R.N., B.S.N.
Patients treated: Couples, singles

MASSACHUSETTS

Boston

Harvard Medical School, Beth Israel
  Hospital
Sexual Dysfunction Unit
330 Brookline Avenue
Boston, MA 02215
617-735-2168

Director: Joanna Perlmutter, M.D.
Patients treated: Couples, singles

MASSACHUSETTS, *Boston (cont.)*

Tufts University School of Medicine
New England Medical Center
Family and Couples Institute
171 Harrison Avenue
Boston, MA 02111
617-956-5747

Director: Derek Polonsky, M.D.
Patients treated: Couples, singles

Boston University School of Medicine,
University Hospital
New England Male Reproductive Center
720 Harrison Avenue, Suite 606
Boston, MA 02118
617-247-6632

Director: Robert J. Krane, M.D.
Patients treated: Couples, singles

MICHIGAN

Mount Clemens

Saint Joseph Hospital
Macomb Medical Commons
43281 Commons Drive
Mount Clemens, MI 48044
313-263-9551

Codirectors: Donald Blain, M.D.; Bernice
Jones, Ph.D.
Patients treated: Couples, singles, groups

MINNESOTA

Minneapolis

University of Minnesota Medical
School
Department of Family Practice and
Community Health
Program in Human Sexuality
2630 University Avenue S.E.
Minneapolis, MN 55414
612-376-7520

Director: Sharon B. Satterfield, M.D.
Patients treated: Couples, singles,
children, families

MISSOURI

Columbia

University of Missouri–Columbia
School of Medicine
Human Sexuality Clinic
Clinic 6, Outpatient
Columbia, MD 65212
314-882-2511

Director: Joseph Lamberti, M.D.
Patients treated: Couples, singles

Saint Louis

Masters and Johnson Institute
24 South Kingshighway
Saint Louis, MO 63108
314-361-2377

Chairman: William H. Masters, M.D.
Director: Virginia E. Johnson, D.Sc.
(Hon.)
Patients treated: Couples, singles

NEBRASKA

Omaha

Creighton University School of
Medicine
Human Sexuality Program
601 North Thirtieth Street, Suite 5830
Omaha, NE 68131
402-280-4325

Director: Emmet M. Kenney, M.D.
Patients treated: All ages and marital
statuses

NEW JERSEY

Piscataway

University of Medicine and Dentistry
of New Jersey–Rutgers Medical
School
Sexual Counseling Service
University Heights
Piscataway, NJ 08854
201-463-4273, 463-4485

Director: Sandra Leiblum, Ph.D.
Patients treated: Couples, singles

NEW YORK

Bronx

Albert Einstein College of Medicine
Department of Obstetrics and
  Gynecology
Division of Human Sexuality   .
1165 Morris Park Avenue
Bronx, NY 10461
212-430-2655

Director: Sheila Jackman, Ph.D.
Patients treated: Couples, singles

Brooklyn

Brookdale Hospital Medical Center
Human Sexuality Program
Linden Boulevard at Brookdale Plaza
Brooklyn, NY 11212
212-240-5977

Codirectors: Norman S. Fertel, M.D.;
  Esther G. Feuer, R.N.
Patients treated: Couples, singles

State University of New York
  Downstate Medical Center
Center for Human Sexuality
450 Clarkson Avenue
Brooklyn, NY 11203
212-270-1750

Codirectors: Marian E. Dunn, Ph.D.;
  Peter Dunn, M.D.
Patients treated: Couples, singles

Glen Oaks

Long Island Jewish–Hillside Medical
  Center
Human Sexuality Center
P.O. Box 38
Glen Oaks, NY 11004
212-470-2761

Director: Maj-Britt Rosenbaum, M.D.
Patients treated: Couples, singles, groups

Manhasset

North Shore University Hospital
Department of Obstetrics and
  Gynecology
Division of Human Reproduction
Sexual Dysfunction Program
300 Community Drive
Manhasset, NY 11030
516-562-4470

Director: Gerald M. Scholl, M.D.
Patients treated: Couples, singles

NEW YORK *(continued)*

Manhattan

Cornell University Medical Center
  Human Sexuality Teaching Program
Payne Whitney Clinic
New York Hospital–Cornell Medical
  Center
525 East Sixty-eighth Street
New York, NY 10021
212-472-6277

Director: Helen Singer Kaplan, M.D.,
  Ph.D.
Patients treated: Couples, singles

Helen S. Kaplan Institute for the
  Evaluation and Treatment of
  Psychosexual Disorders
30 East Seventy-sixth Street
New York, NY 10021
212-249-2914

Director: Helen Singer Kaplan, M.D.,
  Ph.D.
Patients treated: Couples, singles, groups

Jewish Board of Family and Children's
  Services
Sex Therapy Clinic
120 West Fifty-seventh Street
New York, NY 10019
212-582-9100

Director: Clifford J. Sager, M.D.
Patients treated: Couples, singles,
  adolescents

Lenox Hill Hospital
Psychosomatic Clinic
100 East Seventy-seventh Street
New York, NY 10021
212-794-4840

Director: Don Sloan, M.D.
Patients treated: Couples, single women

Mount Sinai Medical Center
Department of Psychiatry
Human Sexuality Program
19 East Ninety-eighth Street, Room 9A
New York, NY 10029
212-650-6634

Director: Raul C. Schiavi, M.D.
Patients treated: Couples, singles

NEW YORK, *Manhattan (cont.)*

New York Medical College
Sex and Marital Therapy Unit
215 East Seventy-third Street
New York, NY 10021
212-772-8700

Director: Don Sloan, M.D.
Patients treated: Couples

New York University Medical Center
Program in Human Sexuality
550 First Avenue
New York, NY 10016
212-427-0885

Director: Virginia A. Sadock, M.D.
Patients treated: Couples, singles

Stony Brook

State University of New York at
    Stony Brook School of Medicine
Sex Therapy Center
Stony Brook, NY 11794
516-246-2066, 246-2464

Director: Joseph LoPiccolo, Ph.D.
Patients treated: Couples, singles

NORTH CAROLINA

Durham

Duke University Medical Center
Sex Therapy and Education Program
P.O. Box 3263
Durham, NC 27702
919-684-5322

Codirectors: John F. Steege, M.D.;
    Anna L. Stout, Ph.D.
Patients treated: Couples, singles

Winston-Salem

Bowman Gray School of Medicine
Marital and Family Therapy Clinic
300 South Hawthorne Road
Winston-Salem, NC 27103
919-748-4281

Director: Sallie Schumacher, Ph.D.
Patients treated: Couples, singles,
    children, adolescents

OHIO

Cincinnati

University of Cincinnati Medical
    Center, Jewish Hospital
Department of Psychiatry
Human Sexuality Center
3216 Burnet Avenue
Cincinnati, OH 45229
513-872-5895

Coordinator: Kayla J. Springer, Ph.D.
Patients treated: Couples, singles

Cleveland

Case Western Reserve University
Department of Psychiatry
Sexual Dysfunction Clinic
Hanna Pavilion
2040 Abington Road
Cleveland, OH 44106
216-444-3426

Director: Stephen B. Levine, M.D.
Patients treated: Couples, singles, adults,
    late adolescents

Cleveland Clinic
Sexual Dysfunction Unit
9500 Euclid Avenue, Desk 68
Cleveland, OH 44106
216-444-5815

Director: Lawrence M. Martin, M.D.
Patients treated: Couples, singles

Toledo

The Toledo Hospital
Human Sexuality Center
2142 North Cove Boulevard
Toledo, OH 43606
419-473-4189

Director: Malati Multani, M.D.
Patients treated: Couples, singles

PENNSYLVANIA

Lancaster

Saint Joseph Hospital and Health Care
Center
Human Sexuality Center
250 College Avenue
P.O. Box 3509
Lancaster, PA 17604
717-397-3115

Director: Mary Kearns Condron, M.S.
Clinical Supervisor: David E. Nutter,
M.D.
Patients treated: Couples, singles

Philadelphia

Hahnemann Medical College and
Hospital
Van Hammet Psychiatric Clinic
112 North Broad Street, Sixth floor
Philadelphia, PA 19102
215-448-8821

Director: Ilda V. Ficher, Ph.D.
Patients treated: Couples, singles, groups

Jefferson Medical College
Department of Psychiatry and Human
Behavior
Jefferson Psychiatric Associates Sexual
Function Center
1015 Chestnut Street
Philadelphia, PA 19107
215-928-8420

Director: Salman Akhtar, M.D.
Patients treated: Couples, singles

Medical College of Pennsylvania
Eastern Pennsylvania Psychiatric
Institute
Department of Psychiatry
Outpatient Clinics
3200 Henry Avenue
Philadelphia, PA 19129
215-842-4209, 842-4296

Director: Edmond Pi, M.D.
Patients treated: Couples, singles,
families, groups

PENN., *Philadelphia (continued)*

University of Pennsylvania School of
Medicine
Division of Family Study
Department of Psychiatry
Marriage Council of Philadelphia
4025 Chestnut Street
Philadelphia, PA 19104
215-382-6680

Director: Martin Goldberg, M.D.
Patients treated: Couples, singles

RHODE ISLAND

East Greenwich

Kent County Memorial Hospital
Franek Clinic, Inc.
4601 Post Road
East Greenwich, RI 02818
401-884-3530

Codirectors: Bruno Franek, M.D.;
Marilese Franek, M.Ed.
Patients treated: Couples, singles

SOUTH CAROLINA

Charleston

Medical University of South Carolina
College of Medicine
Department of Psychiatry and
Behavioral Science
171 Ashley Avenue
Charleston, SC 29425
803-792-2971

Director: Oliver Bjorksten, M.D.
Patients treated: Couples, singles

TENNESSEE

Memphis

University of Tennessee College of
Medicine
Department of Psychiatry
Special Problems Unit Sexual
Dysfunction Clinic
66 North Pauline, Suite 633
Memphis, TN 38105
901-528-5489

Codirectors: William Murphy, Ph.D.;
Peter Hoon, Ph.D.
Patients treated: Couples, singles

TEXAS

Galveston

University of Texas Medical Branch
Department of Obstetrics and
  Gynecology
Sexual Dysfunction Treatment Clinic
Ambulatory Care Center
Ninth Street and Strand Avenue
Galveston, TX 77550
409-761-7023, 761-7026

Director: L. C. Powell, Jr., M.D.
Patients treated: Couples, singles

Houston

Baylor College of Medicine
Baylor Psychiatry Clinic
1200 Moursund Avenue
Houston, TX 77030
713-799-4856

Director: James W. Lomax, M.D.
Patients treated: Couples, singles, groups

University of Texas Medical School of
  Houston
Department of Reproductive Medicine
  and Biology
P.O. Box 20708
Houston, TX 77030
713-792-4796

Chairman: Emil Steinberger, M.D.
Patients treated: Couples, singles,
  children, elderly

UTAH

Salt Lake City

University of Utah Medical Center
Department of Psychiatry
Sexual Problem Clinic
50 North Medical Drive
Salt Lake City, UT 84132
801-581-7951

Director: Nyla J. Cole, M.D.
Patients treated: All types

VIRGINIA

Falls Church

Johns Hopkins Medical Institutions
Fairfax Hospital
Department of Psychiatry
3300 Gallows Road
Falls Church, VA 22046
703-693-3626

Director: Thomas N. Wise, M.D.
Patients treated: Couples, singles;
  by referral only

WASHINGTON

Seattle

Northwest Hospital
Diagnostic Clinic for Sexual
  Dysfunction
1550 North 115th Street
Seattle, WA 98133
206-364-0500

Director: Jeanette J. Chen, Ph.D.
Patients treated: Men only

University of Washington School of
  Medicine
University Hospital
Sexual Dysfunction Clinic
4701 Twenty-fourth Northeast
Seattle, WA 98105
206-543-0936

Codirectors: John L. Hampson, M.D.;
  Susan M. Tollefson, R.N., M.A.
Patients treated: Couples, singles

WISCONSIN

Milwaukee

Good Samaritan Medical Center
Clinic of Urology, S.C.
Sexual Diagnostic and Treatment
  Clinic
2040 West Wisconsin Avenue, Suite
  401
Milwaukee, WI 53233
414-344-3700

Director: Stuart W. Fine, M.D.
Patients treated: Men of any age (medical
  and psychological evaluation of
  impotence), couples when warranted

SELECTED BIBLIOGRAPHY

BACH, GEORGE R., and WYDEN, PETER. *The Intimate Enemy*. New York: William Morrow & Co., 1969.

BARBACH, LONNIE GARFIELD. *For Yourself.* New York: Doubleday & Co., 1975

BEAL, EDWARD W. "Money and Sex: Parallel Areas of Marital Conflict." *Medical Aspects of Human Sexuality* 14, no. 1 (January 1980): 50–61.

BERGES, EMILY TRAFFORD; NEIDERBACH, SHELLEY; RUBIN, BARBARA; SHARPE, ELAINE FIRST; and TESLER, BARBARA WEINBERG. *Children and Sex*. New York: Facts on File, Study Group of New York, 1983.

BERNARD, JESSE. *The Future of Marriage*. New York: Bantam Books, 1976.

BERNE, ERIC. *Sex in Human Loving*. New York: Pocket Books, 1976.

BITTMAN, SAM, and ZALK, SUE R. *Expectant Fathers*. New York: Ballantine, 1981.

BLUMSTEIN, PHILIP, and SCHWARTZ, PEPPER. *American Couples*. New York: William Morrow & Co., 1983.

BRAKE, MIKE, ed. *Human Sexual Relations*. New York: Pantheon Books, 1982.

BRANDEN, NATHANIEL. *Honoring the Self*. Los Angeles: Jeremy P. Tarcher, 1983.

BRECHER, EDWARD M., and the Editors of Consumer Reports Books. *Love, Sex, and Aging: A Consumers Union Report*. Boston: Little, Brown & Co., 1984.

BREMER, FRANCES, and VOGL, EMILY. *Coping with His Success*. New York: Harper & Row, 1984.

BURR, WESLEY R. "Satisfaction with Various Aspects of Marriage over the Life Cycle: A Random Middle-Class Sample." *Journal of Marriage and the Family* 32 (February 1970): 29–37.

BUTLER, ROBERT N., and LEWIS, MYRNA I. *Sex after Sixty.* New York: Harper & Row, 1976.

CLARK, ALEXANDER L., and WALLIN, PAUL. "Women's Sexual Responsiveness and the Duration and Quality of Their Marriages." *American Journal of Sociology* 71 (1965): 187–196.

CLIFFORD, RUTH. "Sex as a Chore." *Medical Aspects of Human Sexuality* 13, no. 5 (May 1979): 56–61.

COMFORT, ALEX, ed. *The Joy of Sex.* New York: Crown, 1976.

CUBER, JOHN F., and HARROFF, PEGGY B. *Sex and the Significant Americans.* Baltimore: Penguin Books, 1966.

DICKS, HENRY V. *Marital Tensions.* London: Routledge & Kegan Paul, 1967.

DOHRENWALD, BARBARA SNELL, and DOHRENWALD, BRUCE P., eds. *Stressful Life Events.* New York: John Wiley & Sons, 1974.

EDWARDS, JOHN N., and BOOTH, ALAN. "Sexual Behavior in and out of Marriage: An Assessment of Correlates." *Journal of Marriage and the Family* 38 (February 1976): 73–81.

———. "The Cessation of Marital Intercourse." *American Journal of Psychiatry* 131, no. 11 (November 1976): 1333–1336.

EDWARDS, JOHN N.; FRANK, ELLEN; KUPTER, DAVID J.; and DECKERT, GORDON. "Viewpoints: How Prevalent Is Lack of Sexual Desire in Marriage?" *Medical Aspects of Human Sexuality* 15, no. 9 (September 1981): 73–83.

EYSENCK, H. J. *Sex and Personality.* Austin: University of Texas Press, 1977.

———. "Personality and Sexual Behavior." *Journal of Psychosomatic Research* 16 (1972): 141–152.

FELDMAN, HAROLD. *Development of the Husband-Wife Relationship.* Ithaca, N.Y.: Cornell University Press, 1967.

FELDMAN, PHILIP M. "Hidden Expectations in Marriage." *Medical Aspects of Human Sexuality* 16, no. 4 (April 1982): 61–74.

FINKLE, ALEX L. "Sex Problems in Later Years." *Medical Times* 95, no. 4 (April 1967): 416–419.

FORD, CLELLAN S., and BEACH, FRANK A. *Patterns of Sexual Behavior.* New York: Harper & Bros., 1953.

FRANK, ELLEN; ANDERSON, CAROL; and RUBINSTEIN, DEBRA. "Frequency of Sexual Dysfunction in 'Normal' Couples." *New England Journal of Medicine* 299, no. 3 (July 1978): 111–115.

FREUD, SIGMUND. *Sexuality and the Psychology of Love.* New York: Collier Books, 1972.

FROMM, ERICH. *The Art of Loving.* New York: Harper & Row, 1956.

GADPAILLE, WARREN J. *The Cycles of Sex.* Edited by Lucy Freeman. New York: Charles Scribner's Sons, 1975.

GAGNON, JOHN H. *Human Sexualities.* Glenview, Ill.: Scott, Foresman & Co., 1977.

GAGNON, JOHN H., and SIMON, WILLIAM, eds. *Sexual Conduct: The Social Sources of Human Sexuality.* Chicago: Aldine Publishing Co., 1973.

GINSBERG, GEORGE. "Men's Reactions to Wives' Sexual Assertiveness." *Medical Aspects of Human Sexuality* 14, no. 4 (April 1980): 15, 47.

GOLDBERG, MARTIN. "Sexual Survey #27: Current Thinking on Loss of Marriages' Sexual Vitality." *Medical Aspects of Human Sexuality* 13, no. 10 (October 1979): 63–68.

———, moderator. "Roundtable: Handling Sexual Refusals in Marriage." *Medical Aspects of Human Sexuality* 10, no. 6 (June 1976): 30–46.

HALL, ELIZABETH. "A Conversation with Erik Erikson." *Psychology Today,* June 1983, 22–30.

HARBIN, HENRY, and GAMBLE, BRIAN. "Sexual Conflicts Related to Dominance and Submission." *Medical Aspects of Human Sexuality* 11, no. 1 (January 1977): 84–89.

HARTMAN, LORNE M. "Relationship Factors and Sexual Dysfunctions." *Canadian Journal of Psychiatry* 24, no. 7 (1980): 560–562.

HOON, P.; WINCZE, J.; and HOON, F. "A Test of Reciprocal Inhibitions: Are Anxiety and Sexual Arousal Mutually Inhibitory?" *Journal of Abnormal Psychology* 86 (1977): 65–74.

HUNT, MORTON. *Sexual Behavior in the 1970's.* New York: Playboy Press, 1974.

JAMES, WILLIAM H. "Marital Coital Rates, Spouses' Age, Family Size and Social Class." *Journal of Sex Research* 10, no. 3 (August 1974): 205–218.

———. "The Honeymoon Effect on Marital Coitus." *Journal of Sex Research* 17, no. 2 (May 1981): 114–123.

JOHNSON, FRANK; KAPLAN, EUGENE A.; and TUSEL, DONALD J. "Sexual Dysfunction in the 'Two-Career' Family." *Medical Aspects of Human Sexuality* 13, no. 1 (January 1979): 6–17.

KAPLAN, HELEN SINGER. *The New Sex Therapy.* New York: Brunner/Mazel, 1974.

———. *Disorders of Sexual Desire.* New York: Brunner/Mazel, 1979.

———. *The Evaluation of Sexual Disorders.* New York: Brunner/Mazel, 1983.

——— [interviewed]. "You Earn More: The Sexual and Psychological Implications." *Savvy* 2, no. 11 (November 1981): 82–86.

KERNBERG, OTTO. "Mature Love: Prerequisites and Characteristics." *Journal of the American Psychoanalytic Association* 22, no. 4 (1974): 743–768.

———. "Barriers to Falling and Remaining in Love." *Journal of the American Psychoanalytic Association* 22, no. 3 (1974): 486–511.

————. "Boundaries and Structures in Love Relations." *Journal of the American Psychoanalytic Association* 25, no. 1 (1977): 81–114.

KINSEY, ALFRED C.; POMEROY, WARDELL B.; and MARTIN, CLYDE. *Sexual Behavior in the Human Male.* Philadelphia: W. B. Saunders Co., 1948.

KLIMEK, DAVID. *Beneath Mate Selection and Marriage.* New York: Van Nostrand Reinhold Co., 1979.

LEDERER, WILLIAM J., and JACKSON, DON. *Mirages of Marriage.* New York: W. W. Norton & Co., 1968.

LEVINSON, DANIEL J. *The Seasons of a Man's Life.* New York: Alfred A. Knopf, 1978.

LIEF, HAROLD I. "Sexual Desire and Responsivity during Pregnancy." *Medical Aspects of Human Sexuality* 11, no. 12 (December 1977): 56, 57.

———— [interviewed]. "The Role of Sex in Marriage." *Medical Aspects of Human Sexuality* 10, no. 10 (October 1976): 42–56.

LUCKEY, ELEANORE BRAUN. "Number of Years Married as Related to Personality Perception and Marital Satisfaction." *Journal of Marriage and the Family* 28 (February 1966): 44–48.

MC LANE, MICHAEL; KROP, HARRY; and MEHTA, JAWAHAR. "Psychosexual Adjustment and Counseling after Myocardial Infarction." *Annals of Internal Medicine* 92 (1980): 514–519.

MALEN, RICHARD, and CORNFELD, RICHARD B. "The Ambitious Husband and the Wrecked Marital Relationship." *Medical Aspects of Human Sexuality* 13, no. 6 (June 1979): 53–71.

MANCINI, JAY A., and ORTHNER, DENNIS K. "Recreational Sexuality Preferences among Middle-Class Husbands and Wives." *Journal of Sex Research* 14, no. 2 (May 1978): 96–106.

MASTERS, WILLIAM H., and JOHNSON, VIRGINIA E. *Human Sexual Response.* Boston: Little, Brown & Co., 1966.

———— [in association with Robert J. Levy]. *The Pleasure Bond.* Boston: Little, Brown & Co., 1975.

MAY, ROBERT. *Sex and Fantasy.* New York: W. W. Norton & Co., 1980.

MICHAEL, R. P., and ZUMPE, D. "Potency in Male Rhesus Monkeys: Effects of Continuously Receptive Females." *Science* 200 (1978): 451–453.

MONEY, JOHN. *Love and Love Sickness.* Baltimore: Johns Hopkins University Press, 1980.

MUNJACK, DENNIS J., and OZIEL, JEROME L. *Sexual Medicine and Counseling in Office Practice.* Boston: Little, Brown & Co., 1980.

MURSTEIN, BERNARD I., ed. *Theories of Attraction and Love.* New York: Springer Publishing Co., 1971.

OFFIT, AVODAH K. *The Sexual Self.* New York: Congdon & Weed, 1983.

OLSON, DAVID H., and LAUBE, HERBERT. "How Different Types of Marital Interaction Affect Sexual Functioning." *Medical Aspects of Human Sexuality* 16, no. 5 (May 1982): 64–76.

ORTHNER, DENNIS K. "Leisure Activity Patterns and Marital Satisfaction over the Marital Career." *Journal of Marriage and the Family* 37 (February 1975): 91–102.

————. "Patterns of Leisure and Marital Interaction." *Journal of Leisure Research* 8, no. 2 (1976): 98–111.

PASINI, W. "Sexuality during Pregnancy and Post-Partum Frigidity." Chap. 68 in *Handbook of Sexuality,* edited by J. Money and J. Musaph. Amsterdam: Excerpta Medica, 1977.

PFEIFFER, ERIC. "Sexuality in the Aging Individual." *Journal of the American Geriatrics Society* 22, no. 11 (November 1974): 481–484.

————. "Sexual Behavior in Old Age." In *Behavior and Adaptation in Later Life,* 2d ed., edited by Ewald W. Busse and Eric Pfeiffer. Boston: Little, Brown & Co., 1977.

PFEIFFER, ERIC, and DAVIS, GLENN C. "Determinants of Sexual Behavior in Middle and Old Age." *Journal of the American Geriatrics Society* 20, no. 4 (1972): 151–158.

PFEIFFER, ERIC; VERWOERDT, ADRIAAN; and DAVIS, GLENN C. "Sexual Behavior in Middle Life." *American Journal of Psychiatry* 128, no. 10 (April 1972): 82–87.

PINEO, PETER C. "Disenchantment in the Later Years of Marriage." *Journal of Marriage and Family Living* 23 (February 1961): 3–11.

POZE, RONALD SERWER, and POZE, PHILIPPA J. "Sexual Avoidance." *Medical Aspects of Human Sexuality* 12, no. 4 (April 1978): 130–142.

RENNE, KAREN S. "Correlates of Dissatisfaction in Marriage." *Journal of Marriage and the Family* 32 (February 1970): 61.

ROGAWSKI, ALEXANDER. "How Children Affect the Marital Relationship." *Medical Aspects of Human Sexuality* 10, no. 6 (June 1976): 48–62.

ROLLINS, BOYD C., and FELDMAN, HAROLD. "Marital Satisfaction over the Life Cycle." *Journal of Marriage and the Family* 32 (February 1970): 20–28.

ROSSI, ALICE. "Transition to Parenthood." *Journal of Marriage and the Family* 30 (February 1968): 26–39.

RUBIN, LILLIAN. *Women of a Certain Age.* New York: Harper & Row, 1979.

SAGER, CLIFFORD. *Marriage Contracts and Couple Therapy.* New York: Brunner/Mazel, 1976.

————. "The Role of Sex Therapy in Marital Therapy." *American Journal of Psychiatry* 133, no. 5 (May 1976): 555–558.

SHEEHY, GAIL. *Passages.* New York: Bantam Books, 1973.

SOLBERG, D. A.; BUTLER, J.; and WAGNER, N. M. "Sexual Behavior in Pregnancy." *New England Journal of Medicine* 288 (1973): 1098–1103.

SOLNICK, ROBERT L., ed. *Sexuality and Aging.* Los Angeles: University of Southern California Press, Ethel Percy Andrus Gerontology Center, 1980.

STOLLER, ROBERT J. *Sexual Excitement.* New York: Simon & Schuster, 1979.

SWENSEN, CLIFFORD H., JR. "Post-Parental Marriages." *Medical Aspects of Human Sexuality* 17, no. 4 (April 1983): 29–52.

TOLOR, A., and DI GRAZIA, P. V. "Sexual Activities and Behavior Patterns during and following Pregnancy." *Archives of Sexual Behavior* 5 (1976): 593.

UDRY, J. RICHARD. "Changes in Frequency of Marital Intercourse from Panel Data." *Archives of Sexual Behavior* 9 (1980): 319–325.

UDRY, J. RICHARD, and MORRIS, NAOMI. "Relative Contribution of Male and Female Age to the Frequency of Marital Intercourse." *Social Biology* 25, no. 2 (1978): 128–134.

VERWOERDT, ADRIAAN; PFEIFFER, ERIC; and WANG, H. S. "Sexual Behavior in Senescence." *Geriatrics,* February 1969, 137–154.

WESTOFF, CHARLES F. "Coital Frequency and Contraception." *Family Planning Perspectives* 6, no. 3 (Summer 1974): 136–141.

WESTOFF, LESLIE ALDRIDGE, and WESTOFF, CHARLES F. *From Now to Zero.* Boston: Little, Brown & Co., 1971.

WILLI, JURG. *Couples in Collusion.* New York: Jason Aronson, 1982.

INDEX